Praise for Polly Evans's
Unforgettable Travel Adventures

FRIED EGGS WITH CHOPSTICKS

"Funny and fascinating. . . . and
many, many wry observa n't
the China that visitors t
Beijing are going to see *nstitution*

"Evans writes travel lit at ground level: noisy, colorful, and
entirely delightful. Comparisons to Bryson, Cahill, and
Theroux would not be unwarranted." —*Booklist*

"Highly readable ... *Fried Eggs with Chopsticks* is gutsy
and funny." —*South China Morning Post*

"Funny and astute, this is an engrossing portrayal of one of
the world's most fascinating countries." —*Wanderlust* (UK)

"Offering a fresh take on travel writing, *Fried Eggs with
Chopsticks* is honest and a lot of fun." —*Trip* (UK)

"A charming, insightful and humorous view of life
on the roads and rails in the People's Republic of China."
—*That's Shanghai*

"An entertaining companion for armchair travelers who enjoy
women's magazine-style writing." —*Publishers Weekly*

IT'S NOT ABOUT THE TAPAS

"A highly likable debut ... As unpretentious as a tapas bar,
and as brimming with savory morsels." —*Kirkus Reviews*

"A fast-paced but reflective memoir about Evans's six-week bike pilgrimage around Spain, complete with sherry binges, mongrel-dodging and watching *Lois y Clark* in dumpy motels." —*People*, "Great Reads: Travel"

"Sampling everything from prawns to paella, Evans discovers one of the best payoffs of traveling by bike: she can eat more without gaining a pound." —*Shape* magazine

"Evans' derisive wit ... is in the best tradition of xenophobic sarcasm, parliamentary put-downs and Monty Python moments.... I found myself more than willing to go along for the ride." —*San Francisco Chronicle*

"This book is great! ... An action-packed story of determination, gall, and joie de vivre ... in an ongoing tapestry of history and scenic beauty crafted by an author of supreme talent." —*Mountain Biking Magazine*

"Bicycle enthusiasts rejoice! ... Evans spices the account of her agony with amusing tidbits from Spanish history, culture, and cuisine. It's hard not to admire her nerve and gutsy spirit." —*Library Journal*

"A hilarious account of an epic adventure around bike-mad Spain." —*Daily Express* Book of the Week (UK)

"This true triumphant tale will appeal to anyone who's eager for adventure." —*OK!* (UK)

Also by Polly Evans

IT'S NOT ABOUT THE TAPAS

FRIED EGGS WITH CHOPSTICKS

About the Author

Polly Evans studied modern languages at Cambridge University before joining the editorial team at a leading London publisher. After four years she moved to Hong Kong, where she worked as a journalist before embarking on a bicycle journey around Spain. This became the subject of her first book, *It's Not About the Tapas*. Polly is also the author of *Fried Eggs with Chopsticks*, which describes her journey around China. She now lives in London where she is at work on her next book, *On a Hoof and a Prayer*, about her attempts to learn to ride in horse-mad Argentina.

Visit her website at www.pollyevans.com.

KIWIS *might* FLY

POLLY EVANS

DELTA TRADE PAPERBACKS

KIWIS MIGHT FLY
A Delta Book

PUBLISHING HISTORY
Bantam UK edition published 2004
Delta trade paperback edition / April 2007

Published by
Bantam Dell
A Division of Random House, Inc.
New York, New York

Extract from *Future Indefinite* by Noël Coward published by Methuen Publishing, copyright ©
The Estate of Noël Coward. Extract from *Voyage of the Beagle* by Charles Darwin used by
permission of Wordsworth Editions. Extract from *The New Zealand Dictionary* by Elizabeth and
Harry Orsman used by permission of New House Publishers. Extract from *View From the Summit*
by Sir Edmund Hillary, published by Doubleday, reprinted by permission of The Random
House Group Ltd. Extracts from the *New Zealand Herald* and the *Southland Times* used by
permission of Print Media Copyright Agency, NZPA Content Services, New Zealand.
Extracts from *The Journals of Captain Cook* published by The Hakluyt Society
used by permission of David Higham Associates.

Every effort has been made to obtain the necessary permissions with reference to copyright
material; should there be any omissions in this respect we apologize and shall be pleased
to make the appropriate acknowledgments in any future edition.

Library of Congress Cataloging-in-Publication Information:
Evans, Polly.
Kiwis might fly / Polly Evans. — Delta trade paperback ed.
p. cm.
ISBN-13: 978-0-385-33994-0 (trade pbk.)
1. New Zealand—Description and travel. 2. Evans, Polly—Travel—New Zealand. 3. Motorcycle
touring—New Zealand. 4. New Zealand—Social life and customs. 5. Men—New Zealand.
6. Masculinity—New Zealand. 7. Sex role—New Zealand. I. Title.
DU413.E83 2007
993.04—dc22   2006022851

Delta is a registered trademark of Random House, Inc.,
and the colophon is a trademark of Random House, Inc.

Printed in the United States of America
Published simultaneously in Canada

www.bantamdell.com

BVG   10 9 8 7 6 5 4 3 2 1

For my godson, Alistair,
and my nephew, Zac

Acknowledgments

The people of New Zealand really are immensely helpful—almost fanatically so, in fact—so I should probably start off by saying a big thank-you to all four million of them for their gestures of friendliness that made my journey so memorable.

Special thanks to Ian and John Fitzwater at Adventure New Zealand Motorcycle Tours & Rentals (www.gotournz.com) for providing me with a fantastic bike and for their faultless recommendations of the best roads, the most comfortable hotels, and the most outstanding restaurants.

Thanks to Gordi Meyer, who looked after me in Auckland, took me for a very exciting ride in a police car, and bravely gave me the telephone numbers of his friends around the country.

Sir Henry Every very kindly spent many hours tracking down members of the New Zealand branch of his family and providing me with contacts, so many thanks to him, and to his relatives Chris and Adrienne Rodgers and Richard and Phyllis Bruce for their hospitality.

For their company, comfortable beds, and insights into strange Kiwi ways, thanks also to Mary, Bill, and Tiggy Farrell, Eileen Birch, Morris and Fay Wharekawa, Lawrie and Carol Chandler, Pete and Skiff, the Hansen family, Frano Barker and Michael Keith, Lee Matson, Dave and the shearers, Frances and Brian Ward, Brendon, Veronica, and Sandy Park, Kyle and Marion Mewburn, and to Sheena Ashford-Tait and Duncan Ashford for the night in the camper van.

Andrea Brunetti at Dainese and Dan at Chiswick Honda kitted me out in a fantastic set of black leathers that, dare I say it, were really rather attractive. Well, I thought so anyway.

And to Jane Gregory and Broo Doherty and all at Gregory and Company, and to Francesca Liversidge and everyone at Transworld, thanks as ever for their friendship, enthusiasm, and professional expertise.

Contents

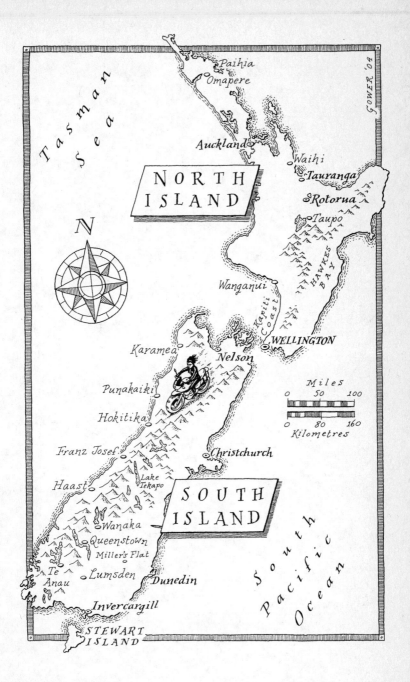

GOWER '04

Tasman Sea

Paihia
Omapere

Auckland

NORTH ISLAND

N

Waihi
Tauranga

Rotorua

Taupo

HAWKES BAY

Wanganui

Kapiti Coast

WELLINGTON

Karamea

Nelson

Punakaiki

Hokitika

Miles
0   50   100

0   80   160
Kilometres

Franz Josef

Christchurch

Haast

Lake Tekapo

SOUTH ISLAND

Wanaka

Queenstown

Miller's Flat

Te Anau

Lumsden

Dunedin

South Pacific Ocean

Invercargill

STEWART ISLAND

KIWIS
might
FLY

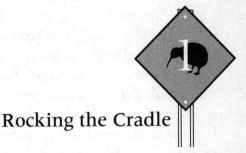

Rocking the Cradle

"SO," SIÂN, MY NEUROLOGIST friend, asked brightly, "are you going to wear one of those motorcycle helmets that covers the back of your head up to your fourth cervical vertebra, so that if you crash you're left quadriplegic, or are you going to get one of those higher-cut ones so that you're killed outright instead?"

My stomach lurched. I was deeply afraid.

It had all started a few months earlier, when I'd read a survey that claimed the ordinary Kiwi bloke was about to turn up the toes of his gum boots. He was, apparently, hanging up his sheep shears and moving to the city. A new masculinity was rearing its pretty, hair-gelled head. Men were waxing their backs. In ten years, said the survey, the traditional, hirsute New Zealand man would be dead.

The early New Zealanders had been virile and vigorous. The Maori were fearless warriors. Then the Europeans had arrived after arduous journeys across thousands of miles of treacherous ocean. The life that awaited them was hard.

New Zealand men grew up to be strong. They slaughtered whales, panned for gold, and felled timber. They learned to play rugby. Fearlessly, they drank home-brewed beer. Then something went wrong. The environment changed; the species had to mutate. Volcanic eruptions? Tectonic shifts? An over-boiling of the primordial soup? No. It was none of these things. It had more to do with washing machines from Japan.

With the arrival of airplanes and domestic appliances, the fences came unstuck for the traditional New Zealand man. What did it matter if he could mend a tractor using three bits of old wire and a pot of distilled sheep dung when spare parts were lined up at the local Kawasaki store? The real Kiwi bloke was fast becoming redundant.

The curious thing was that nobody seemed to be making much of a fuss about his demise. When other creatures have faced extinction—when the tiger threatened to roar no more, or the red-legged frog looked fit to croak—the conservationists beat their chests like gorillas whose trees just got the chop. But when the Kiwi bloke, an almost-human species, began to shuffle off to the big brewery in the sky, nobody seemed much bothered. One or two insensitive souls even breathed a quiet sigh of relief.

There was nothing else to do. Somebody was going to have to travel to the other side of the globe, to delve deep into the New Zealand countryside, to sniff around on sheep farms and poke about in rural pubs and ask the question: Is the Kiwi bloke *really* about to breathe his last?

It was cold and raining at home in London; in New Zealand it was summer, the perfect time to hunt out a shy species on the verge of extinction from its spectacular alpine hideaways and wave-swept beachside lairs. It looked as though that somebody might have to be me.

I thought I'd tour New Zealand on a motorcycle. Kiwi men were known to be fond of machinery; these were the guys who were meant to be able to strip down the engine of their truck on a Sunday afternoon and have it working again by Monday. If I rode a motorcycle, I thought, and, better still, if I shoehorned myself into the tightest set of black motorcycling leathers I could find, I should stand a greater chance of luring these timid men from their hunting grounds and watering holes. If I was really lucky, I might even persuade one or two of them to speak.

I enrolled in motorcycling classes. Working on the basis that there are fewer maniacal cars out to kill a learner motor-cyclist in the countryside than in town, I decided to take lessons in the depths of rural Derbyshire.

I shared my first day's training with two sixteen-year-old boys who had just been given their first mopeds. We learned that cool kids ride safely. The two boys set off around the traffic cones on their gloriously gearless scooters. I got less than a yard before the 125cc training bike coughed, gave a little shudder, and stalled. I tried again.

"You gotta treat the clutch gently," Oz, the instructor, admonished me. He was a big, grizzled man with stubbly gray facial hair and well-worn leathers. "Handle it like, well"—now he looked embarrassed—"we always say like you'd handle a woman."

He shuffled and grinned. I raised an eyebrow. Not only was I expected to ride this piece of killer machinery, now I was meant to build a meaningful relationship with it as well. I tried again. The bike hiccuped, coughed, and stopped.

I rented a 125cc bike—the largest I was allowed to ride

without actually passing a test—for a week. My relationship with my clutch still had some way to go. On the first day, I dropped the bike in a traffic circle, where I created an outraged, horn-tooting traffic jam. Half an hour later, I had some problem selecting a suitable gear as I turned right on a steep hill. I stalled—again. The bike teetered, toppled, and crashed to the ground. An elderly couple in a little red Peugeot 106 stopped at the intersection, he in his flat cap, she with a woolen neck scarf. They peered with some distaste out of their window at the helmeted figure lying on the pavement in distress and, quickly concluding they wanted nothing to do with such a creature, shot off, leaving me there all alone.

No, wait, it's only me, I wanted to shout after them from beneath my helmeted disguise. I don't have tattoos. I have no idea how to do a wheelie. I don't batter old women at bus stops or boil their bones into soup. . . .

But they had disappeared as fast as third gear could carry them.

I went back to Two-Wheel Training for more lessons. Two characters called John, who was very round, and Kieran, who was very skinny despite consuming a remarkable number of pies, put me through my paces.

"What do you think you're doing you're going to get yourself killed *get out of the path of that oncoming truck*," Kieran would bellow with some excitement through the radio earpiece.

"Get up to speed get up to speed get up to speed if you wimp out like this *you'll fail your test*," John would counter as the headwind buffeted my leather-clad limbs at a quite terrifying forty miles an hour.

One day I accidentally missed the road and drove up onto the sidewalk instead; another day I dropped the bike and snapped off the brake lever twice in one hour.

Test day dawned. I hadn't slept. My palms were clammy. I could scarcely eat. I had entirely forgotten that taking driving tests was quite so terrifying.

The examiner's name was Simon. He was a small, mild-mannered man with blond hair. He looked like the type of person who would be kind to small children and cats. In normal circumstances, he would have seemed pleasant and unassuming. As it was, I viewed him with the same warm feelings I would entertain for a hungry grizzly bear.

Simon strapped a radio to me. He relayed instructions through my earpiece; I gingerly turned left out of the test center. Simon came behind in pursuit on his vast white steed of an examiner's bike. We turned left, we turned right, we turned right, and we turned left. I remembered to stop at the red traffic light. I managed the hill start without sliding backward into Simon's hulk of a machine. I U-turned without falling off the bike and executed a neat little emergency stop. We turned left, and then, just when I had almost stopped shaking with fear, I noticed: My blinker was flashing. That last turn had been at least a minute or so back—and motorcycle blinkers don't cancel themselves when you turn, as car ones do.

"Bugger bugger bugger bugger," I muttered all the way back to the test center.

I had failed.

I couldn't retake my test for three weeks and spent most of that time trying to come to terms with the horrible reality: I had to go through it all again. I started to have nightmares about the diminutive Simon, whose body took on grotesque, outlandish forms. His short limbs stretched to inhuman, entwining, entrapping proportions; his gentle blue eyes widened to become garish cobalt orbs with the piercing glare of a wolf who thinks you've eaten his elk. The Simon of my dreams stood and snarled, orange lights flashing left and right about his diabolical, distended head.

"Ha-ha-ha-ha-ha," he cackled demonically through my anguished subconscious. "You left your blinker flashing, blinker flashing, blinker flashing. . . ."

The problem was that I had already bought my ticket for New Zealand. I *needed* to pass this next test. I considered bribes, threats, body doubles, but had to conclude that Simon hadn't looked terribly susceptible to corruption. There was nothing else to do: I had to try, once more, to do a U-turn without falling off the bike. I had to attempt to ride on the road and not on the sidewalk. I had to remember to turn the blinker off. It was a tough call. Vowing never again to undertake a project so high-risk that I needed to pass an exam before I could embark upon it, I returned to the test center.

John the instructor, usually a garrulous character, was strangely quiet as we rode there. As we waited for my turn to take to the road, even he was looking faintly green. It was Simon's day off, so another examiner took his place. We struck out for the country lanes, traffic-free. After ten minutes or so of winding rural roads, I was almost enjoying myself. We came into the city, sat in a rush-hour traffic jam for a while, and then it was all over.

"I'm happy to tell you you've passed," said the examiner.

John's entire capacious body slumped with relief. I was so elated that I nearly—but not quite—hugged him.

To celebrate, I headed instead to the nearest Dainese gear shop and acquired a suitably fetching set of leathers and boots. I confirmed my rental of a 650cc Suzuki Freewind with Adventure New Zealand Motorcycle Tours on the other side of the globe. Clutching my license, newly inscribed with a little picture of a motorcycle, I packed my bags and boarded the plane.

Motorcycles are like twitchy thoroughbred racehorses or large dogs with big teeth: It's not a good idea to let them know that you're scared. They can sniff out fear at a hundred paces. At the merest hint of adrenaline they become frisky, jumpy, and prone to bolt.

When I arrived at Adventure New Zealand Motorcycle's depot just outside Auckland to pick up my motorcycle, I was therefore determined to disguise the fact that I was consumed by terror. It wasn't just the bike; I didn't really want Ian and John, the two brothers who owned the company, to know how frightened I was either. I hadn't thought it circumspect to admit to them exactly how inexperienced a motorcyclist I really was. There was something about the way their Web site proclaimed "We are fiercely proud of our range of bikes ... all of our bikes are in as-new, showroom condition" that stopped me letting on that the day I picked up their glorious, gleaming blue-and-silver Suzuki was, well, the first day I'd ridden a motorcycle without learner plates. It was the first time I'd been on the road without an instructor in radio contact telling me how to stay alive. It was the first time I'd ridden a bike anything approaching this big.

I arrived in a taxi; as the driver headed off down the road, I felt my last link with the safe world of four wheels disappear. A man called Paul wheeled out the bike I was to ride for the next few months. I blinked. I let out a tiny squeak. I breathed a little faster. This bike was *huge*. It was a monster. It looked like the kind of beast that might just take umbrage with a bumbling novice motorcyclist and buck her from this world into the next. How on earth was I meant to build a meaningful relationship with *that*? It didn't look like a bike that would like to have its clutch gently squeezed or lovingly massaged. It looked like a machine that would be more into wild animalistic pumping.

Paul looked happy, delighted to be handing this piece of killer machinery over. Paul had no idea of the lunacy in which he was unwittingly complicit. I did my best to look cool, but underneath the tight black leathers I was pouring sweat.

Six hundred fifty ccs hadn't sounded all that big when I was back home, safe and warm, sitting in front of my computer looking at online photographs of motorcycles and fantasizing about roaring along deserted roads, past hillsides covered in swaying golden tussocks, up winding mountain passes with panoramic views, alongside rugged white beaches thumped by wild, crashing waves. Six hundred fifty ccs looked rather more frightening in the flesh.

I tried to delay the inevitable as long as I could. I spent a good while unpacking my luggage and loading it into the panniers. I found the bike wouldn't balance on its stand very well once it was loaded with luggage, because it was on a slight slope. I tried to wheel it over to a flat piece of pavement. It was so heavy, I couldn't shift it. Paul blithely sauntered over to help. For some reason, he still didn't look concerned.

"That's it, you're on your way." He grinned in a carefree manner. "See ya."

"See ya," I squeaked back. I was trying hard to sound relaxed, but my voice came out high-pitched and strangled. I put the key in the ignition and turned the throttle gingerly. The bike gave a mighty man-eating roar.

There was a little hill down the driveway onto the main road. I inched my way down, convinced that at any moment the bike was going to lunge into life and hurl me to my death under the wheels of a passing Volvo.

"Urrrrrrrrrr," it purred, sounding frighteningly like a panther preparing to pounce.

Riding this bike was a ludicrous idea, it now occurred to me. It wasn't just averagely silly—people actually die when they fall off motorcycles. Forget the extinction of Kiwi blokes; right now it looked as though I myself might be about to bestow a favor on the human race by removing my own insane genes from the evolutionary pool, by finishing myself off before I'd gotten around to reproducing. I was horribly vulnerable. I was grossly incompetent. I ought to have taken the bus.

But there was no bus. The taxi had left half an hour ago.

"Come on, bike," I muttered, trying to sound powerful. "You're in my hands now."

And with that, I opened the throttle, let out the clutch, and stuttered off down the road.

I was heading north to Paihia in the Bay of Islands. From there I was planning to visit Waitangi, the controversial birthplace of modern-day New Zealand and, therefore, the cradle of Kiwi man. Then I'd head back down to Auckland before heading south.

I puttered slowly for the first few miles. After twenty minutes or so, I was forced to accept that the bike was spinning along quite effortlessly. As long as I didn't have to do anything scary—such as stop at a red light—all was well. I started to look at the digital display in front of me in an attempt to figure out what the various gauges were trying to tell me. My speed was obviously that big number in the middle—a whopping forty-seven miles an hour at present. And that line down the side with notches on it seemed to be the gas gauge. Except that there wasn't any mark on it. The bike, surely, had gas in it. It was moving, after all. I screwed up my eyes at the display. Then I noticed: The three notches at the bottom of the red "empty" box had turned to two. The tank was nearly empty. Goodness, I thought, perhaps that purring noise had not been the bike preparing to pounce but the anguished rumbling of its half-starved tummy. Clearly, the beast had to be fed—and soon.

I had just a minute or two earlier passed through a small township called Warkworth. I turned around, managed to execute a successful left turn at the traffic lights, and found a gas station.

I stopped the bike. It didn't crash to the ground. I swung my leg over. Still no disasters. I filled up with gas, paid at the kiosk, and left.

Things didn't run so smoothly for long. At the intersection to get out onto the main highway, the traffic light was red. I stopped in the line of traffic. The light turned green. I can't even remember what happened next: As tends to happen after traumatic events, such as when one witnesses the annihilation of one's entire family at the hands of a crazed gunman, my mind has obliterated the memory. But, somehow, the bike bunny-hopped, I let go of the handlebars, and the whole she-bang crashed to the ground.

I stood and stared in horror at the vast machine lying prostrate on the asphalt. I'd had it for less than an hour and already I'd managed to drop it. My terror, which had in the last fifteen minutes or so subsided to a small puddle somewhere in the region of my toes, now welled up again and washed over me with the force of a tsunami. I looked around in desperation. There was no way I could pick the bike up by myself. Let's face it, an hour ago I hadn't even been strong enough to wheel it across Adventure New Zealand Motorcycle's parking lot. There seemed little point in even trying. Surely one of these drivers would rush to my aid in a moment; they'd help me lift the bike so the traffic could move on. But the drivers just glared at me and waved their hands in flurried, impatient shrugs. There was a tooting of horns. I was entirely mortified. I felt physically sick. I willed the ground to swallow me whole.

Finally, after what was probably just seconds but seemed like about half an hour, a woman laden with shopping bags full of groceries ambled over.

"Can I help you with that?" she asked, dumping her plastic bags on the ground. A small bottle of bleach toppled out onto the road.

I grabbed the handlebar; she heaved from behind. The bike didn't so much as budge. We tried again. We wheezed and we puffed. My sweat—a heady combination now of exertion, fear, and abject humiliation—had given up oozing and dribbling and developed into a full-force flood. And then, as if by magic, the bike lifted itself. I looked around. A vast Maori man, whose tattooed biceps bulged from his tank top, stood behind me. His vest stretched taut over pulsating pectorals. He seemed to have lifted the bike with a tiny effort from just one finger.

"Er, thanks," I said.

I looked up at him fearfully. What was he going to say? I braced myself for his brutal, scathing observation that I shouldn't be playing with dangerous boys' toys, that if I must play with something, I should be riding a nice little girl's scooter. I winced thinking of the way in which he would growl that my incompetence was threatening the safety of everyone else on the road. I cowered and looked back down at the road.

"Nice bike," he said, and laughed.

"Er, yes, well, I only just picked it up from the rental shop," I stumbled, red-faced.

The man sauntered into the middle of the road. He was still beaming—he seemed to find the whole awful episode wildly entertaining. He held up his hand to the cars. The traffic stopped. And then, when it was completely safe, he waved me out onto the highway.

"Ride safely now!" he called as I wobbled away shamefaced and vowing that never, ever, however desperate the circumstances, not even if aliens dropped out of the sky and obliterated every other town on the planet, would I show my face in Warkworth again.

It took me five hours to ride the 155 miles to Paihia. Long lines of frustrated traffic strung out behind me as I puttered pathetically along, but I didn't care; I just wanted to stay alive. Just north of Whangarei, I stopped for bacon, eggs, and coffee at a roadside café.

"You want mulk un thet?" asked the girl behind the counter.

"I'm sorry?"

"*Mulk?*"

I had no idea what she was talking about. The girl was of the plump, cheerful kind. Her hair was scraped back in a devil-may-care attitude, one that refused to be flustered by bobbly bits and wayward locks. Underneath the once-white apron, her clothes positively howled: *I am not a fashion victim!* The girl laughed at the strange foreigner, drew breath, and gave it one last go.

"Would you like *mulk* in your *coffee?*"

So it looked as though it wasn't just the bike that would be giving me problems in this strange land twelve thousand miles from home. It wasn't just the men—who were so laid back they wouldn't bat an eyelid if a tractor grew wings—that were a little bit odd. It looked as though I wasn't going to be able to speak to anyone in this peculiar aberration of English either.

When, eventually, the tiny waterfront town of Paihia appeared, I was giddy with relief. I had survived day one. It wasn't until the next morning, when I woke up with astonishingly stiff buttocks, that I realized what kind of workout five hours' terrified bottom-clenching can provide.

Paihia is the main township of the Bay of Islands, a remarkably pretty place whose warm climate and array of waterborne activities today draw the vacation crowds. I had been here once before, when I came on vacation to New Zealand to escape the chaos of the magazine publishing office where I worked in Hong Kong. On that trip, I had gone out into the ocean on a small boat owned by a Kiwi bloke named Captain Bucko; we had dived amid the rusting wreckage of a ship that had met its end in these waters many years before. We had swum through crumbling iron doorways into decrepit caverns where packed shoals of tiny shimmering fish parted to allow us through. Back outside, as we moved slowly through the water along the length of the wreck, a huge, solitary stingray had undulated beneath us. From a crack in a rock, a moray eel had poked out its head and granted us a toothy grin.

Back on dry land, I had lain on the beach at the nearby township of Russell and strolled through the forest. I hadn't, however, troubled my head with historical detail—and history is something that this part of New Zealand has in just as rich abundance as its rippling, wriggling marine life.

It was in the Bay of Islands that Charles Darwin first set

foot on New Zealand soil in December 1835. He stopped here on his five-year voyage aboard the *Beagle*, during which he also visited the Galápagos Islands, whose fossils were later to lead him to his theory of evolution. Darwin was less than enchanted with what he found.

"[New Zealand] is not a pleasant place," he wrote in his journal. "Amongst the natives there is absent that charming simplicity which is found in Tahiti; and the greater part of the English are the very refuse of society."

He might have had a point. From the 1790s onward, European and American sealers and whalers had been coming here for rest, booze, and sex with the local Maori women. Their ships were often crewed by escaped convicts, thieves, and thugs. Some of these stopped off in the Bay of Islands and opened shops and brothels. Drunkenness and debauchery pitched and rolled; the now-paradisiacal township of Russell became known as the "hellhole of the Pacific."

With so many of those Kiwi blokes in need of spiritual assistance, the early Kiwi missionaries set up their first base here too. Samuel Marsden, the Anglican chaplain of New South Wales, brought God to the Bay of Islands in 1814. He was frustrated by his failure to turn the Australian convicts and Aboriginals into good Christians, so decided to try his luck with the Maori instead. The gospel was first preached on New Zealand soil on Christmas Day of that year. "Behold, I bring you tidings of great joy," Marsden proclaimed before disappearing back off to Australia as fast as the wind would carry him and leaving his minions to sort out the mess. Marsden's legacy lasts to this day: The main street of Paihia is still named after him.

The missionaries did their best to spread the word, though sometimes the message was lost in translation. "The chief was at this time rather notorious from having lately hung one of his wives and a slave for adultery. When one of the missionaries remonstrated with him he seemed surprised, and said he thought he was exactly following the English method," Charles Darwin recounted in his journal, *The Voyage of the Beagle*, after visiting a tribe at Waiomio with his religious friends.

In some unfortunate cases, grog got the better of God, and sex won over souls. In less than twenty years, three missionaries had been given the sack: one for adultery, one for drunkenness, and the third for what Marsden, with delicious prudery, mysteriously labeled "a crime worse than either."

But the Bay of Islands was not merely an early settlement for lusty whalers and fast-succumbing missionaries. It has a more notorious place in history, for this was where the Treaty of Waitangi was signed. Waitangi lies just up the road, a mile or two from Paihia. It was here that, on February 6, 1840, the British resident, Captain William Hobson, convinced a number of Maori chiefs to cede to British sovereignty.

It was because of the Treaty House at Waitangi that I had come north at all. This was, albeit controversially, the site where the Maori and British peoples joined together as one nation, the place where their cultures merged and where the country "New Zealand" was created.

The next morning, I was out of bed early and, after a fortifying coffee and muffin in a waterfront café, I wandered up the road to Waitangi. In contrast to the bitterness and bloodshed that the treaty has provoked over the years, the Waitangi Treaty House is well tended and squeaky-clean. At the visitors' center, an audiovisual display tells the story of the founding of New Zealand as we know it. It is a rose-tinted, sugar-coated tale. The narration theoretically comes from a Maori and goes something like this: *Once upon a time our people arrived* in Aotearoa in a great big canoe. They had lots of nice sex, and after a few generations the country was inhabited by many different tribes of happy, cuddly brown warriors.

Then one day a big ship came along with pretty white goblins inside. It was like a dream. The white men brought pottery and pigs and sheep and guns. But as more and more white men came to hunt the whales and seals around our shores, things started to get messy. The white men were frequently drunk and took a shine to our women. We needed protection.

Luckily for us, the missionaries came and taught us how to love each other. But we still yearned for the hand of good government. And so when William Hobson came to save us, not only from the randy whalers but also from the garlic-breathing Frenchmen who were at that time eyeing up our land, we thanked our newfound God for our luck. Just think, if the British hadn't come along, we might all be mincing about in berets and saying "bah" at the end of our sentences and that wouldn't do at all, eh.

On the sixth of February, 1840, the nice Captain Hobson put up a tent in his garden and invited all his friends the tribal chiefs to come and sign the Treaty of Waitangi, which meant that the Maori people could be protected by the fair and just government of Great Britain. Our peoples were joined. Our nation was born. And everyone lived happily ever after.

Or something like that. I forget the exact words.

In practice, it wasn't quite so simple.

To start with, the treaty wasn't signed by all the chiefs. Second, the Maori version of the treaty—which ostensibly granted British sovereignty and protection to the Maori people and guaranteed possession of their fisheries and resources in exchange for allowing the British Crown sole rights to buy their land—didn't say the same thing as the English version. The Maori had no concept of land ownership and often didn't realize what selling it really meant. They had no idea of the numbers of Europeans that would come: Te Whatrepouri, the tribal chief who sold Wellington, later complained that he had only expected nine or ten Pakeha (which is believed to derive from the Maori word "pakepakeha," meaning pale-skinned fairies) to come and live there. Oops.

After the treaty was signed, the British settlers frequently abused the agreement and took Maori lands by force even when the Maori didn't want to sell them. The bitterness and disagreements continue to this day, with the Maori still fighting, now through the official channels of the Waitangi Tribunal, for compensation for the land that was taken from them.

So why did the British bother? New Zealand was a long way away, trade was flowing freely, and Britain was up to its eyes in troublesome colonies already.

One reason was that the French were sailing about New Zealand's shores with a proprietary Gallic glint in their eyes. In 1837, the adventurer Baron Charles de Thierry had even been so bold as to plant his flag on eight hundred acres in Northland and to proclaim himself the "Sovereign Chief of New Zealand"—and there was nothing more certain to inspire the British into action than the opportunity to outdo the French, especially after that irritating business just a few years earlier when Napoleon's head had grown too big for his bicorn and he'd even dared dream of marching his cheese-fueled armies into Britain itself.

The missionaries, too, were trying to persuade Britain to annex New Zealand. They didn't like the French much either, because they didn't want their Anglican missions ousted by the Catholics. Their repeated prayers for a great big storm to come and sink the nasty papist French ships had come to naught. Maybe God was paying them back for their misdemeanors with other men's wives. So, just to be on the safe side, the missionaries hedged their bets with God and teamed up with the money-minded men of the New Zealand Company as Plan B.

The New Zealand Company was created by a group of colonialist entrepreneurs in England. They reckoned that since the Industrial Revolution, when machines began to take over from manpower, Britain had too many people. Profits were declining and poverty was increasing. What better solution, then, than to create another Britain, a "Britain of the South," and ship some of the excess bodies over there to a better life ... oh yes, and to make lots of nice money for their very own coffers by establishing that "the Crown" alone was allowed to buy land from the Maori? Having purchased the land at a favorable rate, they could then sell it on to the new European settlers at a profit.

The powers of London's great Colonial Office were unconvinced. All those arguments hadn't brought New Zealand any nearer. So the pro-annexation brains brought out their trump card.

The British traders, whalers, and grog-sellers had effectively turned the place into a British colony already, they said, but one fueled by booze and corruption. The local people were being raped, pillaged, oppressed, subordinated. Britain had a moral duty to step in and restore order.

The ancient sages of the Colonial Office shuddered into wakefulness. *Moral duty?* "Well, if you put it like that, I suppose we'd better colonize the poor souls," they said. And so they did.

*   *   *

I left the fantastical World of Waitangi and walked the short distance back to Paihia, over the little bridge where the Waitangi River meets the sea. This part of New Zealand, way up in the north, is subtropical in climate. The summer isn't too hot, the winter scarcely happens at all, and the vegetation shoots, sprouts, and spawns. To my right the river wound through mangrove swamps and lush forests to the thundering, tumbling Haruru Falls beyond. To my left lay the clear turquoise ocean, scattered with scores of islands deep green with foliage and lined by golden-yellow beaches. Among them fishing boats bobbed on the wake of ferries that motored along the path between the red and green buoys. Dive boats, sailing boats, and brightly colored kayaks puttered between the islands.

Coming into Paihia, I walked along the packed wet sand by the water's edge. The beach here wasn't littered with bodies. It was a narrow stretch of saffron yellow, at the back of which a small grassy hump rose up and gave way to a tree-lined strip of lawn. The occasional sunbather lay on a towel on the grass and read, a couple of children made sand castles, but most of Paihia's visitors were an active crowd who preferred to play on the waves than to lie about and watch them. A lean teenager strolled along the sand, throwing a ball into the sea for a dripping, delirious black-and-white Border collie that shook itself vigorously each time it emerged from the ocean. The boy's long blue board shorts, hanging low beneath his tapered waist, were drenched by the dog's spray and clung to his thighs.

The restaurants and cafés lining the Marsden Road were half full. Chilled-out vacationers sipped a coffee to energize them for that afternoon's boat trip or grabbed a bite to eat to replace any calories they'd inadvertently lost while kayaking that morning. Others looked as though they had settled themselves in for the day. They worked their way gently through a few bottles of chilled New Zealand wine and slurped oysters fresh from the ocean.

I went back to my motel, plugged my laptop into the phone socket, and checked my mail.

"I assume you have by now tamed the beast and have started work on the men," wrote my friend Sarah.

I stared at the screen sadly and sighed. I hadn't tamed anything at all. The bike was still sitting abandoned in the parking lot, its headlight glaring at me menacingly through the window.

Back home my friends were safe and warm in their offices, earning money the comfortable way. They had visions of me sweeping along New Zealand's winding roads, an indefatigable Amazonian roaring with adventure and derring-do. They knew nothing of the pitiful reality. They didn't know that I was sitting in a cheap motel with flowery wallpaper and a threadbare carpet, drinking complimentary tea with too much tannin from the only cup I could find that wasn't chipped, gingerly boiling water in a yellow-plastic, lime-scale-encrusted kettle.

I dug deep for grit, courage, and a tiny white lie.

"Currently engaged in a bit of a power struggle, but victory imminent," I e-mailed back. I looked through the window and fixed the bike with a steely glare.

"Tomorrow," I told it in my most commanding tone, "you and I are hitting the road."

Size Matters

NEW ZEALAND IS A small country with a tiny population, yet it's obsessed with doing everything big. It's not just the motorcycles; the flora and fauna, too, are fixated by that most masculine of concerns: size.

Take the moa, the now-extinct flightless fowl that were indigenous to New Zealand and roamed the forests quite happily until the Maori came along and ate them all. The moa were huge. Because prior to European contact New Zealand had no mammals, except for a couple of indigenous bats and the rats and dogs that the Maori had brought from Polynesia, the moa was hunted by nobody other than the Haast eagle. While we're talking size, the Haast eagle—which itself died out five hundred years ago—weighed twenty-two pounds and had a wingspan of ten feet. When it spotted prey in the form of a tasty moa, it would dive from trees at fifty miles an hour. The bone-splintering impact as it smashed into its target was such that even the largest moa were felled. The eagle would then use its powerful talons, the same size as lions' claws, to crush and pierce the necks of its victims.

But even the Haast eagle and its mate would take several days to peck their way through a moa. Shaped like an out-sized ostrich, with flecked brownish feathers and a slender arching neck, this behemoth of a bird could grow to heights of more than thirteen feet. Its eggs weighed 220 pounds. A moa's legs alone would have risen high above the heads of the men who hunted it. One can only imagine the barbecue they would have needed to build to roast the drumsticks.

The kiwi bird is little better. The female—a brown bird about the same size as a chicken but with thin, spindly legs, a long, foraging beak, and useless stubby wings that don't fly—insists on laying an egg so big that her tummy sometimes drags along the ground. She has to stand in cold water to re-lieve the pain; in the final days before laying she can't eat at all because so much of her belly is taken up by her egg, which grows to *six times* the size of eggs of other birds the kiwi's size. Big may be beautiful, but this is ridiculous.

No sooner had they set foot on New Zealand soil than the early Kiwi blokes, too, became obsessed by size. Everything needed to be not just better but bigger than its equivalent back home. Settlers in nineteenth-century Christchurch grew nine-pound carrots.

"The carrots were not like ordinary carrots, they out-carroted carrots," Edward Gibbon Wakefield, founder of the New Zealand Company, apparently commented when he first arrived on fertile New Zealand soil, winning at once the world record for the number of times you can fit the word "carrot" into a single sentence.

Down in Dunedin they managed to produce a twenty-one-pound beetroot and a fifty-five-pound cabbage. And all without genetic modification.

People grew bigger too. In the late nineteenth century, New Zealand children, growing up on farms, tended to eat more protein than their European counterparts—and their hair apparently grew longer. "After two years in Auckland," wrote one woman, "my hair, from being thin and weak, is now so thick that I can scarcely bear its weight."

And then there are the kauri trees. These soaring giants can live for thousands of years and grow upward of 160 feet tall. The rest of the forest—the abundant tree ferns, the towering palms, the tall stands of lush, dense grasses—appear in photographs to be mere shrubs next to these gargantuan kings. The kauri's towering columnar trunk seems perfectly in proportion with the boughs that sprout from its tip. It's not until you look at the pictures more closely that you realize just how massive this plant really is; it's not until you notice the people that the extent of its mighty trunk becomes clear. The speck of blue tucked under what seems to be a spray of bracken turns out on closer inspection to be a rain jacket worn by a grown man; the fronds above him are the branches of a full-sized ponga tree.

The kauri trees are so large, in fact, that in the late 1800s an entire family—two parents and *thirteen* children—set up home in one. It sounds a desperate thing to do, I'll agree, but in the early days of colonial New Zealand the government hadn't come to grips with state-funded housing projects, and it must have seemed a good idea at the time. The story goes that in 1882 an Irish immigrant, Richard Shepherd, took up a grant of land at Totara North, a few miles from Paihia. A huge kauri tree was growing on the land; on closer inspection Richard found that it was rotten in the middle. Since the family was living in tents and could find no other way to put a roof over its head, Richard and his wife, Rose Ann, scraped out the moldy wood, constructed a ceiling, and built seats around the outside of the new "room." As the family expanded, Richard built another story with several bedrooms. The family lived in the tree for fourteen years.

As well as providing shelter for innovative homemakers, these trees also helped create one of New Zealand's earliest industries—the timber trade—and in doing so planted the roots of the tough Kiwi bushman. It was to the Waipoua Kauri Forest, directly across from Paihia on the west coast of Northland, that I was heading today, to take a look at the magnificent trees that had encouraged such hardiness in the men who labored to destroy them.

The Maori had always used the kauri trees for building canoes, paddles, weapons, and other instruments, but they never developed the wholesale plunder that the Europeans would later embrace. The first tree was felled up here in Northland by Europeans as early as May 1772, when the French expedition leader Marion de Fresne needed replacements for the foremast and bowsprit of one of his ships. Despite the successful selection and felling of a tree by his men, and the backbreaking dragging of the timber for many days across the forest toward the sea where the ship lay at anchor, these new spars were never used. Word reached the timber-felling crew that de Fresne and twenty-five of his party had been attacked and eaten by the Maori. (Their bones were apparently made into forks and flutes.) The rest of the party abandoned their loot, leapt aboard their ships, and fled.

Despite these inauspicious beginnings, Europeans were

exporting timber from New Zealand from the mid-1790s; a hundred years later, in 1891, forty-two million feet of timber were shipped abroad.

It wasn't an easy life for the men who lived in the forest. In the early days before chain saws, the work was done entirely by hand. Once the huge trunks had been cut, the timber was transported by teams of bullocks and judicious use of dams: When enough water had built up, a trip rope was tugged. This sent a roar of water plummeting downhill, hurling the strategically placed logs to the booms—fences made of logs chained together—many miles below.

The loggers lived in bush shanties—makeshift huts with nikau palm roofs and rows of bunks. The working week was generally fifty-eight hours of backbreaking labor, ten hours a day Monday to Friday, eight hours on a Saturday. Many of the men would remain in camp for up to six months at a time, saving their wages, before taking a week or two off to blow the lot on a drinking spree in town.

I wanted to see the trees whose size and toughness had bred such resilience in those early Kiwi bushmen. I was digging deep for strength and tenacity myself. I dressed in my leathers once more. Wearily, I clipped on my panniers. Taking deep breaths, I pulled on my helmet, then my gloves. And then, when I really could procrastinate no longer, I climbed onto the bike, turned the key in the ignition, and gave the throttle a little twitch.

"Grrrrr," said the bike.

I frowned. Was that a growl?

"Now listen here, bike," I hissed through my visor, directing a stern expression at the handlebars. "Don't you try any funny business with me. You're just a heap of metal and plastic. You don't have a say. *I'm* the one who's in control."

The bike gave a little hiccup of disbelief. I fixed it with another hard stare and inched out onto Marsden Road. Having successfully executed a wobbly left turn, I chugged off down the road, trying not to knock down any Kiwi blokes—or birds— as I went.

I only had to ride sixty miles or so to the Waipoua Forest, and things went quite smoothly at first. It was perfect motorcycling weather: dry and still, not too hot, not too cold. The roads were comfortingly quiet, which was something of a relief, since this meant that if I were to suffer a moment of gross incompetence, the chances of another vehicle finding itself unwittingly involved in my idiocy would be considerably fewer. This in turn would reduce the importance of just how many cervical vertebrae my helmet covered.

A slow-speed accident should be okay. My leathers had rock-solid, built-in armor in the knees, down the shins, and on the shoulders and elbows. In addition, the kind people at Dainese had thrown in a back protector—a funny contraption worn like a rucksack under your jacket. It's meant to stop you from breaking your back if you're thrown from your bike following an altercation with the controls. My helmet—or one of its kind—had apparently been tested by having metal spikes hurled at it from a great height and had survived. So, I reckoned, if I fell off all by myself, and if I was going slowly enough, I stood a good chance of survival. A couple of months strung up in the hospital with all my limbs in traction, maybe, but hopefully I wouldn't actually die. If I drove headlong into an oncoming sheep truck, however, the outcome might be rather less rosy. So empty roads were good roads.

After an hour or so, the fields on either side of the road

with their smatterings of trees and small copses here and there came to an end, and the forest became lush and dense. The road began to twist tightly now through the trunks and roots of the mature, dark-green trees that towered over me. I arrived at a small row of cars parked along the side of the road. This was the entrance to the path that led to Tane Mahuta, the largest kauri tree still living in New Zealand.

It was only now that it occurred to me that I was not very suitably attired for walking in the forest. Fully armored tight black leathers are all very well for falling off motorcycles; for an afternoon's hiking, they're not quite the thing. Fortunately, just by the parking lot there was a woman serving up burgers from a pie cart.

"Could you possibly look after my leathers and helmet for an hour or two?" I asked after I'd parked my bike alongside the cars.

"No worries," she replied. The New Zealanders are obliging like that. In England, they'd glare at you and assume the helmet contained a bomb. In New Zealand, the helmet might well harbor a bomb, but New Zealanders live sheltered lives and haven't figured that out yet.

And so, newly attired in shorts and sneakers, I marched off down the path to admire the trees.

It may seem strange to travel all that way just to look at a very old tree, but Tane Mahuta is special. It is sublimely, monumentally tall. Stretching high, soaring more than *160 feet* into the sky, Tane Mahuta towers over the Waipoua Forest.

I stood and stared. Tane Mahuta's trunk extended high and straight. For perhaps sixty feet it reached up into the sky, a vast, curving wall of pale-brown bark unhindered by branches. Then, from the top, the branches sprayed out from the central core, shooting thousands of tiny green oval-shaped leaves.

The branches were twisted and gnarled; some were broken. They looked spindly and vulnerable compared to the solid expanse of trunk that supported them, their raggedness betraying the tree's great age. Even for those of us who know nothing about trees, this was a phenomenal, breathtaking sight. It was a fabulous tree that sprouted character from every crack in its ancient bark. I loved it.

Tane Mahuta is reckoned to be about two thousand years old. Really, it was humbling just to think about. This tree put out its first roots at around the same time as Jesus Christ lived. And here it was, still growing away in a forest in the north of New Zealand, where I could touch it—or even attempt to hug it—quite freely.

There used to be even bigger trees than this one, but they fell victim to the lucrative timber industry and the gum trade that sprang up when kauri gum was found to make good varnishes; it was acquired much of the time by bleeding live trees. The kauri trees had a hard time of it. Happily, just before the whole lot was plundered, the government stepped in with its protective hand and one's no longer allowed to chop them down. This is good for the trees but sounded the death knell for that early incarnation of Kiwi bloke, the logger. The kauri trees were here to stay, but *he* was going to have to move on.

I walked back to the tiny roadside parking lot, climbed back on the bike, and wended my way a little further down the winding road to visit another tree, Te Matua Ngahere, the Father of the Forest. This one isn't as tall as Tane Mahuta, but it is stupendously, staggeringly fat, with a girth of more than fifty feet. If you laid three grown men in a line from head to toe along the ground, they'd just about stretch the same width as its gargantuan trunk. I've never been a great one for staring at boughs and branches and things, but here I just stood and gawked. It was sensational. It was just so *big*. So very New Zealand.

By the time I'd finished staring and clambered back on my bike once more, a light drizzle had started, adding to my nervousness—wet roads are slippery when you only have two wheels. I was going painfully slowly around the hairpin bends; an agonized camper was trailing behind me. It was embarrassing, really, to be riding this huge, glamorous motorcycle and to be going more slowly than an enormous, lumbering Britz rental camper. What were the couple inside saying to each other?

"What d'you reckon, Gladys," George from Utah was probably asking his wife, "this woman in front's going about as fast as Auntie Marjorie on her walker?"

"Nah," Gladys would have replied. "Auntie Marjorie's way faster."

They would have been quite right to question my competence. I should have been carving up the bends at wild angles, my armored kneepads skimming the asphalt. I wasn't.

As they labored behind me, I had to consider that I might have been better advised to drive a camper myself. The idea of having four wheels rather than two appealed. After all, I'd never heard of anyone falling off an RV. I could play CDs on the stereo. I could garner a whole new insight into New Zealand culture by listening to talk radio. And—the most seductive thought of all—with all those cupboards and closets, I could carry all the clothing I liked.

We lumbered on farther, around another bend, then another. Every couple of seconds I checked my mirrors—couldn't the camper just pull over into a turnout? Wouldn't its inhabitants find they fancied a stroll in the woods, a few minutes of tree-admiration? Couldn't they just get off my tail?

Clearly not. Minutes ticked by. We crawled on. My discomfort was intensifying now. Really, I was going pathetically slow. I wished I could just work up a little more courage, just take the corners at something approaching a respectable speed. Another motorcycle passed on the other side of the road. With a roar and a jaunty little tilt, it spun around the bend. My heart sank lower. There was no doubt about it: As a motorcyclist, I was utterly hopeless.

In the end, the ignominy of going more slowly than an RV got the better of me. The humiliation had to end and, as I didn't dare go any faster, the only option was to pull over and let it pass. The problem was that, on this windy road, there weren't many passing places. I would have to make a snap decision, and my balance wasn't really up to impulsive actions. I came around a bend and saw a small clearing to the left. I pulled over; it was covered in gravel. The motor home sailed past as I braked. The bike skidded on the gravel and I crashed to the ground.

A Dutch woman appeared as if from nowhere.

"Are you all right, are you all right?" she hollered, wringing her hands. I assured her that my body was fine, even if my pride had just taken yet another almighty battering and the plastic top-box holder on my motorcycle had sustained a fearsome crack.

"We must move the bike, oh my God it is heavy, where is my husband, Christoffel, *Christoffel*, CHRISTOFFEL!"

At this point, a portly Dutch gentleman trotted briskly out of the bushes (I have no idea what he was doing in there) and, between the three of us, we managed to heave the bike and its ridiculously weighty luggage to an upright position and wheel it out of the road before it came to grief under the wheels of another camper.

"You must rest for at least ten minutes," the Dutch woman instructed me in no uncertain tone. "You are looking very pale."

And with that, she and Christoffel disappeared.

I waited on the roadside for about three minutes; after that, I got bored and, checking carefully to make sure the Dutch couple were nowhere in sight, decided to disobey orders and go on my way.

That night I had been invited by some friends of friends of a friend to stay with them just outside the forest in the township of Omapere. (New Zealand, by the way, doesn't *do* villages. The word is just too, well, small.) New Zealand is like that—there aren't very many people, so they're all immensely hospitable both to one another and to outsiders. Everyone you meet gives you the phone numbers of at least five friends they insist you call upon as you pass through. The result of this is that your friendship circle soon branches and sprouts to quite unmanageable proportions.

"You absolutely must phone my friend Jemima if you're passing through Otago," they say, riffling through their address book. There's some confusion as they scour through the crossings-out. First there was the telephone number from when Jemima lived in Hamilton, when she was married to that layabout Phil who drank too much. Then, after an almighty showdown when she came home from work one day to find Phil naked and in a compromising situation in the kitchen with Grace from the dairy, she moved out and acquired a new number, but it changed again when, after much inner searching, she found herself and settled down in a new-age commune on the beach with a woman named Joy.

And then you find that Jemima's lover, Joy, is the best school friend of Rosemary, who used to be married to Joe, who is an old friend of Bill, the New Zealander who works in the pub in Clapham.

"It's extraordinary," Eileen, my hostess for the evening, said later as we drowned the rigors of the day in a glass of wine, "the way that in New Zealand, you can never go to a single social function without finding that one of the people you meet is the friend of another friend of yours." That's just one of the effects of living in a country with a population of just four million. And they all have to be nice to each other. You never know, you see, whether the motorist you just waved your fist at for cutting into your lane is going to turn out to be your boss's best friend Kevin. There's a popular joke that, had Jesus Christ been born in New Zealand, tongues would have been wagging: "Virgin my arse! I knew her in school."

Eileen talked about the local area and the problems that the widespread poverty in these parts creates. This part of Northland was one of the first areas to be settled by the Maori, and there's still a high concentration of Maori living here. In the eight hundred years between their ancestors' arrival in canoes and the appearance of the first Europeans, the Maori had organized themselves into tribes. They lived off the land, hunting birds and rats and planting crops such as kumara, a sweet potato, which they had brought from Polynesia.

After Europeans began to settle here, though, Maori culture rapidly declined. With the arrival of guns and Western diseases against which the Maori had no immunity, the numbers of Maori in New Zealand dropped from an estimated sixty thousand in 1858 to about forty-two thousand forty years later. Interbreeding saw the numbers of pure-blood

Maori dwindle further still. As the Pakeha culture and technology became dominant, the Maori over the decades left their tribes and ancestral lands and moved in large numbers to the cities. There, removed from their traditional cultural and family structures, they failed to flourish in European-style schools and workplaces.

Determined that the Maori should conform to Western models of education and culture, early Pakeha authorities forbade the Maori language to be spoken in schools. When Maori students floundered, it was assumed that this was because they were genetically predisposed to stupidity.

"The unemployment's as high as eighty percent around here," explained Eileen, who has lived in the area for more than twenty years; her sons, though British-born, both went to local schools and speak fluent Maori. We had settled down in her sitting room; outside, a storm was brewing. The trees' branches whipped and the wind wailed. "We're now starting to see third-generation unemployment, where neither the individual, nor his father, nor his grandfather has ever really held down a job." The side effects of this are poverty, disempowerment, crime, and domestic violence.

"The Maori people were warrior people. Now they have nothing. And the violence is a symptom of that," said Eileen. Back down the road in the Waipoua Forest, she said, they'd had to employ security guards to oversee the parking lots after break-ins became rife.

Before European contact, the Maori had channeled their so-called toughness into tribal warfare. On November 15, 1769, a few weeks after arriving in New Zealand, Captain Cook commented in his journal that the locals were certainly engaged in frequent warfare, "for the people who resided near the place where we wooded and who slept every night in the open air placed themselves in such a manner when they laid down to sleep as plainly shewed that it was necessary for them to be always upon their guard."

Their warrior heritage is played out in the haka, that frenzy of eye-rolling, chest-slapping, tongue-protruding, stamping, roaring dance, one particularly fearsome version of which is performed by the New Zealand national rugby team, the All Blacks, before every game they play across the globe.

But rugby and tourism are now just about the only outlets for traditional Maori warrior crafts. There are no more moa to hunt in our high-tech consumer world. The Maori have moved on, away from their tribes and into the cities, but in many cases their change of environment has led not to adaptation and strength but to virtual cultural collapse.

The next morning I packed up the bike and administered my own sticky, scrappy form of surgery to my top-box holder's crack with a roll of Eileen's packing tape. To be honest, I was starting to feel sorry for the bike. As the big-biceped man in Warkworth had said, it was a nice one, and I was hardly doing it justice. It was five days since I'd picked it up, and I'd only worked up the courage to actually ride it twice. I'd managed to drop it more than once. It was bruised and battered. Its accessories were scratched and cracked. I would have quietly apologized and muttered a promise to try harder from now on had it not been for the fact that Eileen might have heard, and I didn't want her to think that the solitary nature of my journey had reduced me to talking to a machine.

I headed off back through the forest once more. Because I'd traveled south to see the kauri trees yesterday and then back north to stay with Eileen, today I had to ride through the tight bends again as I was heading down to Auckland. It was turning out to be something of a torturous route.

Matters weren't helped by the very spirited wind that was still blowing strong from the storm that had brewed overnight. This is something nobody ever tells you about before you visit New Zealand. It would appear that the New Zealand Tourism Board has conspired with every Kiwi who has ever traveled abroad to make out that the weather in New Zealand is consistently fantastic. Before issuing passports to New Zealanders, they probably make them swear an oath never to let on that really, in actual fact, the weather in New Zealand can be quite foul.

Unlike the trees I was riding through, I am slight of stature. With the fierce crosswinds shrieking, just holding the bike on the right side of the road left me in severe danger of garnering a little definition to my biceps.

For several miles I sang "Rudolph, the Red-Nosed Reindeer" at full volume into my helmet in an attempt to convince myself that I wasn't scared. It didn't work. The wind was howling around me; I was clinging on for dear life, riding so slowly that the lines of traffic were building up behind me again.

At Matakohe I stopped to visit the Kauri Museum. I wandered around rooms full of slabs of wood and logging machinery, ate lunch in the restaurant, and gazed dolefully out of the window at the tree branches being buffeted about in the gale.

A couple of miles further down the road, I stopped at a tiny one-possum town to fill up with fuel. I drove neatly up to the pump, put the bike on its stand, and carefully climbed off on the pump side. But I didn't quite manage to get my leg over: My foot knocked the bike and, unbalanced by the weight of my luggage and its rather short stand, it toppled over, trapping me between itself and the pump. I flailed my arms uselessly around, but the situation was hopeless. I couldn't move the bike even an inch. I was stuck.

"Are you all right there?" A girl poked her head out of the shop doorway. She looked bemused.

No, of course I wasn't all right. I was pinned to a gas pump by a vast hulk of a motorcycle. She wandered over, grinning now, and helped me to hoist the bike upright so that I could finally fill the tank and hobble ashamedly away, etching a black mark against the name of another New Zealand town that I would never dare to visit again.

I had intended to check out the great tourist attraction of Sheepworld on my way into Auckland. It sounded like a hugely entertaining place where you can watch a sheep-shearing demonstration and—get this—you are even allowed to feed the lambs. But by the time I got there I'd been battling with the wind, the bike, and the demands of gas stations for several hours too many for such delights to entice me. I was exhausted, terrified, and badly in need of a long, hot bath.

Instead, I pressed on into the city and a short while later pulled up outside the Sebel Suites, where I was to spend the next few nights in unaccustomed luxury. I briefly considered carrying my own bags—I think motorcyclists are meant to be able to do that kind of thing—but quickly realized that after the rigors of the day, the effort would have been too much. I parked the bike illegally by the hotel door and went in to summon the immediate aid of the bellboy.

City Boys

THE REST OF NEW ZEALAND is very mean about Auck-landers. The city's nearest rivals in Wellington say you'd find more culture in a pot of yogurt. South Islanders shudder should they even have to pass through. The mere idea of walking across Queen Street's couple of lanes of crawling cars sets their hill-hardened legs a-tremble. The traffic! The crime! The pollution! They beat their T-shirt-clad chests. Then they start to froth at the mouth as they splutter that Aucklanders are greedy and self-obsessed, half of them can't even speak English, they're brash, they're brazen, they're, they're, they're ... RUDE!

For Auckland has committed the ultimate New Zealand crime. It laughs in the face of Tall Poppy Syndrome, the dic-tum that requires no one stands out from the crowd. It's here that the transformation of Kiwi Bloke into Sensitive New-Age Guy (SNAG) is most apparent. With its influx of Asian and Polynesian immigrants, Auckland is the most multicultural, cosmopolitan city in New Zealand, and it picks up new ideas first. The men here dare to dress in well-cut suits. They have the audacity to make money. With terrible indecency, they then go and spend it. They built the Sky Tower.

Of course, if you come from any other city across the globe, Auckland seems like a big, friendly green garden. You're kept waiting in lines in shops because the cashier is *chatting* with the person in front. The Viaduct Basin, glitzy and glamorous enough to make the average rural New Zealander fall facefirst into his herd of sheep, is really quite a groovy place to hang out. Indeed, it was where I had booked a room.

Ten years ago, Auckland's Viaduct Basin was lifeless. A derelict part of the city's port, its stagnant water was filled with toxins from the old fish-processing plants and sewage discharges. Then, in 1995, Sir Peter Blake and his crew brought home the world's most prestigious yachting title, the America's Cup, from the U.S.

Blake was an archetypal Kiwi bloke. He was building sailing boats in his backyard before he reached his teens. He epitomized the Kiwi sense of adventure and sportsmanship: As well as winning the America's Cup for New Zealand twice, he won the Whitbread around-the-world race and the Jules Verne Trophy for the fastest nonstop navigation of the globe. His trademarks were his lucky red socks—he apparently wore the same pair throughout the entire 1995 America's Cup Challenge. Presumably he wasn't wearing them that sad day in December 2001 when he was shot and killed by pirates during an environmental expedition in the Brazilian Amazon. The whole of New Zealand mourned his loss.

They knew nothing of the tragedy that was to come, though, when in 1995 Blake and his crew returned triumphant to New Zealand's shores with the America's Cup. New Zealand reveled in the victory with its characteristic David-versus-Goliath jubilation. When New Zealand defended the Cup in the next challenge, five years later, the glamorous sailing event came to Auckland. The Viaduct was chosen as the site for the America's Cup Village; the waterfront areas that surrounded it became attractive to private investors, who built expensive apartment complexes and upscale bars and restaurants over-looking the marina. There are plenty of men here, but they're wealthy bankers dining alongside the boat crowds who pose on the decks of their yachts. In the Viaduct Basin, there's not a black T-shirt or a gum boot to be seen.

My hotel room was so sleek that, for a brief moment, I wondered whether I had to bother with the world outside at all. The furnishings were minimalist and chic. There was a groovy little kitchen area that was a far cry from the peeling Formica and chipped cups of my motel room up in Paihia. This, after all, was Auckland, where image counts.

With a level of excitement that I'm now slightly ashamed to recount, I whipped open all the drawers and cupboards to find out what thrills were lurking within. Inside a very stylish chrome drawer at the bottom of one of the units, I found a little dish-washer. On the opposite wall, a built-in closet hid a washing machine and dryer. Desperately eager to play with all my new appliances, I threw open my panniers. With wild abandon, I hurled my laundry into the washing machine, chucked in the complimentary detergent, and, with a gleeful flourish, pressed the button marked *POWER*. There was a glorious gurgle and a deeply satisfying churn. And then, realizing that if I was to play in the kitchen area I'd need accessories, I went out to in-vestigate another facet of New Zealand culture—the super-market.

I like going to supermarkets in other countries. It's strange, because I don't find going to the supermarket at home very enthralling at all. But overseas, even in places like New Zealand, which are eerily similar to England in many ways, the supermarkets have different smells, packages of curiously shaped animal parts, and brightly colored fruits that surely didn't come from any tree on planet Earth.

I loaded my very conventional groceries onto the conveyor belt: some recognizable peaches, bananas, and tomatoes, a loaf of bread, some butter and some ham, and a six-pack of beer.

"ID," grunted the teenager at the checkout.

"I'm sorry?" I thought I'd misheard.

"ID *please*." She glared. Here was one person who had been smoking behind the bike shed the day they taught helpfulness at school. But what was unbelievable was not that I had found a churlish New Zealander. More incredible was that I was being ID-checked for buying a six-pack of beer. I was thirty-two years old; the minimum age at which you're allowed to buy alcohol in New Zealand is eighteen.

Naturally, I was entirely delighted and would have kissed the surly checkout girl had it not been for the sturdy conveyor belt that stood between us, and her rather oily skin. With joy in my eyes, I fished out my driver's license from my wallet and gleefully handed it over.

The checkout girl looked blank. She had clearly never seen a British driver's license before. She screwed up her pimply nose.

"D'we take this?" she said to the bag-packing boy, who at least had the decency to look embarrassed. He, it seemed, knew an old hag when he saw one. Behind me in the line, a couple of Kiwi blokes grinned.

My sense of humor, however, was fast fading. It was quite entertaining to be asked for ID, but to be refused beer would be an entirely different matter.

"Yes you do," I informed her with the authoritative tone that comes only with age, with the experience of having had to lie convincingly many times before. "It's a driver's license. And there's my date of birth"—I jabbed my wrinkled finger at the spot—"1970."

The girl looked vaguely confused—she didn't have thirty-two fingers to count with—and ran the beer over the scanner.

Alcohol consumption is something of an issue in New Zealand. Most people will tell you the Kiwis drink an awful lot. In fact, they take a shockingly low twenty-third place in the world, according to a recent survey of alcohol consumption. The legal age for buying and consuming alcohol in public places was only reduced from twenty to eighteen in 1999. At the same time, the ban on supermarkets selling beer was lifted, and pubs and liquor stores were, for the first time, allowed to trade on Sundays.

The fact that this relaxation in the law only happened a few years ago, and that there was considerable opposition to it, suggests that New Zealand, rather than being populated by alcoholics, is actually discouragingly wholesome. In a few remaining districts—such as West Auckland, and Geraldine and Invercargill on South Island—supermarkets are still barred from selling alcohol, and it's the local residents who have voted for the prohibition. During my trip, there was an ongoing debate in the papers about the worrying fact that *Coronation Street* (one of New Zealand's most popular television shows) might be socially damaging because so much of the action takes place in the Rovers Return Inn.

New Zealand has always had a strong core of puritans. In the early days of European–Maori contact, male-dominated crew culture ruled—whalers, sailors, gold-diggers, and the like—and they tended to drink rather a lot. In mid-nineteenth-century Auckland there was one conviction for drunkenness for every eight people living there. Meanwhile, the Wellington beaches were so littered with bottles that Governor Fitz-Roy remarked that it was unsafe to walk there. (This FitzRoy, incidentally, was the same man as the Captain FitzRoy who steered Darwin and the *Beagle* to these shores back in the 1830s.)

But toward the turn of the century, the nature of employment changed and the crews started to die out. The number of European families moving to New Zealand not for sporadic work but in search of a clean, green life rocketed, and the moral zealots found fertile ground. It was around this time that the crusade for the prohibition of alcohol began in earnest.

In 1917, a law was passed requiring pubs to close at six p.m.—and they didn't reopen in the evening until 1967. It didn't stop people drinking, of course. It just made them determined to drink more quickly and led to the so-called six o'clock swill, whereby men left the workplace at five and then dedicated the next hour to guzzling as much booze as they could squeeze into their fast-burgeoning bellies. But beer was often watered down, so that drinking enough to become intoxicated became a feat of physical fortitude in itself. The anti-drink brigade attempted to further discourage consumption by forbidding drinkers to buy rounds. In some areas, the temperance movement was more successful still and managed to ban alcohol altogether; nationwide prohibition was only outvoted by a tiny majority. Still, despite their efforts, the old crew concept that a true man can hold his beer persists in twenty-first-century New Zealand, as it does else-where.

The following night, I had the chance to see for myself whether New Zealand men can handle their drink. A friend of mine, Gordi, is a policeman in Auckland. He was working the night shift and had offered to take me along in the patrol car. It was a Saturday night a few weeks before Christmas, a fine opportunity to see whether Aucklanders were *real* men—or whether they were, God help us, a lily-livered aberration of masculinity who couldn't hold their drink.

"This is the radio," said Gordi, picking up a small black box at the end of a spiraling wire. "If ever Dave and I are out of the car and it looks like we're in trouble, you press this button and then let go, and someone will speak to you. Our call sign is AVI three."

Now, hold on a minute. Who said anything about *trouble*? I had been quite excited about going for a ride in a police car, but I hadn't counted on actually having to *do* anything. I hadn't considered that I might be called upon to make split-second life-or-death decisions. What constituted trouble, anyway? Was I to call for help at the first sight of a bad-tempered burglar—or should I wait until Gordi and Dave were both lying in pools of blood while the crazed psychopath who had done them in stalked over to the car in which I was cowering, the iron cross-bar raised above his head ready to batter me to a pulp? I could see him now, leering through the window of the car, yellowish drool dribbling down his sagging, stubbled jowls, his eyes blood-shot, his breath misting up the glass, and the heady stench of alcohol oozing in toward me....

"Yes, fine. No problem," I said to Gordi blithely.

It was all right for him. Gordi is a big guy. At six foot two and weighing in at something over two hundred pounds, he's not carrying a lot of fat. He spends most of his spare time running up and down basketball courts and rugby pitches. When he comes up in fights against bad guys in the street, he usually wins. Dave, his partner, was smaller and younger: Tonight was just his fifth day of being a policeman. He wasn't carrying Gordi's weight, but beneath his pale-blue policeman's shirt he looked suitably lithe. If two fit men like Gordi and Dave found themselves in hot water, what on earth would become of *me*? I was thankful to be wearing my sneakers. At least running away was an option.

Sitting in the backseat, I explained the purpose of my New Zealand odyssey to Dave.

"Great," said Dave, "so what kind of bike are you riding? A nice little two-fifty?"

"Well, no. Actually, I'm riding a six-fifty," I said with what I hoped sounded like intrepidity and daring.

"And she's only just passed her test," muttered Gordi from the driver's seat, through what seemed to be a clenched jaw. I slunk slightly into my seat. I hadn't really needed reminding of that. There was a weighty silence from the boys in blue.

As we patrolled the bars looking for trouble, we came upon Steve. He was arguing with the bouncers of a bar, who didn't want to let him in. He was a short, thickset Polynesian man with long, tousled hair in a rough ponytail. There was a protracted scene as first the bouncers, then his friends, and finally the police tried to persuade him to go home. It must have gone on for twenty minutes, maybe longer. And then he urinated on the sidewalk. Steve didn't much like being arrested, and it took a while to wrestle him into the handcuffs and into the car as he screamed obscenities. Down at Auckland Central, swear words emanated at high volume from his cell, accompanied by bone-crunching crashes against the cell door.

"He's going to hurt himself," I said anxiously.

"Well, he's not going to hurt the door," said Dave.

Here, it seemed, was a man who couldn't hold his drink. In Steve's case, it wasn't so much that he was sensitive and new-age; he didn't look like the type who ought to have been drinking sparkling water instead. It was more that he'd gotten his warrior heritage in a muddle. He had failed to understand that it was no good fighting handcuffs and a solid metal door. He desperately wanted to be tough but was having some trouble channeling his fighting spirit. Here was a man who might have been happy had there still been moa to hunt, but who hadn't quite figured out how to adapt his masculinity to the twenty-first century. He hadn't cottoned on to the fact that this need to find an outlet for aggression in a sedentary industrial world was the very reason why they invented rugby.

As Gordi and Dave sorted out the formalities surrounding Steve's arrest, I sat behind the glass partition and watched as the other miscreants came in. It was fascinating. Through that clanging metal door came the whole array of Saturday-night Auckland, all out for a good time, all making a glorious mess of it.

A twenty-something aircraft engineer in very high spirits probably should have been drinking mineral water or, at the very most, Sol with a wedge of lime. A bottle of the Mexican lager would have nicely complemented his beige chinos and striped linen shirt. Give him a few years and a couple of gray hairs and he'd be an expert at changing diapers. In the meantime, however, he had been out drinking with his mates at the Viaduct, where he had commandeered a scissor lift and driven

it along the pedestrian waterfront. He explained to the officers that, in fact, the scissor lift's owners had broken the law
by having left the machinery in some kind of illegal state.

"Do you really want to charge this guy or should we hire
him for a training session?" the desk sergeant in charge of booking prisoners asked the arresting officers. The young engineer
seemed to know the ropes, cheerfully surrendering the contents of his pockets and belt. The desk sergeant asked him if
he'd been arrested before.

"Yes, once."

"When was that?"

" 'Bout two years ago."

"And what was that for?"

The guy laughed and shrugged affably enough. "Aw, same
kinda thing really. Just being an idiot."

Everyone nodded in agreement.

A teenage graffitist was cooperating and behaving himself.
There was absolutely nothing macho about him. He hadn't
even been *trying* to drink. He looked like a nice enough kid.
The desk sergeant asked for his home phone number, "just so
we can call your parents and let them know where you are."
The boy closed his eyes and shuddered. He looked palpably
sick.

Gordi and Dave had finished their paperwork and we went
back out to the streets. The next candidate for the cells was,
quite simply, mad. A down-and-out with long, shaggy facial
hair and wildly dancing eyes, he stank like an old goat. He
wouldn't leave a boardinghouse when asked to do so; this was
the third time in a week that the police had been called out to
collect him. But he was a very happy man who laughed all the
way to the clink.

After that came a newly immigrated Kiwi bloke: an Afghani

boy, aged twenty, who had been living in New Zealand for a little more than a year. He called out the cops because he was being tailed in his car. It turned out that he knew the kid who was following him: They'd been friends for the last year.

"Er, yeah." He shuffled his feet and grinned when asked if he knew the boy in the car behind. "Yeah, I knew it was my friend, but he wouldn't answer his cell phone when I called, so I got scared and called the police."

You total fuckwit, I wanted to shout at him. Do you have shit for brains? But being terribly restrained, I didn't. His license was in order and he hadn't been drinking. He was let off. Perhaps there's no charge for utter idiocy.

The radio crackled into action once more. This time it was an incident of domestic violence. Gordi hit the sirens; the car eagerly leapt forward and we hurtled with great enthusiasm down the street. Cars parted before us, peeling off to the sides and screeching to a halt in the gutter. We jumped lights, scorched around corners, streaked through the city streets. It was immensely exhilarating. As we tore around the final corner, Gordi called out, "You all right in the back?"

All right? I hadn't been so enthralled since I hugged the two-thousand-year-old tree.

"Oh yes," I replied, as the car slowed down outside the house to be visited. "I liked that a lot."

Gordi and Dave laughed, unclipped their seat belts, and got out of the car.

Inside, Carla and Mike had been having an alcohol-fueled argument about the volume of the music: Mike kept turning it up and Carla kept turning it down. Carla reckoned that, in the course of the argument, Mike had shoved her. So she called the police to sort out the fight. Here were a couple of fine examples of people who didn't deal well with the demon drink. Their house was down-at-the-heels; thin wooden partitions divided the rooms. Cheap pictures in peeling gilt frames decorated the walls—a fluffy white cat in a pink haze, a mass-produced print of the city of Nelson.

Clearly, there wasn't a great deal of domestic violence here, just a couple of tragic drunks. We left them to it, then a few minutes later were called back. This time it was Mike who had called the cops, because Bill, Carla's cousin, had apparently pushed him. We found Mike sitting in the kitchen, looking sorry for himself, very drunk, in a satin robe a little too short to be entirely attractive. What Mike didn't know was that the back of the robe had got tucked up into the bottom of his briefs. He was probably in his midforties. He droned on about how Bill had assaulted him. Carla and Bill and another cousin, Olly, sat looking morose in the living room, spaced out, glazed over. The six brain cells they possessed between them had been fried long ago.

Bernie, the sergeant, was also there this time and suggested that, as it was three a.m., perhaps they should go to bed.

"Which is your bedroom, Mike?"

"Yeah, this one."

"Okay, Mike, I want you to go to bed now."

"Yeah, I'm going."

But he wouldn't go. "It's him, Officer, he assaulted me," he kept whining.

"Now, come on, Mike, go to bed," said Bernie. "You realize if we have to come back here again we're going to have to take you down the station.... This is your last chance.... Come on, Mike, go to bed now."

It was like shepherding an overtired small child who has too much orange soda in his bloodstream. Eventually Mike went into the bedroom; Bernie shut the door and tried to persuade the tranced-out living-room crowd it was bedtime for them too. Then Mike reappeared, a pitiful expression on his face.

"Please, Officer, I need to go to the toilet."

Mike returned from the bathroom; Carla went with him into the bedroom.

"Will you be okay in there with him, Carla?" asked Bernie. "Is he going to give you any grief about this?"

"Aw, don't you worry, I know how to handle *him*," Carla fairly spat.

"I ain't never hit no woman, I ain't never, er, done anyfing to no woman," Mike's sad whining droned from beyond the bedroom door.

We waited in the garden just to make sure they'd really turned in. Lights went on and off and on again, but finally the house went quiet.

Until ten minutes later, when the radio kicked in once more. This time it was the neighbor who called: Mike, Carla, and Bill had broken out into a fresh bout of fighting.

We swung around, and as we arrived in the street Mike hurtled past us on his mountain bike. When we caught up with him, he burst into loud, sorrowful sobs.

"Aw, you're not crying, are you? You big baby," said Gordi.

"I'm not a baby," bawled Mike, and then he started to wail, "You've ruined my life. I wanted to become a security guard, but now you've ruined my life."

Honey, nobody's ruined your life. You never had one, I wanted to tell him.

"A real Kiwi bloke?" I asked Gordi as we drove to the police station, with Mike blubbing in the back. Gordi frowned.

"Hey, Mike, where were you born?" he asked. But the answer

was not the one he wished for. Mike was the true progeny of New Zealand: a genuine, full-blooded example of Kiwi manhood.

The surveys were correct. This was a species in crisis. As for me, well, I'm not sure what it says about the state of my social life, but that was the most stimulating Saturday night I'd had in years.

I went to sleep that night to the sounds of wild revelry on the Viaduct down below my hotel window. When I woke on Sunday morning, things weren't much quieter—this weekend, racing was scheduled. I sat in my fluffy white hotel bathrobe, looked down on the action from my supreme vantage point, and, feeling entirely content with the world, drank my coffee. It was a jovial scene, the perfect backdrop to my sleepy, Sunday-morning breakfast.

This wasn't the America's Cup per se but one of the rounds of the Louis Vuitton Challenger Series that preceded it. The racing had been canceled yesterday due to the high winds, but today the yachts, their support crews, the patrol tugs, police rib boats, corporate gin palaces, and tourist rafts were heading out beneath the early-December sun, their horns blasting with merry optimism. Along the waterfront, the staff in the bars and restaurants had swept up the debris from the party crowd who had gone home to bed just a couple of hours ago and were now serving breakfast and short blacks, as New Zealanders call espresso.

Thinking I'd better get in on the action, I dressed in my very own sunglasses and shorts and wandered up Queen Street to buy jandals. For the Kiwis, masters of casual dress, even jandals—flip-flops to the rest of us—are verging on the dangerously formal, a bit of a wimp's way out. In this country they frequently eschew shoes altogether and walk around barefoot, even on city streets and in shopping malls.

"Why are the children not wearing shoes?" I'd asked Gordi on my first trip to New Zealand two years ago as we'd wandered around the supermarket picking up provisions. He looked totally blank.

"Shoes? Why should they wear shoes?" Judging from the expression on his face, I might as well have asked why they weren't wearing chain mail, or codpieces, or some other outmoded form of protective dress.

"Well," I replied primly, "they might cut their feet."

"Teach 'em to toughen up," said Gordi. And that was the end of that.

For myself, wearing jandals was as far as I was prepared to go. My feet, after all, are English and soft.

Newly decked out, I headed back to the Viaduct, where I had arranged to meet some friends of a friend—Mary, Bill, and their son, Tiggy—for coffee. Mary and Bill are both psychotherapists. It struck me as an unusual occupation for New Zealand, where the people don't give the impression they'd spend their cash on any kind of talking cure. New Zealanders, I was still convinced, were supposed to be tough and taciturn, not given to such luxuries as therapy. I asked Mary and Bill if this was the case. They laughed; they had more business than they were able to handle.

"You see, immigration is very traumatic," Mary explained, "and everyone here at some point came from somewhere else."

"But surely that's generations back for most people?" I asked.

"For some, yes, but the trauma still surfaces in later generations," Mary said.

It was an interesting idea. I thought about those nineteenth-century loggers, those men who sailed halfway across the world looking for a new livelihood, then spent months on end living in rough shanties in the rain-drenched forests, hacking at those vast trees by hand. I couldn't really imagine them going into therapy to talk about the upheaval. Yet, a few generations later, their great-grandchildren were doing just that. They'd moved on from that exterior toughness, from that obvious physical struggle, and seemed to be wrestling with something else. Maybe that summed up the transformation of the Kiwi bloke. Where he used to be silent and stoic, nowadays not only can he talk about his feelings but he pays a therapist to analyze them.

Later, I asked Gordi about New Zealanders and therapy. He looked astonished and grunted. Perhaps he was of the old school.

Along the Viaduct, the sun was shining. Christmas carols blared while ice-cream vendors tapped their toes to the tune. Santa mopped the sweat from his brow as he and his elf hunted for their lost reindeer. A couple dressed up as a clockwork soldier and a clockwork fairy woodenly strutted about, laughing and chatting with onlookers, and hopeful street performers blasted out what was turning out to be a great Southern Hemisphere favorite, "Winter Wonderland."

Except, of course, that it was summer. It was a very curious thing, beneath the blazing hot sun, that all the Christmas songs the performers sweltering in their Santa outfits chose to sing were the snowy ones.

"Dashing through the snow, in a one-horse open sleigh,"

trilled a group of girls in tiny red hot pants and Christmas hats.

A less alarmingly dressed man with a guitar was dreaming of a white Christmas. He could keep dreaming.

The strange thing is, there are plenty of perfectly jaunty Southern Hemisphere Christmas songs that you'd think might suit a hot day at the waterfront better. There's Sticky Beak the kiwi, who volunteered to oust the reindeer and escort Santa through the Southern Hemisphere himself.

Or how about:

> On the first day of Christmas
> My true love gave to me
> A pukeko in a ponga tree.

But for some reason New Zealanders seemed to be fixated on the snowy cold-weather theme. The shop fronts were festooned with cotton-ball snow and silver-glitter frost. The Christmas cards were white and wintry. And when I asked people just why they persisted in evoking sub-zero temperatures in the middle of summer, those very same people who had just helpfully enlightened me with the information that Europe is dark, dank, overcrowded, and full of criminals, that the Queen's a fossil and Prince Charles's ears stick out, and that Britain is a terrible place because you can't buy proper Marmite, shuffled their feet and said, "Yeah, well, it's our colonial heritage, eh."

That afternoon, I booked myself a place on the ocean-rafting trip out into the Hauraki Gulf to see the start of the semifinal race. With great anticipation for the adventure ahead, we piled onto the boat—a couple of Italian guys with bronzed faces and floppy, sleek black hair, a Brazilian couple, a foursome of skinny, tanned German girls, and me—and wrapped ourselves in our calf-length black waterproof coats and bright zip-up life jackets. And then, just as we were about to leave, a rotund figure bounced down onto the jetty. Santa was dressed in a vast sack of red velour. The white fur cuff of his hat almost perfectly matched the real bushy beard that sprouted across his face, reaching thickly from one ear to the other. Stretching the straps of his life jacket to their fullest capacity, he heaved himself into the boat and settled his capacious belly into one of the back rows of seats.

"Have you been good?" he bellowed as he smeared white pasty streaks of zinc-oxide cream across his nose, forehead, and cheeks. Then he beamed his biggest Santa smile; the boat's engines roared to life and, with a wave and a ho ho ho, we set off across the waves.

It's weird, I know, because this wasn't really Santa but some strange man dressed up in a silly red costume with a pillow stuffed down his front, but his presence on the boat was somehow entrancing. Many years had passed since I'd last had a chat with Santa and, in an admittedly infantile way, I was delighted to see him. What with the police car, the sirens, the boat trip, and the interaction with Santa Claus, this was turning out to be a fun-packed weekend. Everyone else might be rude about the city, but I was beginning to think that Auckland was truly tremendous.

It was another windy day and the boat, a high-powered in-flatable, hurtled unforgivingly over the choppy sea. We flew from our seats as we took off from the crest of each wave and then winced as we crashed down hard onto the water below. I clung to the handrail in front of me but couldn't work out how best to sit—ramming my legs against the seat in front saved me from taking off and therefore from the spine-crunching crashes, but after ten minutes my legs were covered in huge, swollen bruises.

"Oh, bloody hell," Santa whispered from behind me. After the first couple of minutes, his ho ho hos had become distinctly plaintive. Now they'd petered out altogether. The three furry pom-poms that ran down his chest and belly became damp with the salty spray and started to droop, then to drip.

Eventually, we arrived at the start line and were told that the racing had been postponed due to the high winds. Our driver steered us instead into the sandy bays of the gulf, to check out the yachts of the well-to-do and to let our now even whiter Santa muster up a little festive cheer.

"Merry Christmas, merry Christmas," he boomed, standing up and waving regally from behind the inflated yellow sides of the dinghy. Women with perfectly manicured toenails condescended to smile. Their children laughed and waved back.

"Have you been good?" Santa's voice rang out across the choppy waves.

"Yeah, of course," the kids chorused back. And then, because they'd learned from their go-getting Aucklander parents that brash is good but barefacedly brazen is better, they called out, "Got any presents?"

Santa's hands were stout and work-hardened. A small, faded tattoo beneath the thumb and forefinger of his right hand peeked out from the fluffy white cuff of his baggy velvet sleeve and betrayed the fact that his companions in life had not always been reindeer and elves.

Santa had, in a former life, been a sailor. He'd served in the New Zealand Navy for twenty years, based right here in the

Hauraki Gulf. I don't know if he knew the names of all his reindeer, as I never tested him, but he was pretty good on the names of the hulking gray frigates moored outside the naval base. He seemed to know all about virtually everything else we passed as well; islands and lighthouses, dinghies and yachts, he was on first-name terms with all of them. It sounded as though Santa, once, had been quite a Kiwi bloke. The faded tattoos indicated that he might once have been halfway tough. But what had happened? Now, instead of hanging out with hardy seamen, he was spending his days with elves. He had swapped his sailor suit for a red velvet Santa outfit and was spending his summer in a shopping mall in a suburb south of Auckland—that's to say *in public*—sitting children on his knee and dispensing presents from his sack. Was Santa's descent from down-to-earth bloke to fairy-tale figure a sign of what was happening to New Zealand men in general? If so, he didn't seem to have much of a problem with it.

"I'm having the best summer of my life." He grinned. "Anyway, what're you doing here?"

I told him I was writing a book about Kiwi blokes and riding a motorcycle round the country.

"Ah yeah?" said Santa. "What kind of bike you riding?"

"Oh," I said nonchalantly, trying to be cool, "a Suzuki Freewind—six-fifty cc."

Santa raised his bushy white eyebrows. "So you're pretty experienced on motorcycles then?"

"Um, well, not exactly," I replied. "Actually, I just passed my test."

Santa's beard-clad jaw dropped a couple of inches. "Christ, you must be nuts," he muttered darkly.

On the way back, I figured out that the solution to the leg-battering, spine-shattering problem was simply to stand in a kind of squat with my thighs against the back of the seat and to let my legs take the impact. After I'd gotten the technique perfected, the trip was pretty fun. The racing may have been postponed, but our driver made up for it by spinning us around at high velocity in tight circles and figure eights just to ensure we'd had our money's worth. The Kiwis, after all, are never ones to take your money from you without making sure you've been scared silly.

I said good-bye to Santa, and he gave me a kiss. I'd never been kissed by a Santa before, and I'm not at all sure Santas are supposed to indulge in that kind of thing.

Men in Sheds

IF YOU OVERLOOK THE FACT that a building had inconveniently fallen down on the main road out of town, and the fact that the traffic was gridlocked on Auckland's southern highway following an accident, I managed to leave the city the following morning without incident. This was due in part to the very rigorous luggage cull that I had exercised the night before.

The *cafetière* for one and the packet of Lavazza Espresso, bought to save me from lackluster starts to the day in small-town hotel rooms, hit the reject pile. They would have to sit for the next few months relegated to the bottom of a newly bought America's Cup carryall in the back of Gordi's wardrobe. So would the trail-running shoes. Neither the funky white flared jeans nor the Earl Jeans denim jacket for which I had nearly taken out a second mortgage made it to the final cut. The small stash of educational literature would have to be read on the flight home. The generous supply of underwear wouldn't be coming on the road with me either: A couple of pairs of panties and a tube of travel wash were going to have to do. I was paring things down to the barest of minimums. This was a survival kit, in a situation where survival was far from assured.

Such stern measures, however, had the necessary result. The bike was now transformed into a different beast. No longer did I quake at the thought of a traffic light turning red; now I could, after a fashion, handle the bike. It was leaner and lither, and my terror slowly, slowly started to subside.

I was heading southeast, to Waihi, at the bottom of the Coromandel Peninsula. Famous for its gold-mining past, the town might be a good introduction to the so-called crew culture, give me an insight into the hardened men who followed the gold rushes, who worked hard, lived hard, and drank hard. In short, they *were* hard—and their legacy has been imprinted on New Zealand's masculinity ever since.

I rode for an hour or so in a sufficiently competent manner to ensure that I neither dropped the bike nor attracted the attention of the local constabulary. I stopped to fill up with gas, and managed it without making a major fool of myself. As I was dispensing my fuel, a truck driver sauntered over to my pump.

"I'm really sorry if I was following you too close," he said.

Actually he had been rather close, and I'd been wondering why he didn't just get on with it and pass me. It wasn't until we were at the gas station and I saw the vast, double-articulated truck he was driving that I understood.

"No, not at all," I replied, in keeping with the Kiwi spirit of helpfulness. "I'm sorry I was going so slowly. It's the wind. It makes me nervous. Why don't I wait till you're done here and let you go out first so that I don't hold you up again?"

"Aw no, don't worry. There's no way I'll keep up with you through the gorge," he replied.

Gorge? I gulped. Oh my goodness, was it going to be all tight little bends and steep hills like the road through Waipoua Forest? How embarrassed would I be if I really did go more slowly than a double-articulated truck? I climbed back on the bike. Bracing myself, I turned the throttle. The bike let out an all-devouring roar, and together we hit the sweeping bends.

Waihi is a couple of hundred miles and a whole world away from Auckland. Here the 1870s meet the 1970s. Of the twenty-first century, there's nothing to be seen. The main street, like an immaculate American Wild West, was deserted. In its heyday, in the early 1900s, Waihi was one of New Zealand's most prosperous gold-mining towns. The Martha Mine, named after a relative of one of the early prospectors, opened in the late 1870s and for a while was one of the most productive mines in the world. Eight thousand people lived here. Today, there was scarcely a soul about.

The roadway, brand-new and perfectly black, swept to either side of a central island littered with yellow flowers. Above them loomed wrought-iron lampposts complete with flag masts from which fluttered wholesome Christmas images, white doves and futile supplications for peace on earth. The one-story wooden buildings seemed to hark back to earlier times with their outmoded painted lettering: "Guinness Appliances," one bright-red billboard announced, jutting in triangular splendor from its blue-painted shop front, "100% Your Electric Store." Next door stood a sand-colored building with a corrugated-iron awning, below which hung in a mixture of capitals and italic lettering: "*Waihi* DRY CLEANERS *and* LAUNDRY." On the other side of the electrical store was the public library, its pale blue weatherboard, rectangular dark-blue-framed picture windows, and colonnade along the rooftop an architectural reminder of Waihi's prosperous prospecting days at the turn of the century.

The library displayed a notice in its window advertising that it offered Internet access. I went in to check my e-mail.

"Oh. It's busy at the moment," said the woman at the desk, looking over to the girl furiously typing at the library's one computer. "It will be free at half past twelve."

That was forty-five minutes away. I went to the café next door, ate a large slice of moist, rich carrot cake, drank coffee, read the local paper. I wandered around the visitor information center at the end of the street; I went to the greengrocer's and bought fruit. An hour later—ample time, I thought, for the girl to have finished her typing—I went back to the library. A different person, a mustachioed man, was now hammering at the keyboard. The woman at the desk looked at me reproachfully.

"I told you half past twelve," she said. "Now there are no free slots till three."

I thanked her and decided to forgo contact with the outside world for a day or two. The sole computer in Waihi was clearly in hot demand. Instead, I continued my tour of the town.

On the corner by the traffic circle, the Rob Roy Hotel showed none of the bawdiness it would have known back in the bad old days of the gold rush. Its weatherboard was bright white. Between the veranda posts, painted signs swung and creaked in the breeze: "Accommodation," "Games Lounge," "Bedrooms from $20." The hotel is now a backpackers' hostel. In the past, miners from all over the world would have come here in search of fame and fortune. Now Japanese and Germans brewed instant noodles where once crowds of diggers came in search of beer and girls.

Further along gleamed the garish red-and-white candy-stripe awnings of KFC. The grinning face of Colonel Sanders leered from a giant replica paper cup on top of a pole like a strangely wholesome Big Brother surveying the empty streets below. But even he seemed to wear a slightly bemused, questioning expression.

"This is a very pleasant, pristine town," he seemed to say, "but where are all the people? Who is going to eat my finger-lickin' chicken wings? Where's the fun? Where's it all happening?"

It wasn't here.

After its closure in 1952, the Martha Mine reopened in the 1980s and is still operating today. This one mine produces over one million New Zealand dollars' worth of gold and silver each week. I went to visit it. I thought that perhaps at the mine—the gleaming, glittering life force of this rather quiet town—I would find a pulse.

The viewing platform lay on top of a hill on the outskirts of town. Through the grid of fencing and the six rows of barbed wire that determinedly kept visitors at their distance, the Martha Mine descended in giant, sandy steps to a vast, drab quarry bed below. Up and down the pathways that were formed by these terraces, trucks and diggers hummed, their bright-orange and yellow paintwork dulled by the dust. Against the lush rolling hills that rose and fell in the background, the mine was a lusterless blot. It resembled a very large sandpit, an endless, dreary building site. Though, presumably, there were men sitting inside the cabs of those brightly colored machines, there wasn't actually a person to be seen. The mine seemed entirely mechanized, lacking in humanity, in any kind of real life. Gold was still being dug here, but these men didn't need to be hardy. They could sit in a nice warm cab with a cup of coffee and a bun, I presumed, shouting back at talk radio as they worked.

It was strangely disappointing. With hindsight, I'm not quite sure what I was expecting. I suppose it was unrealistic to hope that dazzling nuggets of glistening gold would be piled up on the roadside. Deep down, I think I knew that gold doesn't actually come out of the ground that way. But it might have been nice to see something more inspiring than a big, faceless sandpit. It would have been soothing to glimpse a person or two so that some form of humanity could be introduced to this huge, dollar-wielding dustbowl. I pressed my nose against the wire fence, watched the great yellow diggers trundle up and down, and tried to muster up some enthusiasm. And then, a couple of minutes later, I gave up and went on my way.

Other than creating a big sandy hole in the ground, the rumblings of the new Martha Mine have had one other undesired effect in Waihi. When the mine reopened, the ground started to shift with the unaccustomed vibrations, and the hundred-odd miles of disused underground tunnels from the original mine became unstable. Then, one night in December 2001, they swallowed a house whole.

It was just after midnight, and the Kilgour family—a young couple with three children—was tucked up in bed. At twelve-fifteen a.m. the ground shook, and then, with a judder and a whoosh, their entire house, their RV, and two cars, along with the neighbor's garage and car, dropped fifty feet into a disused mine shaft under their home's foundations. The family was pulled out alive, if somewhat surprised.

The powers that be duly looked into the matter and drew up a list of other properties that might fall into holes in the ground sometime soon.

"But don't you worry," said Josie, the white-haired owner of the bed-and-breakfast I was staying in that night, as she came to the end of this calamitous tale. I was sitting on an armchair belonging to her floral-patterned suite, drinking a cup of tea. "It's only the garden that's at risk. The house itself is quite safe."

"*This house?*"

Josie laughed. Strangely, she didn't look too worried. She seemed to think that the whole debacle of houses vanishing into holes in the ground was a lot of fuss about nothing and the surveyors and their pens were just out to be a nuisance.

I know that New Zealanders are meant to be practical, imperturbable, and unflappable—but I am not a New Zealander. On the contrary, I am prone to the occasional neurosis. And the prospect of my bed for the night disappearing into a crater was as likely as anything to provoke one.

I did my best to look unconcerned. I hoped fervently that Josie was right and it was just the possums in the garden that needed to worry. With an affected air of nonchalance, I sipped my tea and expressed great delight at the fact that her compensation check had arrived in the mail that morning. She still had to move out of her home of twenty-one years—which had, with a stroke of a surveyor's pen, become worthless—but at least she could now pay for the new place she'd found down the street.

That night, on television, they were showing a program called *The Kiwi Male Revealed.*

"I think we're a nation of one-night stands," said a bartender sorrowfully. The TV host went on to inform us that the New Zealand male is one of the most sexually active in the world. Apparently, the average Kiwi man loses his virginity when he's 16.9 years old. The only people doing it earlier are the French, the Germans, and the Americans.

Perhaps this explains the mutation in New Zealand men, I thought. Lots of sex with lots of different partners would speed up change. Wild, licentious sex is brilliant for an evolving species: The man spreads his seed as widely as he can, and the women pick the fittest partners. Genetic variation is rampant, and this allows the species to adapt more quickly to its changing environment. Being a sit-at-home family man who only ever does it with the wife is no good for an evolving species at all.

The program paused for a commercial break. A blond-haired, blue-eyed man in a Santa hat strolled amid the cotton balls and crooned about a winter wonderland. He winked at the three trilling women perched on a snowy log and moving their hands in synchronized, circular waves. It was a commercial for tires. I raised my eyebrows at the television screen. Josie followed my gaze.

"Bah, he's an Australian," she snorted.

The New Zealanders aren't known to be all that fond of their Aussie neighbors. "Any Kiwi emigrating to Australia raises the average IQ of both countries," Prime Minister Robert Muldoon famously commented on the "brain drain" of New Zealanders who crossed the Tasman Sea in search of jobs in the early 1980s. It may be good to have a wide gene pool, then, but to widen it as far as Australia would be nothing short of catastrophic, in New Zealanders' eyes at least.

I felt quite lucky to wake up the following morning and find my bed, together with the rest of Josie's bungalow, the flowery chairs, and the teacups, still above ground. Not having to waste several hours being dug out of a hole by the emergency services meant that I had time to visit Waihi Museum.

Regional museums are lovely places. The big-city galleries have all the funding, the world-famous exhibits, and the information boards created by expensive graphic designers. They serve good coffee. Regional museums are blessed with none of these things. They need to try a bit harder. They have to scrape the barrel.

Somebody with a great love for Waihi had spent many hours in his shed creating an interactive experience that, while not exactly on a level with Mortal Kombat, provided a flicker of a thrill for a moment or two. I pressed a button and the model ore-crushing pistons pumped. In front of the model railway I stood on a mat which lay on a switch which triggered a train to choo-choo around the track. It was wild. There was even a pickled snake in a bottle against which rested a notice: "This snake-in-a-bottle bears absolutely no relevance to our museum. But it is proving a good talking point anyway."

But the real reason people go to Waihi is to look at the pickled thumbs. Here's the story: Back in the bad old days of the original mining company, the miners had no pensions. The only way they could get out of working themselves quite literally to death was to lose a limb, to be declared unfit to work, and to be paid compensation by the company. The smallest limb that counted was the thumb, so aging miners used to lop off their own digits. Somewhat bizarrely, the mining company kept the thumbs in bottles of formaldehyde, and the museum keeps the macabre exhibit on display to this day.

*   *   *

I left Waihi, bade good-bye to Josie and her unstable garden, and headed out on the road east. Today I was off to a small farmholding near Tauranga. Should you ever happen to be passing along State Highway 2 in this direction, do allow yourself a half-hour stop at the Woodturners' Café at Mangatarata. A home-baked muffin in the shade of their courtyard orange tree is just the thing after a hard drive, or an easy drive, or even a vigorous session sitting in the passenger seat changing the CD. Really, any excuse will do.

As I came through Tauranga town and headed up into the hills toward the farm, a fine drizzle set in. The roads became tinier and windier. The surface curled and coiled around tight, steep bends past houses perched high on the hillside; then the blacktop gave out and became a gravel track. This was my first time on gravel roads, and I wasn't remotely enthusiastic about them. I dropped my speed down to about twelve miles an hour, clenched my bottom hard, and prayed to gods of various religions.

The road wound on; the little metal mailboxes on posts at the end of each driveway drifted further and further apart. Morris and Fay, the couple I had arranged to stay with through a local farm-stay organization, lived at number 664. I arrived at the four hundreds; some while later I made out five hundred something in the scratched paintwork. And then the road ran out. I executed a hesitant U-turn and headed back the way I'd come. The numbers on the mailboxes seemed erratic; reading the faded inscriptions at the same time as avoiding the potholes amid the gravel required all the concentration I could muster. At last, I found the turn I'd missed and, very slowly, chugged up Morris and Fay's driveway.

A stocky Maori man with a smattering of facial stubble and

short-cropped hair just starting to gray around the temples appeared at the gate of the house amid a flurry of barking. He was wearing a baggy gray polo shirt tucked into long black shorts and navy socks pulled up around the calves.

"All right, wolf," said Morris to the larger, more energetic of the two dogs, a bright, bouncy young husky called Whisky. The second dog, Buzz, a lazy, lovable mutt who liked to eat, waddled out behind.

Morris and Fay's farm isn't their sole source of income. This is lucky, because they only have eleven cows. On top of rearing these and taking in guests, Fay goes out to work in a legal office in the daytime, and Morris turns his hand to all sorts of impressive things. He's a proud Maori and a wood carver. When I visited, he had just won a contract to sell artifacts on cruise ships. A few years ago he built for his local iwi, or tribe, an eighty-foot Maori war canoe that seats a hundred paddlers. He's a builder by trade, cum farmer, engineer, remote-control helicopter pilot, farm-stay host, and, today, chief chef and bottle-washer. He has beds of worms that convert almost all the household waste, from tea bags to old socks, into "vermicast" fertilizer.

Now that sounded like a terrific idea, I thought. Back at home I had plenty of tea bags and old socks. If I could rear a little bed of worms somewhere in my flat, it would save me from having to put all that garbage in big black bags and cart it off to the trash can. And, as an added bonus, I could become very smug about doing my bit for the environment. I would have earned the right to swan around in brown-leather sandals with hairy legs and unpainted toenails. I could bore people at dinner parties with my righteous waste-disposal stories. It would be terrific. There was only one issue—where in my small third-floor flat was I going to keep the worms? It was all right for Morris—his were a safe distance away in the garden. But I didn't have a garden. I considered the matter for a moment. The kitchen had the advantage of being the site of greatest garbage-production, but I wasn't sure it would in all honesty be a good spot for the worms. What if some of them escaped and found their way into the fruit bowl? The bedroom was out for much the same reason. Really, I didn't want worms in my bed, whatever their ecological benefits. The living room would be all right, but it might upset any visitors who came by for a cup of tea or a glass of wine. Hmmm. It was a difficult issue and one that was going to require more thought.

This ability Morris had to turn his hand to pretty much anything is a quality that New Zealanders call "Kiwi ingenuity." It is very much a part of the traditional New Zealand character (and, apparently, vital if you want to call yourself a real Kiwi bloke). It's all to do with that pioneering spirit: New Zealand is a very long way from anywhere of any consequence, and so, in the days before airplanes, if you wanted something, you had to build it yourself. When the early European settlers came over, they had highfalutin' ideas from their home countries about the luxuries and conveniences they'd like in their new lives, but replacements were several months away by boat. And so they learned to create things, to make do, to use things they did have to build other things they didn't. In keeping with this spirit, some early copies of the *Auckland Times* were printed on a converted washing mangle.

The New Zealanders refer to this proclivity as the "number-eight fencing wire" mentality (the logical question "What about numbers seven and nine?" is one of life's great unanswerables), because there are, apparently, limitless ingenious uses for the stuff. Sir Edmund Hillary used number-eight wire to try to hold down the roof of one of the schools he built on the Nepal–Tibet border. (It didn't work; the roof blew off anyway.) Apparently it can also be used as a crude surgical instrument for holding a sheep's not-so-private parts together after she's given birth. But the "number-eight fencing wire" allusion doesn't just apply to things you can do with bits of wire. It has gone further. Nowadays, reference to number-eight wire covers pretty much any act of ingenious making and mending, witness to the Kiwi tendency to be able to solve problems with very few resources but shedloads of creativity.

Some people might consider that Morris had taken Kiwi ingenuity to unnecessary extremes. Not content with building a mere man-powered war canoe, Morris decided to build a hovercraft. It would be useful, he thought, for getting over to his ancestral land on a nearby island.

The craft sat in the front of his workshop, adjoining the garage, a vast yellow-and-blue contraption. It *almost* worked. There were a few technical details that Morris still had to figure out. He showed me home videos of him and his mate Roy—who also liked to build a hovercraft or two when he had a moment—down on the beach where they took the craft for its first test drive. Like two small boys with a new bicycle, they hurtled around the wide wet expanses of sand. Roy was the more experienced hovercraft handler, and he tried to teach Morris the basics of steering. In vast arcs they glided over the beach, daring each other to zoom ever faster.

In these hills just outside Tauranga, natural selection had favored the number-eight fencing-wire gene. Most of the small farmers around here were full of the entrepreneurial spirit. The neighbors on the next property grew lavender but also fixed washing machines. Their land was a curious blend of beautiful, ordered lavender beds and chaotic piles of rusting drums and crumbling hoses.

Another neighbor took on the task of shooting the cattle when the time was right. This was an area of farming that Morris and Fay found difficult. The problem with having only eleven cows was that they knew them all by name. Their cows were much-loved, sleek, gleaming creatures. When Morris walked up to their paddock, they gamboled over to greet him with the enthusiasm of a litter of puppies. He stroked their noses; they licked his hand. They were very happy cows, who experienced none of the stress of being herded around the place, none of the performance anxiety experienced by those cows who have to eat and eat and eat or face the barrel end of a shotgun when they don't reach their target weight. At Morris and Fay's place, skinny cows don't get culled, because Morris and Fay can't bear to be so unkind.

When it came to shooting their first two cows, Buster (who, on arrival in the paddock, burst straight through the electric fence because Morris had forgotten to turn it on) and Bumper (who bounced off the same fence just as Morris found the switch), Morris and Fay hired a man to come and do "home kill." This is supposed to be easier for the cows. They're happily standing eating hay in their very own comfy paddock when suddenly—bang!—it's all over. But watching the cows they'd named and reared being killed proved too much for their owners. Fay spent that fateful afternoon huddled under the duvet in a state of high emotion, just waiting for the shots to ring out. Morris, being a bloke, managed to stay out of bed, but he didn't like it much either. This, after all, was the man who had been so saddened by the death of his cat that he had kept it in a specially carved box in his living room for two days.

"When are you going to bury her?" Fay had asked in the end, concerned no doubt about the presence of a decomposing feline in her house.

"Just as soon as I've got used to the idea of her being dead," Morris had replied. Here was a man, then, who may be able to turn his hand to anything but who, underneath all those good-bloke credentials, was, well, a little on the sensitive side.

Now they took the cows to the neighbor. That way these hard Kiwi farm folk didn't have to watch.

The afternoon was rainy, so I spent it in Morris's workshop, trying my hand with chisels and planes as I made a koruru. This is the carved head that hangs over the entrance of the Maori meeting house to protect those inside from malignant spirits.

"So what was your grandfather's name?" Morris asked.

Ancestry is important for the Maori, and each carving should be a representation of a person's own life, beliefs, and forebears. (Buying a mass-produced one in a tourist shop won't keep away the demons to nearly such good effect, then.) One of the most vital parts of the Maori identity is one's whakapapa—one's genealogy or family tree—which blends together the past and the future. It's the web of connection that binds all Maori people. Before the Europeans arrived in New Zealand, all Maori history and literature were oral and passed down from generation to generation. Still today, with a little research, most Maori can trace their genealogy back a thousand years to the first canoes.

I told Morris that my grandfather's name was Ron but that everyone called him Yo. This was long before "yo" rhymed with "bro." If somebody had held their palm up in a high five, my grandfather would probably have waved back. Rap, for him, was a short, sharp thwack across the knuckles. He was of the old school. He ate a full English breakfast complete with fried bread every day. He sprinkled sugar on his peas. Every child-hood problem was solved by an Opal Fruit candy.

My grandfather's nickname came from the letters on the license plate of his first car. Apparently, a man once had trouble remembering his surname, which was Jago, and instead called him "Mr. Yoyo." As ridiculous things sometimes do, the new name stuck.

Because his throat had been damaged during his forceps delivery on entry into this world, my grandfather was unable to eat solid food until the age of four. As a result, despite coming from a family that generally measured in at around six feet, he only grew to be five foot six. He made up for his diminutive stature by becoming a big character. He was opinionated, garrulous, and funny. He hated any politician who erred slightly left of center. He loved Derby County, electronic gadgets, the taste of Lake District tap water, and his grandchildren, whose growth he recorded in ballpoint-pen lines, with initials and dates, on the side of the study door each time we went to stay. He frequently roared with laughter. But despite his strong personality, nobody had yet made a statue of my grandfather. Until now.

"Okay, then, this is Yo," said Morris, fishing an old block of wood out of a bin and brushing the dust off. Wielding a pencil, he showed me how to draw lines to denote the curves that would make Grandpa's eyebrows, cheeks, nose, and mouth. And then, plans successfully drawn, we squeezed Grandpa's face hard between the jaws of a vise and went at him with a chisel.

My first attempts were scruffy. Hacking sores, crevasses of wrinkles, divots, and pockmarks littered poor Grandpa's face. But after a few hours, I thought, he was starting to look pretty good. Admittedly his forehead wasn't exactly a regular shape. As Morris put it, he looked like he'd been in a fight. And after I'd applied his moko, or tattoos, he had the odd shaving cut as well. But altogether, he wasn't looking too bad. While we carved, the local radio blared out the snowiest of Christmas songs to entertain us and told us that in downtown Tauranga folk were celebrating the season of goodwill by patrolling the parking meters and feeding in coins to help out late-running Christmas shoppers. It must have been my dumbstruck astonishment that such people existed in the world that made my hand slip. Poor Grandpa took the flak.

"Oh no, Morris! I've sliced a chunk out of Grandpa's cheek," I shouted out in consternation. I wasn't at all sure that Grandpa would feel much like warding off miscreants on my behalf after such gruesome disfiguration.

"Aw, don't worry," said Morris without a hint of panic. "The last girl we had here chopped off *her* ancestor's nose."

And with that, he grabbed a tube of wood glue and deftly administered emergency surgery. Bandaging Grandpa tightly in insulation tape to hold his cheek in place, we went in to supper and *Coronation Street* and left him to sleep off his trauma overnight.

The next day, by the time I had dragged myself from bed and eaten my breakfast, Morris had already been in his workshop for an hour or so, putting finishing touches to Grandpa's facial tattoos.

"I finished Yo for you," he told me as I munched my way through yet another slice of toast. I thanked him between mouthfuls.

"I thought," continued Morris, "that seeing as you talk a lot, it might be in your genes. So I have given him a busy tongue."

Yo now hangs over the doorway of my bedroom, warding off anyone who might wish to enter with impure intentions. His gleaming paua-shell eyes apparently keep watch, while his defiant, protruding, intricately carved tongue jeers at intruders. To be honest, I'm not sure that he should stay there. I think, between his demands and my own, we might narrow the field of potential suitors down to imperceptible proportions. Grandpa wouldn't even consider ceding entry to anyone who hadn't shaved in the last three hours. Ideally, he should be wearing a tie. I, on the other hand, have rather different criteria. In his new role as doorman, Grandpa is strictly on probation.

During his early-morning stint in the shed, Morris had also employed that other great Kiwi characteristic, helpfulness. He had taken the top-box holder off my motorcycle, peeled away the entirely inadequate packing tape that my own fixing abilities had stretched to, and welded fiberglass over the plastic so that the contraption now held firm. For this and his kindness to cows, Morris will surely go to heaven. This could happen sooner rather than later if he keeps zipping around the gravel roads on his motorcycle. He told me of his escapades over coffee later that morning.

"This is my elbow," he said proudly, shaking a vial that he'd just taken out of the kitchen cupboard. It was full of shards of bone. Morris's elbow came to grief when he rode too fast around the gravel corner just down the road.

"I was hoping when they took the bone out I would be able to make a Maori carving, but the bits weren't big enough. But when my brother-in-law lost his leg when a train ran over it, I really thought about asking him if I could have that."

We agreed that, if you must have your leg amputated, it would be pretty cool to make a carving out of it—a walking stick, perhaps. That way you could carry on using your very own leg to walk with.

The rain poured on. Morris lent me a book that someone had given him, *Inventions from the Shed*. Here was an entire book dedicated solely to the crazy things Kiwi men have thought up while sitting alone in their shacks. A man called Ken had invented a motorcycle helmet with a brake light that was triggered by a remote transmitter: When the biker touches the brake with his foot, the light on the back of the helmet glows red so that drivers behind can see more easily that he's slowing down. Then there was Douglas, who had hammered his finger one time too many, so he invented a magnetic finger cap with a groove for a nail. That way, the nail just sits in place next to your protected finger, and you, hopefully, bash the nail and not yourself.

Happily, the rain eased up in time for me to go milking with Alan that afternoon. Alan was a local cow-cocky, or dairy farmer.

"So what do you know about milking cows?" he asked.

"Erm ... nothing," I replied.

I soon learned lesson number one: A good cow is a shitty cow. The more a cow eats, the more it defecates and the more milk it produces. So lots of ordure in a milking shed is a very good thing indeed. By the end of the first hour, I had shit on my hands, shit on my clothes, shit on my face, and shit in my hair. It seemed that these were very productive cows.

"England's got a pretty good rugby team at the moment, eh," Alan remarked.

"So I gather," I said, dredging up one of my very thin scraps of rugby knowledge. "Well, we just beat the Kiwis, didn't we?"

Alan looked a bit put out and went back to milking. The cows, at least, didn't answer back. I mean, what's the point in leaving the Motherland—escaping the nasty fume-belching

Northern Hemisphere and growing *bigger carrots*—if you can't even beat the gutless stay-at-homes at their own game?

He moved on to a less contentious subject. "D'you watch *Coro*?" (*Coro* is Kiwi-speak for *Coronation Street*.)

"Well," I replied, "to be honest I'd never seen it before I came to New Zealand. But since arriving here I've seen it quite a few times."

"Aw," said Alan. "Right."

"Do you watch it?" I asked.

"Er, yes," he said, and blushed.

He showed me how to attach the suckery contraptions to the cows' udders and how to avoid meeting an unwelcome demise from a hoof in the head.

"They do kick a bit—they're female, after all," he said.

The cows filed in and lined up on one side of the shed.

"Give her a whack," shouted Alan from the other end of the shed as an unwilling cow stalled next to me. As if to demonstrate, he then delivered a mighty wallop to the rump of a cow on his right. I hesitated. To march into the cow shed without so much as a conciliatory handful of clover and immediately to start smacking its incumbents on the bottom seemed somehow intrusive. It was their shed, not mine, after all. I was the newcomer. And the cow's brown eyes looked so, well, doleful, so expressively beseeching, "And how did I get myself into this sorry state?" I tapped her gently, as respectfully as one can in such presumptuous circumstances spank a girl on the backside. I felt as though I should somehow apologize.

And so, for a couple of hours, Alan and I milked cows. As the cows on the left filed out into the paddock, we attached the machines, which swung from hoses in the center of the shed, to the cows on the right. By the time a new row of cows had taken their place on the left, the cows on the right were done; they then trotted out and their machines were attached to their opposite number on the other side. Or at least Alan did most of them. While I fumbled ineptly with the first four cows in each row, Alan dealt deftly with the other eight and did all the other little tasks in between. And so it went on. And on. And on. With two hundred cows, Alan reckons he spends a good five hours a day milking them, and the first session's at five in the morning. So, much as I had enjoyed my experience, I decided not to take up milking as a new career.

After the last drop of milk had been squeezed from the final udder, I helped Alan to sluice down the copious quantities of excrement from the floor of the cow shed with a hose of such high pressure that it nearly left me sprawling in the slop. Then we climbed on Alan's quad bike and took a ride through the hilly paddocks to check that the cows were all tucked in for the night and hadn't stuffed themselves silly on clover— this apparently makes them bloated. These cows were picky eaters. They graze in a fresh field every day; after they've been milked they just amble off down the track and go through whichever gate Alan has left open.

"But if I leave the gate open into the same paddock they just came out of, they won't go in. They'll just stand around outside," said Alan.

Tonight was looking as if it could be fun for the cows, as Alan had thoughtfully put a bull in there with them—which leads to an interesting aside about New Zealand puritanism. In the early 1900s, laws were passed that forbade farmers to put cows and bulls together in fields that fronted public roads: Their mating was considered to be an affront to propriety. These regulations weren't shelved until the 1950s.

I spent some time in the shower when I got home, trying to

make sure the steaming jets rinsed every last bit of cow dung out of my hair. As I shampooed for the third time, I considered Alan's credentials as a real Kiwi bloke. He had been wearing a black tank top and gum boots—the species' trademark costume—and had tried to engage me in conversation about rugby. He definitely hadn't been wearing hair gel. He seemed, in fact, to be a pretty good specimen. But even in the short time I had spent with him, I had uncovered in Alan one glaring indicator that all wasn't well for the traditional macho Kiwi man—for what self-respecting bloke would initiate conversation about *Coronation Street*?

As for Morris, well, he had some strong attributes as well. He was very good at turning his hand to anything that came his way, the living incarnation of the Kiwi maxim "If it ain't broke, fix it anyway." He spent many, many hours in his shed. But, oh dear, there was no getting away from that terrible angst over the dead cat. It didn't exactly scream "hard as nails."

I'd only been on the road for a couple of weeks, but early reports were suggesting that the surveys might have been right and the full-blooded Kiwi bloke might be hard to find. There were plenty of guys around who displayed some of the characteristics of the tree-chopping, gold-mining, land-loving New Zealand pioneers, but the advent of technology and the influence of the outer world meant that, so far, I hadn't found any that scored full marks.

It was time to leave Morris and Fay, the cows, the worms, and the shed and to continue with my journey south. Morris decided to accompany me on the road to Rotorua—a fine chance to get out on his own motorcycle, and also to check that I didn't die on the way. Having seen the state of my top-box holder, the poor man was no doubt justifiably concerned about my ability to survive the journey.

The problem with having Morris accompany me on the bike, however, was that I felt a deep sense of performance anxiety. For the first time since my bike test, not all that long ago, I needed to perform. I would have to display at least a minimal level of competence.

The result of all this was that I was forced, for once, to make a bit of an effort with my riding. I actually kept the throttle open just a touch around the bends and thought a little about my riding line and proper leaning. I concentrated on moving at more than fifty miles an hour. When we took the wrong turn on the way to the hotel, I had to do a normal, competent U-turn without allowing myself to wimp out and put my feet down. And here's the funny thing: I actually rather enjoyed myself. At last, I seemed to have reached a turning point—even if it had been imposed upon me.

Morris turned around and rode back home. I found a spot in the hotel parking lot and turned off the bike. There was a shudder and a grunt, and then everything was still.

"So how was that for you?" I asked, unclipping the straps of my helmet and pulling it off my head, feeling rather pleased with my performance. The bike, surely, ought to have been happy about my newfound technique, the way it had been allowed to whip racily around the bends, to hurtle enthusiastically along the straights.

The bike didn't deign to reply. It appeared to have fallen asleep.

Geezers and Geysers

ROTORUA STINKS. THIS IS the area of New Zealand most prone to geothermal activity—earthquakes, eruptions, and such. From deep within the earth's core, sulfur dioxide creeps through cracks and craters in the earth's surface and fills the air with an acrid stench. Amid the smoking volcanoes and seething pools, boiling mud bubbles like a lethally flatulent chocolate fondue. Spurting geysers—steaming, scalding, skin-sizzling fountains—shoot high into the sky. Water oozes at killer temperatures down otherworldly terraces. Pools and lakes take on fantastical hues of blue, green, pink, and yellow; their shores are scorched with an eerie, lunar whiteness. Everywhere you go there's the pervasive stench of sulfur.

It's not just the virility of Kiwi blokes that makes the earth move around here. Maori legend has it that these unusually lively features were brought to the Rotorua area by the prayers of an ancient high priest, Ngatoroirangi. Freezing cold on top of Mount Tongariro to the south, Ngatoroirangi prayed to his gods in the mythical Maori homeland of Hawaiki. The gods answered his prayers by sending fire traveling deep underground.

More recent research has concluded that these features have more to do with New Zealand's location right over the point where the Australian and Pacific tectonic plates meet. The plates that carry the earth's continents all move continually. They migrate a few inches across the earth's surface each year, at about the same speed as fingernails grow. When they meet and push against each other, though, geological fireworks begin. The molten lava underneath the plates breaks through the earth's surface and volcanoes and geysers are created; the rock mass that is displaced as one plate is driven beneath another pushes up mountain ranges. Every now and then, the pressure is relieved through an earthquake. New Zealand experiences a staggering sixteen thousand of these each year—although only about one percent of those are felt by humans.

As regards the development of the original Kiwi bloke, Rotorua attracted a type that considered himself rather superior to the loggers and miners whose environments I had visited further north. The men who came here a hundred-odd years ago wouldn't have known a sweat-soaked T-shirt if one had smacked them in the face. Checked trousers were the style for these fellows, for Rotorua was where the moneyed classes came to play, and they brought with them the dazzling new concept of going on vacation.

In the second half of the nineteenth century, overseas travel was all the rage. To journey to distant lands just for the pleasure of spending many uncomfortable weeks on a lilting, lurching boat and then many more hacking over treacherous roads between bad hotels was a newfangled and highly fashionable concept. It had first been thought up by one Thomas Cook, a former Baptist preacher who believed that the majority of social ills could be cured if the working classes were better educated and drank less booze. On his way to a temperance meeting one evening in 1841, he was struck by the idea that travel could be used to power social reform. He started out by organizing trips around Britain on the railways. Over the years, these trips graduated into world tours to guide those who couldn't quite work up the courage to strike out alone. The package tour was born.

The new craze for travel coincided with the end of the New Zealand Wars in the mid-nineteenth century, which had seen frequent violent clashes over land ownership between the Maori and Pakeha authorities. Suddenly, New Zealand was on the tourist agenda. The empire was booming, passenger steamers made long voyages accessible, and Britain's moneyed classes thronged to see the colonies, to visit friends and family who had opted to settle in "paradise," to find out for themselves what all the fuss was about. Anthony Trollope and Rudyard Kipling both made the journey in the second half of the century. Noël Coward came to Rotorua too, though he showed little inclination to pack his trunks and move here.

"Personally, I felt that to be able to boil an egg in a puddle outside your front door, although undoubtedly labor-saving, was not really enough compensation for having to live immediately on top of the earth's hidden fires," he wrote in *Future Indefinite*.

Rotorua was one of the highlights of any tourist's agenda. Back then the real attractions were the pink and white terraces—two stretches of graduated pools formed over centuries by silica deposits. Big-bottomed ladies in bustles and fashionable gentlemen in frock coats and bushy muttonchop whiskers came from all over the world to see the extraordinary formations and bathe in their warm clear-blue waters.

The visitors brought unprecedented wealth to New Zealand's first tourist hub; tales abound of the carvings at the local villagers' marae (meetinghouse) flaunting eyeballs that glinted with half-sovereigns and shillings instead of the customary paua shells. The tribespeople charged high prices for the ride in the canoe from their village to the terraces on the other side of Lake Tarawera and extorted further fees for the right to photograph or paint the terraces. The Victorian travelers, steeped in their own religious culture, were outraged; they considered such natural wonders to be a gift from God for all to behold rather than private property from which a particular group might profit.

Unused to their newfound wealth, the villagers spent their money on alcohol. Illness and immorality tightened their vise-like grip.

"For years past they have received a constant stream of money from tourists, have been plied with liquor to get up hakas and dances, and have been constantly drunk and idle. As a consequence notwithstanding of all the money they receive, they live in a most wretched style and never have a sufficiency of nourishing food," an editorial in the *New Zealand Herald* criticized in June 1886.

A fate yet more gruesome was about to erupt, however. A few days before this column was published, tourists and guides had seen a phantom war canoe paddle across Lake Tarawera.

"*He tohu tera ara ka horo katoa enei takiwa*: It is a warning that all will be overwhelmed," warned Tuhoto Ariki, an elderly priest. The people's greed would provoke the fire to come out of the mountain, he predicted. He might have been right.

A few days later, on the morning of June 10, Mount Tara-wera erupted, its jets of hot lava reaching high into the sky. The pink and white terraces were annihilated and nearby villages engulfed in a flaming pyroclastic river.

The old priest, incidentally, got his comeuppance for being both a killjoy and way too smart. The Maori people, annoyed with him for having incited the disaster, refused to dig him out from his buried home. After four days of interment under hot lava (during which, we must assume, he had a good opportunity to think about what he'd done), some Europeans finally managed to rescue him. They took him, still alive, to the Rotorua sanatorium. He died there a week later.

Today, Rotorua still has an awful lot of tourists. I checked in to my hotel, had a bite of lunch, and headed out to join the throngs at Te Whakarewarewa, the largest thermal reserve around. They don't let visitors walk through the reserve on their own—apparently, in the past one or two have been foolish enough to slip into the six-feet-deep vats of boiling mud—so I had to take a tour, which was spoiled somewhat by the fact that there were sixty-six people in my group, and a good number of those were rather bored, fractious teenage boys from London who didn't seem to think that learning how the early Maori settlers used flax to make dancing skirts was going to change their lives. We traipsed along the walkways, behind the sturdy wooden fences. "Caution!" commanded a sign nailed to one fence. And then, beneath the big, dangerous exclamation mark inside a yellow triangle, it warned, "Icy conditions." Behind the fence, steam billowed and geysers hissed. It seemed a strange kind of notice to put up in the middle of a blistering inferno, but perhaps, in winter, hell really does freeze over.

In contrast to its alarmingly boisterous natural features, I found Rotorua a bland town. The buildings were low, boxy, and drab. There were too many bus tours. The main street was lined with overpriced souvenir shops. They had Starbucks.

I was woken at one-thirty a.m. by the familiar but unwelcome sound of the Cantonese language being shrieked at many decibels into a cell phone. Since I lived for several years in Hong Kong, this is a noise I'm accustomed to but have never learned to love. I lay and listened for ten minutes, then twenty. By now I was wide awake; the chances of going back to sleep diminished as the time ticked by. In the end I got up and leaned out of the window. There, a few feet away, stood a Hong Kong businessman, dragged unwillingly away on vacation by his wife no doubt, who had had to sneak into the parking lot in the dead of night to carry out his wheeling and dealing. The concept of going on vacation may have been dreamed up 160 years ago, but this guy still hadn't got it. He was clearly a slow developer. He was squat and round, in that way Asian businessmen often are—those that haven't figured out that this is the twenty-first century, when fat no longer equals prosperous but merely means you've guzzled too many cheap burgers. He strode up and down outside my window in what he must have hoped was a proprietary manner, but due to his rather short stature and his excess of flesh he actually looked more like *Chicken Run*'s Babs the knitting chicken out for a constitutional waddle.

I banged on the window. Nothing.

I opened it. "Excuse me ..."

He turned. "SSSSHHHH." He gesticulated at me in irritation. There was a million bucks in the offing and some dumb woman with hair askew was asking him to shut up?

Now hold on a minute, I thought. All I did was hiss "Excuse me" through the window in a very controlled manner. I didn't make much noise. Here was a man making a din to rival a turkey farm the week before Thanksgiving—and *he* was telling *me* to be quiet? Admittedly, it wasn't the first time in my life that somebody had suggested I might shut up, but this man was taking things too far. It was time to temporarily shelve my shy and retiring personality and bring out my busy tongue.

"For God's sake, it's the middle of the night. Stop squawking or I'll hurl both you and your precious phone into a vat of boiling mud," I yelled.

The man looked astonished. To be honest, I didn't actually have any boiling mud on hand, but there was a small geyser in the corner of the hotel parking lot that might have done instead. He decided not to take any risks, glared, flapped his hands at me, and strutted off around the corner so that somebody less forthright could be woken by his hullabaloo.

It was hard, but the next morning, in the name of research, I thought I'd better do my best to understand the experiences of those pioneering vacationers, to appreciate the healing properties of the waters and of Rotorua's famous mud. I checked into the Polynesian Spa.

Before I was even allowed into the treatment room, I was forced to spend an hour wallowing in the thermal pools, which ranged from lukewarm to bathtub-hot. But in contrast to my practice in the bathroom at home, here I didn't lie staring at rows of tiles that forced me to consider whether I might need to spend a Sunday afternoon in the very near future tackling my grouting. In the Polynesian Spa, I looked out over the incredible crimson blooms of pohutukawa trees and the waters of Lake Rotorua beyond. After an hour or so of this, I had to make a sterling effort to rouse myself. It took all my powers of self-exertion to clamber out of the pool and into my bathrobe and then to totter a few light-headed steps into the treatment room. There I lay on a bed and was smeared in detoxifying Rotorua mud, rinsed, massaged, pampered, rejuvenated, reinvigorated. Really, it was all quite exhausting, so when it was over they led me gently into the "Relaxation Room," where I plopped onto a plump white sofa, read a magazine, and drank soothing cups of water for another half hour or so.

As I said, it's a hard job.

Sunday, December 22, goes down as a great day in my motorcycling development. The road passed through pine forests fronted by lush green grass with smatterings of buttercups. It was straight for as far as the eye could see. The sun was shining, the birds were singing in the trees, and there wasn't so much as a wisp of wind.

I'd been buzzing merrily along for about an hour when I realized for the first time that the cars weren't all lining up impatiently behind me as they usually did. They weren't swooping past at the first opportunity with a wave of the fist and a blast of the horn. I looked in my mirrors. Yes, that blue sedan had been there, keeping a respectable distance behind, for at least fifteen minutes. Its driver did not have the cross red face that usually loomed angrily in my rearview. He was not gesticulating with rage or throwing his eyes to the heavens. In fact, his head seemed to be bobbing about in quite a rhythmic manner and—hold on—yes, he seemed to be singing.

I glanced down at the speedometer. The bold, digital display positively blared the triumphant figure: sixty miles an hour. My goodness, I thought, that was really quite fast. I mean, the *limit* was sixty-five. A warm glow of self-satisfaction began to well up within me—and then, hot on its heels, a tiny wave of subversion started to creep through my veins.

Hmmm, I thought, I wonder if I could, er, well ...

I leaned a little lower over the bike and tentatively twitched the throttle. The numbers crept up ... sixty-one, sixty-two. My heart beat faster. A little thrill tingled down to my toes. I started to smile.

I turned the throttle a little further, mutiny now coursing rampant through me. The speedometer read sixty-four, sixty-five, then sixty-six. *I had broken the speed limit!*

"Yee-hah," I bellowed with anarchic jubilation.

"Vroom," added the bike, with what sounded like triumphant approval.

I laughed out loud, intoxicated by the thrill of my transgression.

I was on the way from Rotorua to Taupo, and soon after my exhilarating experience I stopped at the Waiotapu thermal reserve, a spellbinding, supernatural place with bubbling pools of gray, green, yellow, and red, seething streams and boiling mud. I was entirely delighted to find that the sixty or so schoolboys from London with whom I'd been forced to share my previous meanderings were nowhere to be seen. Better still, I was actually allowed to walk around on my own, following the signs that insisted I kept strictly to the walkways and didn't hurl myself in a fit of suicidal rage into a seething sulfuric cauldron. Very obediently, I therefore kept my celebratory skipping to a minimum. There was a limit to how much rule-breaking I could cope with in a single day and, anyway, I didn't really want to spoil my giddy successes by tumbling into a luminous-green pond.

I strolled happily for an hour or so along the wooden boardwalk that wound through this extraterrestrial landscape. Steam billowed and geysers sprayed. Boiling water hissed as it cascaded down rock faces coated in glistening, gray deposits.

Saffron-yellow pools faded into sandier hues, then turned jade green and a deep tomato red. The occasional charred, dry tree poked through the hostile ground at the water's edge. The soil was coated with white.

Really, this was an extraordinary spot. It seemed incredible that right here, in the middle of the civilized world, you could drive a mere twenty miles from town and see this remarkable landscape. The very ground I walked on was rich with expression. It seemed somehow dark with anger, impetuous and volatile. It seethed, hissed, and oozed, moody one minute, explosive the next. The colors of the water, of the scorched earth, of the minerals that bubbled up from the earth's molten core were so vivid as to seem almost unnatural. As I came to the end of the wooden circuit, I stopped and stared at the astonishing sight one last time. Then I went out to find my bike. My journey for the day wasn't over yet. I still had to get to Taupo.

The Queen likes to spend her holidays in Taupo when she comes to tour New Zealand, which, admittedly, is not very often. And while I might not wholeheartedly agree with every piece of royal decision-making, in this the monarchy is spot on. Taupo's a great little town on the northeast shore of the lake; beyond the blue waters towers the dramatic, snow-peaked volcano of Mount Ruapehu, whose last significant steamy, rock-spewing eruption took place just a few years ago in 1995. Still, that was nothing compared to the explosion that actually created the lake, about twenty-five thousand years ago: They reckon an eruption hurled out about two hundred cubic miles of ash, which coated the whole North Island about thirty feet deep. The landscape changed again in 181 AD when civilizations as far away as China and Rome recorded a massive explosion, which created the dramatically hewn hills that characterize the area today.

The welcome I received at Lawrie and Carol Chandler's guesthouse in Taupo was warm even by New Zealand's hospitable standards. Before I'd so much as had the chance to peel off my leathers, Lawrie had the kettle boiling and had pressed on me a plate piled high with two different kinds of cake. This seemed to be usual behavior in the Chandlers' kitchen, if the treatment meted out to the array of passersby who happened to drop in during the next hour was any indication.

It is an interesting phenomenon, this need New Zealanders feel to force you to eat. There are a number of explanations. The first is, simply, that New Zealanders suffer from a terrible genetic defect that obliges them to be nice. You don't find New Zealanders shoving old ladies in the bus line. This puts them at a distinct disadvantage when they travel abroad to places where the aggressive old ladies have learned to perform feats of incredible martial prowess with their walking sticks. It's pretty lousy for the survival of a species too. In the great evolutionary squabble, the pell-mell skirmish to send one's own genes to the top of the selection pile, *nice* isn't a terribly good thing to be.

The second explanation for the force-feeding is that, as I have commented earlier, New Zealanders like things big. Arguably, then, when they see a skinny, wizened foreigner, they might feel the need to fatten her up to their own well-covered standards with platefuls of home-baked cake.

The third explanation is that the Pakeha people of New Zealand might, despite the relentless imposition of their own ways, have unwittingly absorbed a little of Maori culture. The

Maori traditionally insist on eating with their guests before any kind of business can be contemplated.

"Eating is part of the whakanoa or decontamination process that visitors must go through in a Maori situation, to rid themselves of alien tapu [taboo]. Pakeha who refuse the cup of tea and piece of cake not only give offense, they may be thought to be endangering the well-being of their hosts," writes historian Michael King in his book *Being Pakeha Now*.

Fearful of vexing my hosts, I gobbled up every last crumb of cake. Only then was Lawrie able to proceed with more serious matters. In his case, the topic most worthy of debate was motorcycling, for this was a passion of his.

"You see that bike out there? That's my fortieth motorcycle," he said.

Feeling entirely inadequate once more, I explained that I was something of a novice.

"Yeah? Well, that's a great little bike you've got there for a beginner," he said. At last! Here was somebody who didn't accuse me of being mad, somebody who thought I'd made a halfway decent decision.

"It's got good power, that bike, and you can go off-road on it too, and no worries passing," Lawrie went on. And for once, I was able to agree. For that day I had actually passed someone. Admittedly, the vehicle in question had only been a slow-moving RV, but it was a definite step forward. I told Lawrie of my proud feat. He laughed.

"Aw, you'll be passing trucks next!" he said with indefatigable optimism.

Among the visitors to Lawrie and Carol's kitchen during the hour or so that I sat there was Pete, who appeared with a large styrofoam crate full of trout. Taupo is famous for its rainbow trout, which, like pretty much everything else in New

Zealand, seem to be firmly of the opinion that bigger may be better, but absolutely enormous is the best of all. In Taupo, girl trout must like their boy trout big, and natural selection has not been kind to the little guys. I commented on the size of the fish in Pete's box.

"Bah, that's nothing." Carol laughed. "Those're tiddlers."

"But they're twice the size of the ones we get back home."

"Yes, but we *laugh* at your trout. We guffaw. Out loud."

So there we are.

"You're writing a book about Kiwi blokes?" Carol asked. "Well, you'd better go out fishing with Pete here. He's a great fisherman. Pete'll take you with him in the morning, won't you, Pete?"

Pete looked mildly embarrassed. He seemed to find himself in a tight corner.

"Er, well, yes, if you want to," he said, being a polite New Zealander who knows a pickle when he's up to his neck in one. I was slightly sorry to put him in such a position; on the other hand, I really wanted to go fishing. I had never been fishing before, and Taupo was supposed to be a fantastic spot for the sport.

"Er, well, I'd have to stay here two nights if I went fishing. Would that be all right?" I asked Carol.

"Two nights here? Even better. You see, Pete, you'd be doing *us* a favor if you took her fishing," Carol cajoled. "You wouldn't want to do us out of a booking now, would you?"

I added devious manipulation to my list of sins for the day, which so far included breaking the speed limit by five miles an hour and eating all the cake.

The next morning I was up at six-thirty; shortly afterward I was on the bike and heading over to Turangi on the southern tip of the lake, where I was going to meet two Kiwi blokes,

Pete and his friend Skiff. Both Pete and Skiff were from Auckland, but they came down to Taupo most weekends to fish. Pete used to be a medical student but gave it up. He was still young, he reckoned, and there were too many fish in the lake for him to dedicate himself to such an all-consuming profession. So for the time being he was working in the marketing department of a chain of casinos and coming down to Taupo whenever he could. Pete and Skiff's operation was a simple one: a twelve-foot aluminum dinghy, an outboard motor, a depth monitor, and a couple of rods. All they had to do was hook up the trailer and drive off to the fishing spot of their choice with very little maintenance or financial outlay required.

Pete lent me his dark green neoprene waders and boots. They were several sizes too large for me, but they kept out the wind. Compared with the heat of the day before, it was chilly on the lake this morning. Skiff, too, wore waders and a thick fleece. Pete was clearly made of sterner stuff. He sat in the boat with just a red sweatshirt, dark green running pants, plastic sandals, and a baseball cap and didn't give way to so much as a shiver.

Pete and Skiff reckoned that the key to their success lay in their method of jigging: One morning a few weeks earlier they had caught eighty-one fish. Pete showed me how it was done. He simply attached the bait to the hook, stuck the rod out over the side of the boat, let the line run until the weight hit the bottom, and then, he said, all you have to do is wait.

And wait. And wait. Pete and Skiff seemed to think it was a slow morning; I was beginning to harbor serious doubts about my technique. This was my first attempt at fishing. It didn't seem quite as straightforward as I had imagined. To begin with, I had trouble working out when the weight had reached the bottom. It was supposed to go "dum," Pete said. I was supposed to be able to feel the "dum" by holding the tip of my finger under the line as it ran, and ran, and ran. Pete and Skiff's weights seemed to have gone "dum" long ago. My rod, on the other hand, was running out enough line to stretch from one side of the lake to the other and trip up all the poor fish who tried to swim across it.

Waggle, waggle, waggle ... "*Ow!*" an unsuspecting fish was probably crying out as it flitted merrily along and then, catching its fins on my trip wire, found itself somersaulted into an involuntary display of underwater acrobatics.

I waited, and waited some more.

"Probably all the fish are having a good old munch on my line and I'm not even noticing," I said as Pete and Skiff frantically reeled in their catch. Were those little tugs on the line fish or just the weight bumping along the bottom of the lake as the boat drifted? I reeled in a couple of times; there was nothing.

"Nah, don't worry, it's just a quiet morning. When you get a fish, you'll know about it."

Then, suddenly, *woooaaahh!* A mighty tug and the rod strained and bent.

"That's a fish!" yelled Pete and Skiff in unison.

"Wind it in! Now stop! Now pull! Now wind! Pull the rod back and stop winding when the fish pulls or you'll lose it.... Now wind some more.... Now stop again.... Ah, you lost it."

I lost two but on the third attempt struck lucky. A huge, glistening, silver-bellied beast emerged from the water on the end of my line. It was ridiculously exciting, wildly exhilarating. Pete jabbed his knife into the top of the fish's head, into its brain, killing it instantly, then slit its throat to drain the blood and rinsed it out in the lake before putting it in the styrofoam box.

It wasn't actually all that nasty. I'm not generally big on killing my own supper. I like it to come pristinely packed in plastic from the supermarket, free from puddles of blood and not looking too unsettlingly like the gamboling cow, pig, or fish it once was. It has something to do with my cowardly preference for not looking my dinner in the eye, for not having to endure the accusing gaze of the creature I'm about to consume. I expected, therefore, that I would be squeamish when Pete grabbed the writhing, wriggling fish, which had a few minutes earlier been frolicking about quite happily in the lake and hurting nobody, and whacked a knife into its head. Objectively, butchering an innocent fish should seem an unreasonable thing to do. I had already spent some minutes psyching myself up for the kill while I had been sitting in the boat dangling my line over the edge. I had hoped that this mental preparation would prevent me from life-threatening embarrassment, from blinking back the tears and squealing, "Stop, stop, you're hurting it!" when finally the moment came.

In the event, though, I was so overcome by an unfamiliar surge of hunter-gatherer self-satisfaction, I wasn't bothered at all. I was, however, quietly relieved that Pete did the knife-jabbing and not me. It was after all a very big fish and I should think took considerable strength to kill. I'm obviously not one to descend into that weird male hey-look-at-me-I'm-really-tough-because-I-killed-a-gigantic-fish thing. I would never allow the size of my catch to increase with the telling. But, really, it was huge. I have a photograph of myself dangling the poor thing from my finger, which is stuck in its startled, gaping mouth. Its dead, glazed eyes are level with my hip. Its tail ends below my knee. Obsessive? Sad? Oh, all right, I admit it: When I got back home I measured from my hip to just below my knee to see how big that fish really was. The distance was twenty inches, almost two feet, very, very big. Now don't tell me you're not impressed.

My catch was plump and packed with fat, which is apparently a good sign in a fish. Back at the Chandlers', Lawrie put it in the smoker. When it was done, I cut it in half, leaving one portion for Carol and Lawrie, and wrapped the other in newspaper. My friends Sheena and Duncan had just arrived in Taupo in their motor home. They live in Hong Kong and had come over to New Zealand for a vacation. We had arranged to spend Christmas together in Hawke's Bay but had both ended up in Taupo the night before Christmas Eve somewhat by accident. They had offered me an RV supper; I had my own offering.

I arrived at the campsite beside myself with anticipation. I was scarcely able to greet them before I pressed upon them my gift.

"I caught it myself!" I beamed like a man with too much testosterone, stuffing the newspaper package into Duncan's hands.

Duncan didn't look as thrilled as he should. "Caught?" he asked suspiciously, wrinkling his nose. "Oh for God's sake, it's not a fish, is it?"

But once they saw that it was ready to eat, and that I'd even brought a loaf of bread to go with it, they cheered up. The smoked trout was juicy, sweet, and succulent. And I glowed with the primeval satisfaction of a true huntress.

Feeding Frenzy

IT WAS CHRISTMAS EVE. The sun was shining, the pohutukawa trees were blooming crimson, the shoppers in board shorts and shades were putting the final touches to their Christmas shopping. Some were loading their cars and joining traffic jams with fellow travelers heading for a few weeks at their bach, the traditional, usually rudimentary New Zealand vacation home. Others were lighting the barby and settling down with a cold beer on their deck. The New Zealand holiday season had begun.

I had my own plans for Christmas. I was making my way to Hawke's Bay, to a small hotel near Hastings called Mangapapa Lodge, where Sheena, Duncan, and I were going to see who could stuff themselves the silliest with two days of eating, drinking, eating, drinking, eating, drinking, and a little bit of lying by the pool.

The night before, in keeping with the New Zealand cult of helpfulness (or was it a Kiwi bloke's instinctual need to prove his worth with machinery?), Lawrie had offered to check over my bike. I was slightly apprehensive. What if there was something really obvious the matter with it, and I had entirely failed to notice? What if Lawrie came back and said something like "Er, you see, it's supposed to have *two* wheels"?

I waited with bated breath and sweaty palms for his verdict. "It looks okay," he told me when he had finished, "but the chain's a bit loose. Just go to the Suzuki garage a few doors down before you leave in the morning and tell them that Lawrie Chandler sent you." I did; they tightened the chain and checked the tire pressures and didn't charge me a cent.

The great delight of today's journey was that Sheena and Duncan were ferrying my luggage in their camper. All I had to carry was a little bit of money and a map. It was only a couple of hours of very cruisy riding over to Hawke's Bay. The road to start with was straight and flat. Keeping up with the standards set two days earlier, I managed to keep at something approaching a respectable speed and was soon eating up the miles. I was full of seasonal joy and goodwill. I had friends at last, people to talk to. Tomorrow was Christmas and there'd be food and presents. The sun was shining, and I thought I could just feel a little snooze by the swimming pool coming on, perhaps after a glass or two of Hawke's Bay wine.

The terrain steepened and I climbed up and up, over the hills. Coming down the other side, the temperature suddenly, tangibly, rose by several degrees. It was a definite wall of change, the difference between the inland and the mountains, and the coastal heat of Hawke's Bay.

This is the wonderful thing about motorcycles. Looking at a bike from outside, the motorcyclist seems cocooned in aggression, the helmet and armored gear creating a hostile, impersonal barrier against the rest of the world. From inside the helmet, though, it's an entirely different matter. From a motor-cycle, you're so much more in contact with the outside world than you are from within a car. When the air temperature rises, the difference hits you with a discernible wave of heat. A biker is alert to every changing smell, every breeze, every bend in the road in a way that a car driver will never be. Gloriously unladen by luggage, I motored though the vineyards and along the coast road, taking in the smells of the sea.

A couple of fellow bikers roared by on the other side of the road and raised their left hands in greeting. Brimming with new confidence, I waved back and *whoa*! My hand whipped back in the wind, my arm flew high in the sky, my shoulder nearly popped out of the socket. That wasn't a wave, that was some kind of half-crazed, frenzied, limb-dislocating fling. The bike wobbled. Here was a finer detail of motorcycling etiquette that John and Kieran hadn't taught me. Clearly, waving was going to require a bit more practice. With my recalcitrant hand firmly back on the handlebars, I motored on, confidence only slightly dented, and before too long I arrived at Mangapapa Lodge.

Mangapapa Lodge is an old colonial-style homestead. With its white-painted weatherboard walls, wooden verandas, and rolling lawns, it's all a bit *Gone With the Wind*—except that going hungry here was out of the question. Sheena and Duncan arrived in their camper. What with their RV and my motor-cycle, we weren't sure whether our collective wheels were quite classy enough for the super-luxury of Mangapapa Lodge. Our transport sat on the circular graveled drive like a huge white rectangular eyesore with its pizza-delivery sidekick.

"Harrumph! What's an unlikely pair like you doing in a smart joint like this?" our fellow guests' Mercedes seemed to snort down their perfectly polished hoods.

The house and its estate were once home to Sir James Wattie, the eponymous creator of Wattie's baked beans and tomato ketchup. Wattie bought the land to grow fruit and vegetables for his cannery business. Wattie's is New Zealand's answer to Heinz (and, true to the spirit of modern commercial evolution, has now been bought out by the American giant).

The warmer temperatures on this coast that I'd noticed earlier were the very ingredient that helped Wattie and his canning buddies to prosper. For the same reason, Hawke's Bay is also one of the main winemaking regions of New Zealand. It's one of the sunniest places in the country, with warm, dry summers and mild winters. It's the perfect place, in fact, to spend Christmas by the swimming pool.

Our festive spirit was only slightly marred by the unfortunate death of a baby bunny rabbit that had hoppety-skipped with a little more seasonal joy than was good for it into the swimming pool and drowned. We felt sad, very briefly, and had to cheer ourselves up with a good long soak in the spa.

On Christmas Day we ate too much breakfast and then took a short walk up a hill that we thought was called Tomato Peak—due to all those baked beans, presumably—but turned out after a prolonged search for it on the map to be Te Mata Peak.

Te Mata, we later discovered, was a legendary giant, the leader of the coastal tribes of Waimarama. The Waimarama tribes were a bellicose lot and kept attacking the tribes that lived on the plains. So the plains-dwellers hatched a scheme: They'd make Te Mata fall in love with the daughter of one of their chiefs. The problem was that she fell in love with him too and was therefore unwilling to make him endure the agonies of unrequited love. Determined that Te Mata should still suffer in some way, her fellow plains-dwellers made her demand that Te Mata prove his love by accomplishing an impossible task: He had to munch his way through the hills that lay between the coast and the plains. Despite being a giant with a ferocious appetite, Te Mata died trying and his prostrate body now forms Te Mata Peak. Mad with grief, his lover hurled herself from the precipice; the gully at the bottom of the hill is supposed to be the indentation formed when her body hit the ground.

It wasn't a particularly cheerful tale for a Christmas morning. It was right up there with childbirth in a smelly stable without an epidural, in fact. Nonetheless, it encouraged us to approach our own impossible eating task for the day—the consumption of the vast seafood barbecue by the pool at lunchtime followed by a five-course dinner—with a new resolve. After a few too many digestive glasses of wine with lunch, we took a wobbly, giggly bike ride: Sheena and I balanced precariously on the hotel's tandem, while Duncan rode with slightly more control on a bicycle made for one. This was followed by a very big nap, then we heroically battled with dinner.

The next day carried on in style. We kicked off with another vast breakfast, then suffered a bout of indigestion when we saw the bottom lines of our bills on checking out of Mangapapa. We put money matters out of mind with a quick tour of Napier's fabulous art deco buildings—the town was entirely destroyed by an earthquake in 1931 and was rebuilt in the style of the time. At the top of Emerson Street, overlooking the sea, the A&B Building—originally an insurance company's offices but now a bar and restaurant—took command with its distinctive clock tower and coppery-green dome. In the next street, the Daily Telegraph Building spouted unashamed pink fountains beneath its stiffly rectangular, copper-framed windows. Beneath the windows, sharp geometric stripes and zigzags crissed and crossed in flamboyant shades of pink against the white brick backdrop. The Crombie Lockwood Building was pink again, though this time more salmon in shade. At the tops of its columns twirled Mayan flower patterns in paler pink and mint green. The gardens by the coast were dominated by a hexagonal blue fountain, whose turquoise basin blended with the blue of the water below and the darker shades of the ocean beyond. The stripes that ran down its stand reflected almost perfectly the arc of the jets of water that shot high into the clear blue sky.

We wandered around with our Tourism Board brochure and map that numbered the buildings and gave three lines of canned history for each one. And we concluded: Napier was pretty; it was vaguely funky. It was even mildly interesting. But there's only so long that one can admire buildings in various shades of pink, so, after an hour or so of trying to work out whether number fifty-two best fit the description of the candy-pink building with swirly bits, or was it the more orangey-pink building with twisty bits, we felt we had immersed ourselves in 1930s architecture quite enough and instead phoned Ian, a colleague of Duncan's, who took us on a tour of the wineries. There we had to drink some more—just to taste, you understand—and afterward we went to Ian's parents' house, where we ate and drank again just in case there were any small crannies left unfilled in our stomachs. We then headed back to the camper, where, courtesy of Sheena and Duncan, I spent the night sprawled out in great comfort in the bed above the front seats.

Then, suddenly, Christmas was over. Sheena and Duncan climbed into their RV and drove it away. I waved them off with a smile on my face. But underneath the blithe, contented facade, I felt tight and tense. My stomach churned. I began to feel just a tiny bit miserable.

For the whole of the last four weeks, ever since my arrival in New Zealand, I had been working toward Christmas. I knew where I was going. I had a place to be and a date to be there. However lonely the preceding weeks might be, whatever went wrong, I just had to survive until Christmas Eve, when I could laugh and eat and drink with friends. Somehow, I had forgotten to think about what might come next. I had managed to put out of my mind that, after Christmas, I still had to face the long road ahead, to continue my odyssey and attempt to survive.

I wanted to call out after them as they trundled off, laughing and chatting together in their big white box, "Stop, stop, please can I come too?"

But I didn't, because there was still a tiny part of me that couldn't stoop to admitting that I craved company, that I didn't much like the idea of being all alone once more.

Bereft and friendless, I loaded my luggage back onto the bike. It weighed a ton. Half of it might have been confined to the back of Gordi's wardrobe in Auckland, but the remaining bulk still seemed remarkably heavy.

I, too, seemed a little overweight. I squeezed myself back into my leathers. They had always been a snug fit, but now, with the small farmyard of animals that I'd consumed in the last few days, they were precariously tight. The snap on the trousers unsnapped, my newly capacious tummy sagged over the gaping waistband. Being fat was lousy. Being all alone was worse. And so I called Jeremy.

Jeremy Hansen was an ex-colleague from my time in Hong Kong. He had since moved back to New Zealand, where he was working as a radio producer in Wellington. He was spending Christmas with his family, though, right here in Hawke's Bay. He invited me to come and stay. I leapt onto my bike with renewed joy. Now that I had friends to eat with, even my tummy seemed less of a burden.

The Hansen family lived out in the countryside, in rural Hawke's Bay, far away from the coastal bustle of Napier and Hastings. In this part of the country, townships were scattered thin across the land; between them, sheep and cattle grazed on the flat green paddocks.

After twenty-five miles or so, I was starting to get used to being back on the bike. I was just beginning to enjoy the solitude, and the sense of speed along the country roads, when I came around a bend to find myself face to face with a traffic cone.

"STOCK," it announced in big, black, commanding capitals. My serenity evaporated in a flash. Stock? Where? What kind? Would the road around the next bend be slick with the ordure of extraordinarily productive cows? I didn't much like the idea of skidding on *that*. Considering the prospect of being thrown unceremoniously from my bike into a steaming puddle of excrement, I grabbed nervously at the brakes. I slowed down to about walking pace as I carefully, cautiously, rounded the next bend.

There were no cows. Instead, a herd of newly shorn lambs was littered haphazardly across the breadth of the road. There was no way through them, of course. As soon as I rode up close to them, they just let out high-pitched, yelping little baaas and zigzagged wildly around the road. How was I meant to ride through such a great number of skinny little creatures? I ground to a stop.

A car appeared from the opposite direction. I'll wait and see what he does, I thought. The car slowed right down, just as I had done. And then, persevering, it drove in an orderly manner right through the center of the pack, the little lambs obediently peeling off to one side and the other.

I tried the same trick. But I was approaching them from behind, which made splitting the pack more difficult. What's more, these lambs seemed to be able to smell my uncertainty and fear and, because sheep are creatures that like to follow, they took my lead. With just a glance at the wobbling black hulk behind them, the lambs panicked. They bleated frantically and ran helter-skelter down the middle of the road. They leapt and pranced, hopped and bobbed, capered and cavorted chaotically from side to side. They crashed headlong into one another. Lamb pandemonium had broken loose.

Just then, a farmer appeared from behind on a quad bike. From the trailer, a border collie barked with uncontained excitement.

"Please! Please! Please!" he seemed to beseech the farmer. "Please let me go and sort out the mess that this incredibly stupid woman has made."

Personally, I agreed with the dog. His solution seemed a good one. As far as I was concerned, he was more than welcome to leap in, sort out the woolly-brained sheep, and I could just putter through at a leisurely pace after him.

The farmer, though, was having none of it. He drew up level with me on his quad bike and stopped. I raised my visor and smiled at him sheepishly. He didn't smile back. On the contrary, he looked quite annoyed.

"You're going to have to go through," he snapped, terse and glaring.

"What, right through the middle?"

Surely not. If I just plowed through the middle of his flock, a scene of veritable lamb carnage could ensue. It was all right for him. He knew how to handle these creatures. He had probably been born in this field just to the left, had probably been suckled by a sheep, had probably ... yes, well, let's not think about that.

"Yes." He fixed me with a hard stare. "And go *fast.*"

Was he joking? Did he want lamb chops for tea? Did he not realize that I wasn't exactly in perfect control of my motorcycle? Yes, matters had improved exponentially in recent weeks, but still, I didn't entirely trust the bike. Our relationship was certainly becoming more cordial, but still it would only take one solitary lamb to hurl its panicky, out-of-control little self under the wheels, and the bike and its heavy load might well topple—and who knew how many of the farmer's bright-white little lambs would gambol no more?

I tried to do as I was told. For a split second or so, I even considered going fast as the farmer had instructed. But in the end, I just couldn't bring myself to open the throttle and blast straight through. A desperately amateur shepherdess, I edged forward, egging the lambs unwillingly on. One by one, they scampered off to the side. By the time I'd overtaken the leaders, I'd successfully split the herd over about half a mile of road.

The Hansens' house was relaxed and comfortable, slam-bang in the middle of nowhere. It wasn't the kind of place you could find because you had the address. It was the kind of place you could find only if you knew that, after climbing a hill and going around a bend past the gate on the left, it was the house behind the fence on the right. Or something like that.

Jeremy was probably a halfway hard Kiwi bloke once. At least, when I asked him about the whole business with New Zealanders not wearing shoes, he remembered that, as a child, he had run around barefoot for six months of each year, up gravel paths, over rocky roads, and it hadn't ever hurt. That qualifies as tough to me. But then he moved to Asia, bought shoes, and the soles of his feet went soft. Vinny, his boyfriend, isn't all that tough either, but then he's from Hong Kong, not New Zealand, so maybe he doesn't have to be.

We had dinner and conversation. I asked them their views on Maori rights issues—a risky topic at mealtimes, I had found over the weeks, but quite stirring if you enjoy seeing people explode, fathers and sons fight, and plates of potatoes fly across the table. The Hansens did none of these things.

"You should look in the *New Zealand Herald* archive for the story about the taniwha and the highway," Jeremy said. "It's interesting if you want to write about that kind of thing. Quite extraordinary, in fact."

He went on to explain. A couple of months earlier, a major road construction project was stopped because local Maori complained that the works were upsetting Karu Tahi, the one-eyed taniwha—a mythological sea monster—who resided in a swamp that lay in the path of the planned expressway. It seemed incredible to many New Zealanders, both Pakeha and Maori, that the feelings of a mythological beast could, in the twenty-first century, influence an intelligent government to the extent that it actually pulled the plug on a high-investment project. As such, it was considered a good example of the way in which the government, in bending over backward to accommodate Maori culture after more than a century of European domination, takes things too far.

I did later look up the newspaper archives as Jeremy suggested.

"It's cultural, just the same as goblins are part of European culture, it's the same sort of thing," Dr. Ranginui Walker, former professor of Maori Studies at Auckland University, told the *New Zealand Herald*.

"The difference is, of course, Pakeha do not use fairies, goblins, trolls, Santa Claus, God, the angels or saints to prevent motorways being built," retorted the journalist.

The Hansens were down-to-earth folk. They didn't seem the types to be swayed by the whims of goblins and trolls. Jeremy's father is a teacher in the local school; if I wanted to be put in touch with rural folk, Jeremy said, they were the people to ask. I explained my project.

"Ah," said Jeremy's mum. "If you're writing a book about New Zealand blokes, you need to spend some time with some shearers. Cathy's brother Lee runs five gangs, I think. I'll give Cathy a call."

And so it was that the next morning, when the Hansen clan packed up their cars and made their way north to their bach in Tokomaru Bay, I loaded up my bike and cruised off to Wanganui on the west coast, where the shearers were already busy with their blades.

I was low on gas, but reckoned I should have enough to get to a small township called Ongaonga, where there was a pump at the general store. I hadn't stopped to consider how remote rural New Zealand can be. I drove for miles and miles along roads with no buildings, no villages, no people. My fuel gauge sank lower and lower. I came to a tiny township with just a couple of buildings and a pub. They must buy gas somewhere around here, I thought. Maybe one of the five or so locals in this godforsaken village kept a few containers in his shed.

I went into the pub in search of someone to ask. One time-ravaged customer with rheumy eyes and spiky gray stubble sat on a stool at the bar, silently contemplating his ten a.m. beer. Behind the counter, a man in a red-checked shirt looked up as I pushed my way through the door. The stubbly man stared fixedly at his spume-smeared glass. He seemed deeply frightened. He absolutely was not going to make eye contact with this strange female dressed like Darth Vader without the cape.

"Er, yes?" said the bartender, clearly wishing I would beam myself back onto my home planet before I whipped out my light saber and annihilated the lot of them.

"Hi." I attempted to be cheery. "Can you tell me, is there anywhere I can buy gas around here?"

Red-Eyes on the barstool let out a rush of pent-up breath. The bartender's shoulders sank a few inches with visible relief. The weird woman was not going to stay. All she wants is gas. We don't need to serve her. We can be nice. We don't have to break the first commandment of New Zealand by being rude. A National Emergency has been averted.

"Aw, yeah," said the bartender, quite friendly now. "There's a pump at the general store in Ongaonga, six miles down the road."

Six miles. That wasn't far. My gas gauge was still a couple of notches above the bottom of the glaring red "empty" box. I should manage six miles with no problem. I chugged off down the road. And then, a few minutes later, the bike lost power. It spluttered, let out three loud, backfiring bangs, and slid to a very disappointing halt. My stomach knotted up. I felt faintly sick. Now what was I supposed to do, all alone, out here in the middle of nowhere?

I reckoned I must have ridden for about three miles since I'd stopped at the pub; that meant it was another three to Ongaonga. It would take about an hour to walk there. But could I really leave the bike on the side of the road in the middle of nowhere, together with my laptop computer, my cameras, my

Eve Lom facial cleanser, and my Mavala cuticle cream? I put the machine on its stand, got off, and fiddled around with the fuel switches beneath the seat. On a motorcycle, there's a reserve system: As long as you remember to keep the pointer at "on," should you run out of gas, you can turn it to "reserve" and you're given a few miles' grace. I turned the pointer to reserve, tried to start the engine.

"Huh-huh-huh-huh-huh," said the bike.

"Bugger," I replied.

"Huh-huh-huh-huh-huh," the bike repeated as I had another go.

And again.

And again. It didn't seem to be working, but I didn't have any better plan. Now I was starting to get quite cross. I glared at the bike and gave it a little kick.

"Stupid bloody bike," I spat at it. "You and your fickle, deceitful, lying gauge. Some help that was. It was, well, *millimeters* above the bottom of the red box."

Really, though, I wasn't cross with the bike, or with its gauge. I was cross with myself. Remembering to fill the tank with gas is generally considered to be a basic requirement when driving vehicles that are powered by the stuff. As gas-filling idiocy went, this was right up there with getting pinned to the pump up north. No, in fact, this was more stupid. In the gas station on my way down to Auckland, at least there was help at hand. Here, I was in the middle of nowhere, all alone.

"Bugger," I said again, because I couldn't think of anything else to do.

And then, miraculously, just before my bad temper transformed itself into full-fledged, chest-pummeling panic, a little drip of gas from the reserve tank found its way to the engine.

"Phwooooaaaaarrrrr," bellowed the bike with great jubilation.

"Thank you, thank you, thank you," I jabbered breathlessly, flinging my leg over and giving the fuel tank an emotional little kiss. And, with no further incident, I chugged into Ongaonga.

The woman at the general store filled the tank, looked at the pump gauge, and raised her eyebrows.

"You were pretty empty," she said.

"Hmm." I nodded. "I nearly didn't make it."

"Well." The woman grinned. "You wouldn't have been the first. There are plenty who run out of gas on this stretch of road."

And what happened to them? I wondered.

I climbed back on the bike and, hurtling along once more with the confidence induced by a tank brimming with lovely, sloshing fuel, I contemplated the fate of those who had made gasoline gaffes before me.

How far away from the gasoline oasis of Ongaonga had they been when they spluttered to a stop? Within walking distance? Or not? How long had they been stranded there on the roadside, many miles from anywhere? Hours? Days? Weeks? Perhaps desperation had forced them to slake their thirst with the last drops of radiator fluid and gnaw their way through the spare tire. After many weeks, they would have given up hope of rescue and tried walking, stumbling, crawling on bloodied, blistered knees along the long, deserted road to Ongaonga.

Or perhaps, on the other hand, they had decided Ongaonga wasn't worth the effort and had just shuffled off into a neighboring field where a whole new species of Kiwi bloke had spawned. Here, *Homo stupidly-ran-out-of-gasolinus* would have developed the necessary skills for survival in his changed environment. The male of the species would have learned to swing from trees, to silently ambush newly shorn lambs and strangle them with his bare hands for lunch. The female of the species would have broken twigs from trees and from them fashioned knitting needles. Using the fleece of the lamb so manfully slaughtered by her mate, she would have knitted pair after pair of woolly survival socks.

I spent some hours considering these possibilities as I careered along. And then, thankfully, before my evolutionary imaginings could become any more ridiculous, I arrived in Wanganui.

Sorting the Sheep from the Goats

WANGANUI IS NOT EXACTLY the center of the universe, even in a very small universe such as New Zealand, where the tiniest towns find something to be the world capital of. Turangi, where I went fishing with Pete and Skiff, is, somewhat predictably, known as the trout-fishing capital of the world. Meanwhile, Havelock in the South Island bills itself the green-lipped-mussel capital of the world, which seems pretty desperate if you ask me, but it makes them proud, while Fiordland tells tourists it's the "Sightseeing Walking Capital of the World," whatever that is meant to mean. Poor old Wanganui, on the other hand, doesn't seem to be the world capital of anything at all—though this must surely be a unique selling point in its own right.

Wanganui was, however, home to New Zealand's first kiwi fruit. In 1903, the headmistress of Wanganui Girls' College, Isabel Fraser, traveled to China to visit her sister, who was working there as a mission nurse. She brought back with her the seedlings from which all subsequent New Zealand kiwi fruits are thought to descend.

I checked into the Grand Hotel, which wasn't all that grand, and phoned Lee Matson, the brother of Cathy, the friend of Jeremy's mum. He told me he had a gang working up in the hills, about forty miles away on the road out to Raetihi, and I'd be welcome to ride up there and join them.

"You just take the road to Raetihi and it's about halfway there. Well, probably a bit more than halfway, actually. Anyway, there's a woolshed on the left," he said. "You'll find the guys in there."

"Right," I replied somewhat tentatively. I didn't know quite how to tell him that I wouldn't know a woolshed if it jumped out of the bush and said baaa.

"Or should I just come 'round and you can follow me up there?" asked Lee, whose sleuthlike powers of observation must have led him to detect that he was talking to a woman who couldn't find her way out of a paper bag. "I can pick you up from your hotel at eight-thirty tomorrow morning if you like."

I asked what I should wear.

"What should you wear?" Lee's voice rose about an octave in astonishment. I don't think he had ever been asked a sartorial question before, certainly not with regard to shearing.

"Yes, well," I backtracked wildly, feeling that I was giving rather the wrong impression of myself before I'd even begun, "I mean, is it okay just to wear shorts and a T-shirt, or is it going to be cold up there?"

In fact, as I was later to find out, there is a dress code for shearers. They wear special little leather slippers that stop their feet from sliding around on the wooden floor of the woolshed, and a particular style of tight dark-blue trousers.

Presumably the last thing you want when shearing is to find a sheep tangled up in your flares.

The New Zealanders have had many years to perfect their shearing wardrobe. The first sheep came to New Zealand with Captain Cook on his second voyage to the country in 1773. They didn't get off to a very good start.

"Last Night the Ewe and Ram I had with so much care and trouble brought to this place, died, we did suppose that they were poisoned by eating of some poisonous plant, thus all my fine hopes of stocking this Country with a breed of Sheep were blasted in a moment," wrote Cook in his journal on May 23 that year.

At the same time, Cook tried to introduce goats. Before they had a chance to procreate, though, they were eaten for dinner by a Maori chief. So much for the introduction of mammals.

Forty-odd years later, the missionary Samuel Marsden had another go at introducing a four-legged flock to New Zealand. He was more successful. Over the decades that followed, as increasing numbers of settlers arrived and bought land, farming sheep became a popular way to make a living. There were a hundred thousand sheep in New Zealand in the late 1840s. Within twenty years, as increasing numbers of immigrants arrived from Europe, dreaming of rural idylls and symphonic variations on the theme of "baaa," this figure had increased to 8.5 million. The first refrigerated ship carted five thousand dead sheep to Britain in 1882—and what was half a world between friends when a freezer was involved? New Zealand's remoteness no longer mattered. There was a fortune to be made from the export market.

All this changed, of course, when Britain joined the EEC and rather unceremoniously dumped New Zealand, choosing to buy European lamb instead. Amid decades of complicated paperwork that you should only read about if you're having trouble sleeping at night—common agricultural policies, farming subsidies, and the like—the number of sheep in New Zealand dropped from seventy million in the early 1980s to under forty million today. For all the decline, that still means that there are ten sheep for every person in New Zealand.

At eight-thirty the following morning I was standing as arranged outside my hotel, my shorts and T-shirt under my leathers. It was all very well the sheep being nervous, I thought, but I was feeling mildly jittery myself. What would these hardened shearers make of the presence of a soft northerner in their woolshed? What was I going to do when I got there? I could hardly see myself being much help. I couldn't even drive my motorcycle through a bunch of lambs, let alone convince a long-haired ewe that she'd like her locks trimmed.

My mind took an incongruous leap twenty-five years back in time to the day when my mother decided it would be nice if I was no longer a long-haired child but became a short-haired child instead. I'm not sure what her reasoning was—whether she was just fed up with the washing and drying routine, or whether she'd seen a photograph of a very glamorous short-haired child in a magazine and thought she fancied one all of her own. Pretending not to be dictatorial, she sought my approval to her plan. Frankly, I was unconvinced, but I was only seven, so in the end I just agreed. I can still remember sitting in the village hairdresser's, in a padded plastic chair facing a mirror on the right-hand wall, and feeling faintly duped as the scissors swooshed, lopped off my locks, and *completely changed the way I looked*. It was a freaky thing for a seven-year-old. Let's face it, if I can still, to this day, remember the event so clearly, it must have been really traumatic. In some bizarre way, it probably scarred my psyche forever. Just imagine, if I had never been forced to have my hair cut, I might not in adulthood be afraid of daddy longlegs. And if haircutting had had that kind of effect on *me*—who had, after all, been consulted on the matter, if only in a very cursory way—what on earth would be the effect on the sheep, who didn't even get the padded chair and the mirror and the grown-up magazines?

But I was unable to dwell on the underresearched matter of ovine psychology any longer because just then a blue pickup with the name "Lee Matson" inscribed on its paintwork pulled up. I climbed on the bike and followed Lee around the deserted, twisting road that led up over the hills and toward the woolshed. The scenery was spectacular. At first, the road followed the Wanganui River out of town, then broke away to climb through the lush green hills. It was a Sunday morning, and there was scarcely another vehicle on the road. It was a fantastic start to the day.

As it turned out, I could have found the woolshed quite easily on my own, had Lee happened to mention that it was the only corrugated iron hut for miles which would be vibrating to the deafening music that blasted from within, over the cacophony of shearing machinery and bleating.

I followed Lee up the steps. This was a small gang, with just four shearers. Inside, they were bent over at their stations, a sheep clutched firmly between each man's legs or pinioned to the ground under his knee as he sheared as quickly and efficiently as he could. Shearers are paid by the number of sheep they shear, but above and beyond the money, there's pride: Each man's numbers are marked down in the book at the end of each "run" or session of the day, and there's kudos in high numbers. As a result, the work is relentless and concentrated.

As soon as one sheep is shorn and bundled down the porthole to the floor below and freedom, the shearer strides briskly through the swing door on the upper floor, where the unshorn sheep are held, grabs another by the forelegs, and hauls it out. There is no rest, no relaxation, no chat, not until the second the clock ticks on to the end of the run, which lasts an hour and three-quarters or two hours. The rousies—the wool-shed's version of support staff—sweep around the shearers' feet, dividing the wool into the good stuff, A wool, and the raggedy, discolored, underside dreadlocks, B wool. The wool—fortunately—is dry, because the sheep are brought down from the hills a day or two before they're due to be shorn. That way, they don't get wet if it rains, and the farmer can make sure they're not fed in the thirty-six hours prior to shearing: It would be a messy business if a jittery sheep were to lose bowel control.

The run ended; tools were put away. The rousies stood their brooms against a bin overflowing with freshly shorn fleeces. A crate of snacks had been left on top of a bale, and everyone dug in. Lee had a quick chat, made sure everything was going according to plan, and introduced me to the gang.

The leader of the group was Dan, a lean, muscular Maori. Then there was his brother, Matt. They were garrulous characters, hard workers and heavy drinkers who were never at a loss for banter, however bad the joke. The other two shearers were Pakeha. Stu had a shaven head and whenever he wasn't working wore a beanie, with a big easy grin. Graham—the oldest of the shearers and stockier than the rest—was more relaxed about both his shearing numbers and his drinking speed later. There were also two children, Cody and Jacinta, both aged about nine or ten, who kept themselves entertained for hours jumping around in the freshly shorn fleeces and whose familiarity with everyone in the quarters was such that it took me a long while to work out which of the gang had parented them.

I'd have expected the rousies to be tough as old hide, but Amy and Christie really weren't. Then there was Hadley, a student at the University of Otago, who was earning some money during his summer vacation as a wool presser, piling the wool into the pressing machine and baling it up.

James was trying to dag the sheep, which in layman's language means cutting off the shitty bits around the sheep's bottom. He was having some difficulty, however, owing to the fact that his knee was fractured in three places. I never figured out whether continuing to try to maneuver heavy sheep in such circumstances meant that James was extremely manly or whether, more simply, he was stark, staring mad.

And last, but by no means least, there was the cook, whose name, imaginatively enough, was Cooky.

Cooky knew how to do many things with mutton. At lunchtime we had mutton stew; in the evening there were mutton chops. The next day for lunch Cooky roasted a leg of mutton.

"Traditionally we're meant to get a sheep for every thousand sheared," he said, "but we don't usually get that much. Doesn't really matter, anyway, 'cause we'd never be able to eat it all."

Don't they get fed up with eating mutton day in, day out? I wondered.

"The guys are all right, they don't mind, it's the girls that are always whining, 'We want chicken!'" Cooky shrugged.

Lee headed off in his van. The shearers went back to their stations, sharpened, tightened, and oiled their tools for maximum efficiency. They stood at the swing door and eyeballed the sheep on the other side, psyching themselves up for the demands of the next two hours. And then, on the dot of the appointed hour, the stereo volume shot to deafening levels, the shearers marched through the gates, and the rousies started to sweep and sort, and sweep and sort.

"Is there anything I can do to help?" I asked Amy, fearful of standing around like a lemon.

"Aw, well, you don't have to," said Amy, "but if you want you could help with the wool."

She showed me how. She and Christie divided the wool into good and bad with their brooms; I helped one at a time by putting the B wool in one bag and shaking the A wool to separate and blend the fibers. It wasn't bad to start with. The wool, fresh from the lamb's back, was warm and slightly—but pleasantly—greasy with lanolin. Shearers' hands are apparently silken soft on account of the lanolin in the wool that they handle all day—though I have to admit that I'm unable to verify this, as I never held hands with any of them. Less attractively, their left hand also tends to be hideously misshapen with swellings and calluses around the knuckles because of the pressure they exert to hold the sheep down as they shear. Most of these men could no longer straighten their fingers.

"Stop whenever you want to," Amy said cheerfully. "It's pretty hard when you're not used to it."

Hard? I thought. Huh! What kind of sissy do you take me for? Have you *seen* the size of that bike parked up the road, outside the sleeping quarters? That's mine, you know. I don't think you realize quite how tough I really am.

That was the first half hour. From then on, it all went downhill.

You wouldn't think that picking bits of wool up off the floor could be too taxing, but I soon felt as if I'd done a few hours' tiger-jousting in the gladiators' ring. My legs and back ached; I was desperate for a break. But until the clock ticks to the end of the run, nobody rests for a moment. It's just grab, shear, and shove, sweep and blend, on and on and on.

They looked a resilient bunch of people, I thought as I gathered another tedious armful of wool. They looked like the kind of people who would start work at some really ungodly hour in the morning. Christ, they probably started at something completely horrible like eight o'clock. And tomorrow I would have to start with them.

"Erm, so what time do you guys start work in the morning?" I asked Christie. "Early?"

"Yeah, pretty early. We start at five." Christie shrugged. "We work from five in the morning till five at night."

Five o'clock in the morning? Surely she was kidding. *Nobody* starts work at five o'clock . . . do they?

My horror must have shown on my face, because Christie started to grin.

"Yeah, and we get up at four."

Good Lord, I thought. What on earth am I doing here?

I could of course have stopped at any time I chose. I was, after all, a mere hanger-on and entirely unnecessary to proceedings. But somehow, pride prevented me from giving up. What was it with me? I wondered as I squatted for the thousandth agonizing time to pick up a handful of wool, then winced with every creaking bone as I slowly, painfully eased myself back up again. It was this Type A personality thing that had come back to haunt me. It meant that the simple issue of picking up bits of old wool became some kind of weird competition, yet another exercise in overachievement, a point of self-esteem. Why couldn't I be a nice Type B person? Then I could just go and lie on that bale of wool over there and take a nap. But no, I had to contend with pride. They say pride is one of the seven deadly sins. This was about as close as it had ever come to killing me. Christ, everything hurt. Picking up wool was lousy. I really wanted to go home. Excruciatingly, the minutes crawled by.

In the end, of course, five o'clock came. We piled into the van and drove the short distance from the woolshed up the hill to the sleeping quarters. This was another corrugated iron hut with rough walls and sliding doors. Partitions down each side of the building marked off rudimentary rooms: A kitchen, a bedroom with three beds, and a washroom ran down one side; three bedrooms lined the other. Down the length of the space in the middle sat a long table flanked by benches. There was one aging armchair and a huge fridge, its door held shut by an assortment of pieces of wire and bungee cord and labeled in capital letters with black marker, just in case anyone could forget: "BEER FRIDGE."

I'll admit, the prominence of the beer fridge cheered me up considerably. A nice cold beer was just what I needed. It should soothe my aching limbs splendidly, I thought. I didn't know at this stage, however, that the consumption of beer was about to turn into another marathon of machismo.

This gang reckoned they weren't heavy drinkers.

"I just have a can or two in the evening," Dan told me at about six-thirty in the evening, by which time he was well into his tenth. But this, apparently, was nothing. Another gang of ten shearers they work with drank their way through forty-eight cases—that's 576 big bottles of beer—in six days. That works out at an *average* of over eight quarts of beer per person, per night. And then, they get up before dawn and start shearing again at five a.m. And the next day the same. And the next.

The drinking session progressed. I needn't have worried that the shearing gang might regard me with disdain. They were a friendly, generous crew, always ready with a joke, a story, and a never-ending supply of beer. The heavier drinkers didn't have a large can each, they had a twelve-pack on the bench beside them. It saved getting up to go to the fridge as often, I supposed. Still, every couple of minutes one of them needed to replenish his supplies.

"You ready for another?" they'd ask me, enthusiastically hospitable.

"No, no, I'm fine," I'd say, clasping my can. If the alarm was going to ring at four o'clock in the morning, getting up was going to be ugly anyway. After eight quarts of beer it would be downright hideous.

An expression of consternation would cross the face of the man at the fridge.

"You sure?" he'd ask, incredulous, as if I'd just told him a sheep had turned pink.

Then one of the other guys would grab my can and give it a little shake. With abject horror, he would widen his eyes and give a couple of appalled little blinks.

"It's nearly empty!" he'd exclaim, shaking his head with great disapproval. "Better give her another."

By eight o'clock, when the drinking games started, I was beginning to feel distinctly light-headed. I can no longer remember the rules. Definitely there was hand-waggling involved, though, and certain signals indicated a change of direction, or skipping the next person in line.

The kids went to bed. Graham turned in too. I was about to drop asleep at the table but was determined to stay up to benefit from the full shearing experience. I waggled my left hand and my right, concentrating so hard it was pitiful. I really, really didn't want to lose this game and get up at four a.m. with a hangover.

"They say that shearing three hundred sheep uses as much energy as running a marathon," Matt announced during a lull in the session.

"Yeah, but nobody runs a marathon every day, eh," said Dan. "We shear that many sheep every day, seven days a week."

My incredulity was growing. In this particular woolshed, on that day, they were shearing lambs at a rate of about 450 per day each. There's no sick pay and no holiday pay. Yet everyone in that shed seemed to reckon that shearing was an awesome life.

"We wouldn't get this pay doing any other job," said Matt, adding that they take home around ninety cents a sheep. That means that, after deductions, they're making about three hundred New Zealand dollars, equivalent to almost two hundred U.S. dollars, each day. In high season, they work almost every day, their food and lodging is covered, and given that they're sitting in a shed in the middle of nowhere, their chances to blow their cash are few.

"Last year was my first season," Hadley told me, "and I just thought it was awesome. The work-hard and play-hard thing."

"I could never work in an office," Christie said.

But, *honey*, I wanted to tell her, in an office you have comfy chairs and a coffee machine. You can make personal phone calls and send e-mails to your friends. You can chat by the water dispenser about your love life, or the film you saw last night, or what Eric from Accounts did with Eve from HR. But I didn't.

I didn't like to point out to her that if she worked in an office she wouldn't have to get out of bed until it was light, and she would be allowed a cup of tea whenever she wanted one, not just when the clock dictated. She wouldn't have to eat mutton day in, day out; she could sometimes eat chicken or fish. So I asked her instead why she didn't train to be a shearer and earn a bit more.

"Ah no, I'm not tough enough," she said, and grinned.

She was tougher than I was by far. I wimped out and went to bed at midnight. Christie sat up with Matt, Dan, and Hadley, waggling their hands and laughing and drinking well into the early hours.

At four o'clock the following morning, the alarm blasted mercilessly, sadistically, psychopathically into life.

TRRRIIINNNNNNGG!

Oh my God, what's happened, oh it's the alarm, ouch, ouch, it hurts, make it stop, make it stop, my agonized brain shrieked inside my head. My eyes were stuck closed. They refused to open. I hid my head under the sleeping bag.

Christie, with whom I was sharing a room, bashed the alarm quiet. For a few wonderful minutes, we had blissful silence. I started to drop back into a relieved sleep. Just at the moment I reached joyful oblivion, an awful blaring echoed painfully from another room.

BEEPETY-BEEP, BEEPETY-BEEP, BEEPETY-BEEP.

Thump.

And then one that sounded like a siren: WAH-WAW-WAH-WAW-WAH-WAW!

Oh no. My body started to realize the horrible truth. This isn't going away. I'm going to be have to get up.

Crash.

The hut was silent. Nobody stirred. The first alarm came in for round two. TRING-*thud.* And the second, and the third. I was awake by now, but I felt about as much enthusiasm for hauling my traumatized body out from my sleeping bag as I did for volunteering to have my fingernails extracted by torture. And then, at about four-twenty, there was a resonant *ker-thump*. A heavy body had tumbled out of bed.

Shlip ... shlop ... shlip ... shlop. Weary feet dragged unwillingly across the rough, wooden floor. The first slow shuffle reverberated around the hut.

Creeaaak-bump. Christ, even the door was exhausted.

I dragged myself from bed. Everything hurt. All those muscles I'd been introduced to yesterday screamed. I made a half-hearted attempt at brushing my teeth and splashed water on my face. My eyes stung. Nobody spoke. Wordlessly we piled into the van. Hadley had lost the drinking games badly last night; a telltale puddle of vomit lay cold and lumpy outside the door.

Outside, the night was dark, chilly, and uninviting. A very different crew from the jabbering, gabbling, hand-waggling group of last night, we made our humorless descent to the woolshed. The shearers silently tuned their tools; the rest of us slumped blankly on the floor, on the bales of wool, until the dot of five. And then, suddenly, the Spice Girls blasted to life from the stereo.

"Baaaaaa," the sheep bleated.

Zzzzzzz, the shearing tools buzzed.

Shwah-shwah, the brooms swept. The pile of fleeces grew and the wool was pressed into bales as the shearing gang kicked itself once more into the relentless activity of another twelve-hour shift.

The first run, from five to seven a.m., was horrible. Every muscle in my legs and bottom ached—even more than they had done after that first day on the bike. I looked at my watch again and again: Just a few minutes seemed to have passed each time. It seemed like hours. What I really, really wanted was to go back to bed for a couple of hours and then get up very, very gently and slowly with a strong cup of coffee. But here in the woolshed, that wasn't an option.

Finally, at seven, we went back to the quarters for breakfast. My mind was starting to work, albeit slowly. I didn't want anyone to think that I wasn't up to the job, but I really couldn't see that I was going to last the day. I had been here for less than twenty-four hours and I was totally beat. I needed to take some photos—that might take up half an hour of the next run if I really spread them out—but that still left the best part of four runs, or seven full hours of picking up bits of wool off the floor. And that wasn't counting the breaks.

"Um, I think, if it's all right by you," I said to Dan, "I ought to head back to town after lunch, because I need to spend the afternoon writing up my notes."

Despicable liar! What I actually needed to do was to spend the afternoon lying weakly on my hotel-room bed nibbling on chocolate bars between snoozes. But the guys seemed to accept it. And in any case, I had by now achieved my goal. I had checked out the shearers and established that they were the nearest to *real* men that I'd found so far. They were physically fearsome. They wore undershirts over their dark-blue shearing trousers. They weren't scared of sheep. They had done something ingenious with a bit of wire—in their case, they had used it to hold shut the broken door of the beer fridge. They didn't chat unless they were drinking beer, and then only either to emphasize their toughness, in case I'd missed it, or to participate in games that involved the drinking of more beer.

On closer inspection, though, something was amiss even here. There were *children* in the woolshed. Two of the shearers—Matt and Stu, to be precise—seemed to be acting as primary caregivers. Were they real blokes, I now wondered, or were they merely New Men in shearers' clothing? They pinioned sheep and drank beer, for sure—but then quietly, secretly, when they thought nobody was looking, they snuck into corners. They cleared their throats and looked at their feet and then, in very, very low little whispers, they asked *questions*.

Casting their eyes about them furtively, checking that nobody would see, they'd hiss, "Have you brushed your teeth?"

Hiding their mouths behind their hands, they'd pretend to cough but instead growl clandestinely, "Why haven't you eaten your vegetables?"

So, it seemed, the new order had oozed even into the woolshed. Even the shearers were not immune.

Fortunately, I never did pick up any more fleeces. About half an hour into the next run, just when I was thinking that I couldn't spin my photography session out for very much longer, a mustached man in black rugby shorts and a black woolen jersey showed up in the shed. This was Dave, a local farmer, and Lee had asked him if he could spare a couple of hours to show me around his farm. I leapt at the chance.

"Get him to shoot us a wild pig," said Dan, thinking of the welcome change a little pork would make to his diet.

We rode in Dave's van over to the farm; my motorcycle was still parked safely in front of the shearers' quarters. At the farm, we exchanged the van for a farm bike, to which Dave hitched a trailer to ferry his six dogs. Dave drove, I sat straddled on the back. This was rough farming terrain with steep green paddocks. From high on Dave's land you could see both the snow-covered volcanic peaks of Mount Ruapehu to the northeast and Mount Taranaki to the northwest.

We chugged up paddocks, through gates, along rough pathways that gave astonishing views. Dave stopped the bike on one high ridge. The rugged deep-green hills reached to the horizon, their valleys carved out sharply by the volcanic activity that has shaped this region. Looking down at them from on high, the late-morning sun casting dark shadows into their contours, they stretched out like a crinkled sheet of emerald. Then, far away, Mount Ruapehu rose up against the cloudless sky. Its lower slopes were a faint mound of hazy blue; its peak, though, was white, covered in snow even in the summer. With the mountain's base barely discernible against the sky, the flat, ragged summit seemed to float above the green foreground. I was transfixed.

I could now see why people waxed on about New Zealand's natural beauty. It wasn't necessarily because each individual aspect of New Zealand's landscape was, in itself, the most beautiful of its kind in the world. Yes, the beaches were pretty, but they were no better than, say, the beaches in some parts of Asia. The mountains were sensational—but no more staggering than the Alps in Europe or the Himalayas. The lush green pastures, the waterfalls, the lakes—they were all remarkable, but standing alone they seemed no more phenomenal than lakes and waterfalls elsewhere. What was amazing about New Zealand was the constant change. Just yesterday, I had been on the dry, sunny east coast, amid the vineyards and peach orchards. Today, after a drive of just a couple of hours, I was in the emerald-green hills looking at a volcano on the horizon. A few days ago, I'd been strolling among sulfuric lakes that steamed in shades of red, yellow, and green. Tomorrow I'd walk the long, peaceful beach of the Kapiti coast. What was incredible about New Zealand was not, I decided, that each of these things was the most sensational I'd ever seen, but that the scenery changed so frequently from one form of beauty to another that my senses were perpetually alert. With every day, every short journey on the bike, there was a sight that was fresh, new, and constantly surprising.

Dave surveyed his stock—he'd just been away for five days over Christmas and was checking for any problems that might have arisen in his absence. Every now and then he would whip his binoculars from his belt as he spotted deer and goats and, on one occasion, wild pigs. But unfortunately for Dan and his stomach, they were far, far away.

To be entirely honest (and, Dan, if you're reading this, now is the time to skip to the next paragraph), I was glad the pigs were so far in the distance. Wild pigs are not known for their placid behavior when they find themselves looking down the barrel of a rifle. They have a nasty habit of charging. Given that the larger boars can weigh more than four hundred pounds, the force behind their tusks as they bury them into a hunter's flesh can make one a little sore the next day.

"When he decides to charge, he lowers his head until his snout is practically at ground level. From this position the whole power of his massive head and neck can be put into the upward and backward thrust of his razor-sharp tusks. . . . One flick of his big head and a dog that has ventured too close can be disemboweled, or a hunter could have his leg ripped wide open," wrote Ken Cuthbertson, self-professed old pighunting hand and author of *Pighunting in New Zealand*.

Cuthbertson reckoned that this area, around the Wanganui River, provided the best pighunting in the whole of New Zealand. The farmers' clearings were surrounded by miles of hilly, untamed bush. This was perfect for pigs because it was hard for hunters to penetrate. But what's a little hardship to a real man?

Cuthbertson tells stories of courage and derring-do. For

example, there's the tale of Curly Appleton, who used his last cartridge to shoot a pig at close range in the 1920s, while his brother had gone to fetch supplies. Instead of dying, as he was meant to, the dastardly pig spun around and charged at Curly. Fortunately for Curly, he was a real bloke, a man of strength and character. Finding no tree to shin up, Curly leapt onto the pig's back, knife in hand, and flung his oilskin jacket over the pig's head in an attempt to stop him from using his tusks.

"A fearful struggle followed. The oilskin was ripped to pieces by knife and tusk. The boar died, but Curly had a terrible rip and was in danger of bleeding to death. His leg had been opened up from ankle to thigh."

But Curly didn't let the mere loss of a few pints of blood deter him. Stanching the flow with strips of his shirt and passing out occasionally as he went, he crawled back to camp, where he dressed his own wounds and awaited his brother's return. To be a pighunter, then, you needed to be a real man. At least, that's what Cuthbertson seemed to reckon.

These days, pighunters are few and far between. One could argue that this is because there aren't as many wild pigs as there were, so there's a shortage of beasts to butcher. On the other hand, it could be because the modern-day Kiwi is a sensitive soul who prefers to bring home the bacon vacuum-packed from the supermarket.

Leaving the wild pig to snuffle in peace on the horizon, Dave and I climbed back on the bike.

"These are all wether lambs," Dave informed me as we drove through one paddock.

All-weather lambs? What is a not-all-weather lamb? I wondered. Did they have the kind that had to be brought in from the rain in case they rusted or shrank? Dave looked at me as though I were incredibly dim. He may have had a point.

Dave grew up on this land—it used to be farmed by his father. He took me to see a spectacular waterfall, whose churning white waters cascaded down from a great height over a dark-gray cliff face to a peaceful stream below.

"Don't reckon there's too many people have seen that," Dave said. "If it was somewhere less remote, it would be a huge tourist attraction."

"Have you ever been down there?" I asked Dave, gesturing toward the pool below.

"Nah. Don't reckon there's any way you could get down there," he said.

The waterfall was close, yet inaccessible, untouchable, out of reach. Nobody had come along and carved steps into the rock or drilled pegs to hold ropes and handholds so that visitors could climb down in safety. This waterfall just stood alone on this remote patch of land. Its tons of water pounded the rocks below as they had for centuries.

Dave, like the shearers, scored pretty high in bloke points. It wasn't just the rugby shorts and the brimmed hat. Nor the knife in a holster around his waist. Nor the way he replied, when I asked him how old his baby daughter was, "Er, I think she's about six or eight weeks. Something like that." It was more to do with the way he bounded up the hills on his long, lean legs and kept up a running conversation with his six dogs.

"Gedup'ere, Shark!" he'd yell as Shark decided it would be more fun to run alongside the trailer than to travel inside it. Or he'd shout, "Bring back, Ben!" and then give a powerful, much-practiced whistle.

"It's no good them running all the way, because then, when you want them to actually do some work, they're too bushed and all they want to do is lie down," Dave explained.

It was then that I noticed something was not quite right. Just when I was thinking that Dave might be the *real* genuine article, I made a terrible, incriminating observation. Dave was wearing plastic aviator sunglasses.

"Yeah, sorry about the glasses," he said. "Pretty embarrassing, really. I don't like to wear them, but I have to, you see, because of my hay fever."

Hay fever? A Kiwi bloke with an allergy? That is *so* modern, faddy, and fashionable. Heavy with disappointment, I sighed and shook my head. My search was not over yet.

Dave, however, had the last word. As we made our way back down the grassy ridges toward the farmhouse, he spotted a small group of goats trotting across the hillside. Jumping nimbly off the farm bike, he whipped a rifle out of an aluminum box at the back of the seat. (I hadn't noticed before, but I now found that I had more or less been sitting on it.) Silently, but speedily, he stalked down the slope and squatted by a rocky outcrop. There was a moment's concentrated silence, then three loud reports rang out. About two hundred yards in the distance, three of the goats dropped to the ground. A short while later, Dave reappeared, dragging the dead beasts by the legs across the grass, and dumped them in the trailer.

"That'll do for the dogs' dinner," he said.

I managed to fit a roast mutton lunch into my tight schedule, but when the time came for the shearers to go back to the woolshed, I found that my notes were calling very urgently. So I climbed back on my bike and, sore and tired, returned to town.

Back in the sanctuary of my hotel, I lay in the bath, drank cups of tea, and ate all the chocolate in the minibar in an attempt to restore my energy levels. And then, feeling not much better, I limped down the street to the cinema to indulge in another piece of New Zealand culture: *Lord of the Rings*. It was four fifty-five. I thought of the shearers still in the shed and about the quantities of beer machismo would require them to stomach before bedtime. I drank Coke and ate potato chips but fell into an exhausted sleep during the film anyway.

A few hours later, I left Middle Earth and returned to central Wanganui. The muscles in my bottom and the backs of my legs ached so much that the mere act of sitting down made me wince. Bending down to undo my shoelaces was painfully impossible. My feet stung from blisters inflicted by the jandals I had bought in Auckland in order to live the full Kiwi experience.

For sure, even in these soft and sensitive times, the New Zealanders were turning out to be much harder than I had bargained for. Yes, Dave might have had his allergies and the shearers their kids, but still they were stronger than I was by far. My brief attempt to live as a Kiwi had left me a crippled, quivering wreck. A few hours in a woolshed and I could barely walk. A gentle stroll in jandals and my feet were in shreds. Was it so shamefully obvious that my ancestors were neither fearsome warriors nor rugged pioneers but spineless stay-at-homes?

By the time I managed to ease my complaining body from under the blankets the following morning, the gang would have sheared and swept their way through about five hundred sheep. I felt no guilt, just relief, as I hobbled to my hotel-room door, retrieved the complimentary newspaper that lay in the hallway outside, rearranged my pillows to accommodate lounging in bed in a reading position, and settled down to start my day's investigation into New Zealand culture the comfortable way.

After a cup of good strong coffee, I felt sufficiently invigo-
rated to putter gently over to the Wanganui Museum. The
museum's prize possession is a particularly large and impressive war canoe. Its highlight for me, though, was its display of
old Maori rat traps.

According to the yellowing, felt-tip-pen labels, rats used to
be quite a delicacy among the Maori—though, to be fair,
there wasn't much other meat to eat. The only other mammals in New Zealand before the arrival of the Europeans
were bats and a type of dog that had been brought by the early
Polynesian settlers. The reason for this is that New Zealand
separated from the ancient supercontinent, Gondwanaland,
about eighty million years ago—after flora and forests had developed on earth but prior to the emergence of mammals.

Arguably, it was the very lack of mammals in New Zealand that contributed to the overpowering of the Maori by
the mammal-ridden Europeans. The presence of animals that
could be domesticated in Europe made agriculture possible.
Once food could be efficiently supplied and stored by just a
section of society, other individuals were free to pursue activities such as manufacturing and warfare.

Neither bats nor rats could pull carts or carry riders. The
Maori were therefore never given the chance to organize agriculture and society to the level of efficiency of their European
invaders. And so it was the earliest evolutionary processes of
the land itself that led to the relatively slow technological development of the Maori people and their vulnerability to
takeover from the north.

Rats, however, could be eaten, and the Maori devised elabo-
rate contraptions of twigs and flax string to catch them. Here
in Wanganui, somebody with great dedication to the dissemi-
nation of Maori culture had spent many happy hours in his

shed with a pile of sticks and a few bits of string so that the rest of us, too, may learn how they went about it.

The first exhibit was a kind of twig wall with a hole in it. Dangling in the hole was a flax noose. When the rat walked through the hole and by an unfortunate twist of fate—for the rat, though not for the hungry Maori—inserted its head into the noose, it knocked another twig on the ground. This triggered a series of twig reactions that resulted in the noose's tightening around the rat's neck, lifting it up and neatly garroting it. There were several variations on the hanging theme. There was also a twig pit: The rat followed the bait and then fell in the pit to await its fate in a Maori stomach.

Strangling rats for dinner was not something to which I had previously given a great deal of thought, but these traps had been painstakingly re-created by someone who cared about the topic a lot. He or she had even made cuddly little stuffed rats who were imitating various stages of death throes, dangling in nooses and wallowing in pits to better demonstrate the effectiveness of the traps. It was intriguing stuff, and if I am ever stuck on a desert island and need to trap a rat for my tea, my newfound knowledge will certainly come in handy.

Needless to say, the Maori in this area gave up eating strangled rats quite some time ago: The Europeans started breeding sheep and pigs here in the mid-1800s. Unfortunately for the Maori, there was a downside. In order to graze their livestock and build their houses, the Europeans wanted land. And the Maori are still to this day fighting about the way they acquired it.

The first Europeans are thought to have arrived in this area in 1831, when a Pakeha named Rowe, who traded in preserved Maori heads, sailed up the Whanganui River. The Maori didn't much like the look of him, welcomed him with a single, fatal club-blow to the neck, and later tried to sell his own shriveled, smoke-dried head to another white trader.

The Europeans became a little demoralized at this point, but within ten years their greed for land had overcome their anxiety. After some negotiation, the tribal chiefs agreed to hand over some of their territory in exchange for about a thousand dollars' worth of goods including guns, powder, cartridges, razors, soap, blankets, and tobacco. The Maori allowed the Europeans to build a township—Wanganui—on the banks of the river. When the Maori realized what the term "permanent acquisition" actually meant, however, bloody disputes ensued. Although agreement was theoretically reached some years later, dissent festered and has been sporadically bubbling to the surface ever since.

Most famously in recent years, in 1995 Maori protesters occupied Wanganui's Moutoa Gardens, which they said belonged to the iwi (tribe), not to the Crown, for seventy-nine days. They staged another occupation of the gardens in 1999 and then again in November 2002, to protest the granting of permission to a state-owned energy company to take water from the Whanganui River, and to voice complaint about the Waitangi Tribunal's delays in processing their land claims.

What has happened in recent years in Wanganui is an indication of a much larger movement of Maori protest across New Zealand. The decline in Maori population, culture, and language that followed colonization lasted more than a hundred years. Then, in the 1970s and '80s, a Maori cultural resurgence began. Maori-language kindergartens and primary-school streaming were created. The government, over time, instigated a policy of "closing the gap" between the material and cultural well-being of the Pakeha majority and the relative poverty of the Maori.

The Waitangi Tribunal was set up to investigate Maori claims into unfair confiscation of lands. It's a costly and drawn-out process, with each claim taking many years to investigate. Some of the claims are gargantuan in their implications. Take, for example, the claim Wai 388—it sounds innocuous enough until you realize that this is the claim for the Auckland isthmus. The Ngati Whatua tribe that sold the land says the Crown breached their agreement; the Waitangi Tribunal has been investigating the claim for ten years already. Adding to the complication, other tribes refute the Ngati Whatua ownership of the land and therefore their right to compensation, which is forecast to run into many billions of dollars. It wasn't theirs to sell in the first place, they say. And so the process of this claim, and many, many others, goes on. And the taxpayer, who at the end of the day is footing the bill, becomes increasingly disillusioned.

Closing the gap is a slow process. Still today, Maori make up fifteen percent of New Zealand's population but fill half of the prisons. They are three times more likely than non-Maori to be unemployed. Their health is worse too: Maori are twice as likely to smoke, four times more likely to die of lung cancer, and among the Maori population five times more babies die from sudden infant death syndrome than among the non-Maori.

Now, of course, many people—both Pakeha and Maori— think that things have swung too far the other way. The Maori-language streams in schools have higher levels of funding than their English-language equivalent. Inevitably, this creates resentment. In other cases, Maori tribes try to make money out of things that many New Zealanders consider to belong to the country as a whole. For example, in 2000, the Ngati Toa tribe announced that it was trademarking the world-famous "Ka mate!" haka, performed by the All Blacks before their rugby games, and would charge the New Zealand Rugby Union a fee for its use. (In the end, this never happened.) Nepotism abounds. In 2001, a government loan of more than two million dollars was frozen when it was discovered that tribal authorities had built houses for their own families and not for the poorer Maori who really needed them.

It's a complex issue, and a difficult one for an outsider to fully appreciate. But at least, I thought, the New Zealanders have had the courage to confront the issue and to address the problems that colonialism created in the past and has perpetuated to this day.

The Moutoa Gardens were quiet now. Wanganui's hanging baskets bloomed peacefully; the people strolled around the cafés and shops looking distinctly apolitical. It was New Year's Eve. Everyone was gearing up for the party tonight, for the holiday tomorrow. Back home in London, a dozen or so of my friends were getting ready to meet up for dinner, to see in the New Year with food, champagne, and laughter. I was all alone in Wanganui. I went to the liquor store and bought a bottle of wine, then, realizing I didn't have a corkscrew, went into the bar of the hotel and asked them to open it for me. I was clearly a pitiful sight.

"Aw, you can't spend New Year's Eve all alone," said a rotund, cheerful man who turned out to be the manager of the hotel. "You must come down here and join us. We'll be here from eight-thirty, a whole group of us. You *must* come."

I agreed that I would. But by eight-thirty, I was already falling asleep. Oh, to hell with New Year's, I thought. I'm sure they were nice people downstairs; no doubt they could have told me hours' worth of entertaining stories. But tonight I was tired of making friends with strangers. If I couldn't be with real friends, I wouldn't spend the evening with anyone at all. I ran a bath, lay in it, and drank a glass of wine. And then, at half past nine, I went to bed—alone.

Capital Adventure

THE NEXT THING I knew, it was January 1st.

I checked out of the hotel, climbed back on my bike, and rode out of town. I was heading south, toward Wellington, but first I had a pleasant New Year's Day diversion: I was going for a picnic lunch by the beach with Frano, a family friend who emigrated to New Zealand a couple of years ago, and her partner, Michael.

If I were to live in New Zealand, I think this spot on the Kapiti coast would be my location of choice. The beach stretches for mile after mile of fine, packed sand. It's not crowded—the odd person runs down the beach, or walks with their dog, or swims among the waves. Out to sea sits the beautiful bird sanctuary of Kapiti Island. It all feels blissfully remote. And yet this place is a mere twenty-five miles from Wellington. The minute you get bored of being blissful and remote, you can just hop on the train and you'll be in the city, with its cafés, restaurants, shops, and galleries, in a flash. These coastal townships ought to be heaving. In any country other than New Zealand, you would scarcely be able to squeeze between the designer swimwear on the beach. The real estate prices would have soared through the roof as rich city folk rushed to invest in this perfect location. But in New Zealand, there aren't very many people and they don't set much store by designer goods, outside of Auckland at any rate. To sit on the beach in a bikini from Prada would be considered horribly beneath one's dignity here.

We sat around beneath the trees on the grass that lines the beach and ate picnic food. I told them of my sheep-shearing experiences, and we talked about strange New Zealand vocabulary—the origins of the word "rousie," which, apparently, is an abbreviation of "rouseabout," whatever that might mean. The New Zealanders are big on shortening words. A postman is a postie, and while in the rest of the world we struggle to get our tongues around "double-you-double-you-double-you-dot," in New Zealand, ever practical, they shorten it to "dub-dub-dub." "Cocky," a slang New Zealand word for a farmer, is an abbreviation of cockatoo: Originally the term was derogatory, the label the larger farmers gave small free-holders who would buy up a section of land, work it for a couple of years, sell it at a profit, and then move on—like a cockatoo who picks off the best bits and then flies away to pastures new. Nowadays, the word's used for all farmers.

Back at the house, Michael gave me an old copy of *The New Zealand Dictionary* that he had no more use for since he'd bought the later edition. Michael was good with words—he worked at Te Papa museum in Wellington, writing the literature that accompanied the exhibitions. The dictionary was fascinating: As well as explaining all those Maori words that I didn't understand, it was brilliant on New Zealand slang. The letter "D" alone was a mine of information. "Darth Vader's pencil box," I learned, is the Bank of New Zealand head office in Wellington. A "doodackie" is a thingamabob. "Dopiness" is a deficiency disease in sheep. A "donger" is a heavy wooden club used for stunning fish.

Most interesting of all, though, I found while leafing through the pages that the ordinary Kiwi bloke had an entry all of his own.

"**ordinary bloke,** also **average** or **real Kiwi bloke:** The stereotypical New Zealand male, regarded as a well-meaning sacred cow," revealed the dictionary.

Sacred cow? So one wasn't supposed to criticize these guys, then? Oops. But then, I thought, perhaps regarding the Kiwi bloke as sacred was the very essence of the issue. To suggest that he was somehow an immutable institution, something that could never be changed, was in itself unspeakably dangerous, for the key to survival in a species is mutation. Yes, the Kiwi bloke himself might alter his ways, might even die out in his present form—but surely these shifts were vital for the survival of New Zealand man in general. If the Kiwi bloke fails to evolve—the long-faced scientists, those harbingers of doom, wring their hands and shake their heads—an even worse outcome could ensue. For the penalty for *that* evolutionary sin is extinction.

The next morning, after breakfast, I set off for the capital.

When I had mentioned to my new friends, the sheepshearers, that I was going to spend a few days in Wellington, they had looked truly horrified.

"What d'you want to do that for?" Matt had exclaimed as he choked on his twentieth can of beer.

It was a difficult question to answer. The chic cafés? The glamorous urbanites? The art, the culture, the ballet? The world-renowned Te Papa museum? The restaurants with their extensive wine lists? The shopping, the gardens, the harbor? The pretty colored weatherboard houses perched haphazardly on the hillsides?

"Er, well, I s'pose I just thought I ought to, seeing as it's the capital city and that," I mumbled.

Really, though, I was hoping to find in this cosmopolitan hub with its wider gene pool confirmation of my theory that in the cities the Kiwi bloke was mutating faster than in the country. In Auckland, the men's newfound sensitivity had seemed more pronounced. Guys were, apparently, indulging in therapy. Down at the Viaduct I'd seen plenty of potential SNAGs—Sensitive New-Age Guys. If Wellington seemed to be going the same way, the evolutionary theory that variation speeds mutation would hold fast.

And anyway, I *like* cities. I've spent years living in cities. I like the buzz, the anonymity, the fact that you can go to bed at eight o'clock or get up at midday and nobody knows or cares. I like sitting in cafés and watching the city folk strut by. And Wellington, even more than most cities, is just the spot for doing this.

About ten years ago, apparently, Wellington used to be a little on the dull side. Parliament sat and diplomats dithered here, but the place had no soul. Then somebody thought, hmmm, how about we use those funny little beany things to brew something that doesn't taste like yesterday's dishwater?

Until this point, everyone had been convinced that brown powder + hot water = the height of sophistication. But with

Wellington leading the vanguard, a veritable coffee revolution occurred in New Zealand, just as it had in Italy three hundred years before. Powdered coffee was out, cappuccinos, mochaccinos, and double decaf lattes were in. In 1985 there were about seventy-five cafés and restaurants in Wellington. Now there are around four hundred. And the Wellingtonians have been sitting debating the issues of the day in these places ever since.

I checked into my hotel and changed out of my leathers into a T-shirt and shorts. I considered the jandals for about a second, then picked them up and hurled them into the wastebasket behind the TV set. It was no good. They hurt my delicate English feet, and today I was planning to do plenty of walking. I put on my sneakers instead and headed out for a caffeine buzz.

To be entirely honest, there weren't that many people to watch, because Wellington was busy staging its own, very silent version of the "Christmas closedown"—that period between Christmas and the middle of January when many businesses shut up shop altogether so their staff can pack up their cars and drive out to the beach. Most New Zealanders take all their vacation days during this time, in much the same way as Mediterranean countries abandon the office in August. Still, there were enough stragglers to ensure that the shops and cafés, at least, were open.

One coffee and muffin fatter, I started to walk. This is one of the great things about Wellington. You can walk everywhere because—dare I say it?—Wellington is very, um, small.

In fact, it's tiny. It's not like a city at all. In New Zealand, a town qualifies for city status when it has a population of twenty thousand.

Wellington is also very quaint. There's only a handful of

high-rise towers. The main streets—all three or four of them—
are lined with two-story brick buildings. In the residential
areas, the painted weatherboard houses lie piled chaotically
on the hillsides. Their picket fences, gleamingly bright and
white, betray nothing of the tough, battle-worn military con-
notations the city's name suggests.

What is it with New Zealand and military names? I'd gone
from Hastings in Hawke's Bay to Wellington (via a few very
unmilitary sheep-shearers). From Wellington I'd take the
ferry over to Picton, named after the commander of the Fifth
Division at Waterloo. From Picton I'd ride over to Nelson.

It's ironic, really, that a country that is now so well known
for its pacifism should have named so many of its towns and
cities after battles, generals, and admirals. Since the mid-1980s,
New Zealand has been nuclear-free, a stance to which it has
held firm despite the wrath of the world's superpowers: the
ANZUS defense treaty with Australia and the United States
broke down when New Zealand refused access to U.S. war-
ships, while protests against French nuclear testing in the Pacific led to the sinking of the Greenpeace ship *Rainbow Warrior*
in Auckland Harbour.

New Zealand's armed forces, which are primarily involved
in peacekeeping duties in the Pacific region, are minuscule. Its
navy and air force comprise little more than two thousand
personnel each; the army isn't much larger at around 6,500.
There are probably more guns in Brixton. Yet in the past,
New Zealand and the concept of the macho Kiwi man have
been strongly shaped by military events.

It was arguably the First World War that created for the
first time the sense of real nationhood in New Zealand. Previously, New Zealanders had always considered themselves to
be British. It was when the men went to war that it became

clear that they were different from the other nations that made up the Empire. New Zealanders had their own distinct identity.

The "noble New Zealander" was defined by those very characteristics that had already become fashionable during the last half of the previous century as Darwin's theories of survival of the fittest had become accepted. The ideal man was healthy, athletic, and courageous. Now, not only would these attributes pass strong genes on to the next generation, they would help him win the war. But New Zealand suffered terrible casualties—about a quarter of the country's male population of military age was killed or wounded—and the impact on the tiny country cut deep. The "Anzac legend," the mythical fearless Antipodean warrior, was born in Gallipoli and is heralded to this day.

At the dawn of 2003 in Wellington, though, there was not a hint of military fervor. The only reference at all, in fact, to guns and bombs was the writing splayed across the front of a T-shirt in one of the shops on the fashionable Lambton Quay: "I am a bomb disposal expert. If you see me running, try to keep up."

I hadn't seen *real* shops for weeks, so I browsed ecstatically in virtually every one along Lambton Quay. I poked around in Kircaldie and Stains, which, apparently, is New Zealand's answer to London's Harrods. It was nowhere near. In many respects, it was much nicer than Harrods, which is vast and brash. Kircaldie and Stains was, on the contrary, tiny and understated. But it seemed curiously outdated. The lighting seemed too dim, the customers all the other side of sixty. I quickly bailed out and headed instead for Cuba Mall.

Here, the music blared and banged in heavy beats from the open-fronted shops. Stalls of CDs sat outside their doorways on the pedestrianized walkway, while the happening set of Wellington grooved on by. This was about as close as Wellington gets to street culture. There was certainly an attempt here at the urban-warrior look—tank tops and muscles, tattoos and bandannas. But I had the distinct impression that these men weren't really all that tough, that they might not survive more than an hour or two in the bush. They looked the kind that were quite happy to strut around the city streets in their bulky, loose-laced sneakers but might become cross and tearful very quickly should any real mud splatter their perfectly stylish clothes.

That night, I checked out a few of Wellington's nocturnal establishments with Aylmer, a friend of Gordi in Auckland. Wellington nightlife is not at all sleepy and dusty; on the contrary, it's as cosmopolitan and groovy as that of any other capital city. And because the city is so small, most of the bars and clubs are within easy walking distance, which makes a bar crawl easy. You could probably actually crawl it for real if matters took a major turn for the worse.

Because Wellington is so tiny, everyone seems to know everyone else. Aylmer and his friends Delly and Audrey had to stop on the street to greet people every couple of steps. And this was at a time, in the first week of January, when almost everyone was out of town on vacation. What would it have been like when everyone they knew was here? How would they ever walk from one end of the street to the other, even if that street was exceedingly short?

"If I had a brother," Gordi had told me back in Auckland as he wrote Aylmer's phone number on a piece of paper, "Aylmer would be him."

"Why's that?" I asked. "Does he look like you?"

Gordi laughed. "No."

"Does he behave like you?"

"Er, no."

My suspicions mounted. I took a deep breath. "Is it because you love him?"

There was a moment's uncertain silence, a slight shuffling of feet, then, "Er, yes."

Oh, for heaven's sake. He was meant to be my on-the-ground bloke consultant. He was supposed to be a traditional, macho man. I knew he lived in Auckland and was therefore open to the namby-pamby influences of the wider world, but this was hopeless. He couldn't go around *loving* his mates.

Aylmer is a big guy, a Maori bodybuilder. His upper arms have about the same girth as my thighs. He was a police officer for fourteen years; now he works as a personal trainer.

"I used to go to work and people would try to kill me," he said. "Now I go to work and my clients give me a hug."

A dedicated family man (at the age of thirty-eight, he has five children and a granddaughter), he started a support group, SMASH, an acronym for Single Men and Separated Husbands, after his marriage broke up. I got the impression that the group's support activities revolved more around propping up the bar and buoying the profits of the breweries than about sitting around in a circle making affirmations, but membership of the group seemed to be very much sought after. It turned out that Gordi was the group's Auckland representative. This was something he had never told me about. Setting up support groups wasn't what I'd been led to expect from Kiwi men.

I spent the next morning making myself look marginally less feral. My standards, shamefully, had dropped during my weeks on the road. It's a peculiar side effect of travel. For the first few days, I look and behave quite normally. After that, my hair starts to stick out at funny angles and my clothes aren't quite as fresh as they might be—and this creates some concern. This is not the bad bit, though. At least for now I still *care* about looking a mess. The next stage in the descent of this woman is when I stop worrying that I might smell on the basis that I am far from home and unlikely to meet anyone I know. Trips to the laundry become less frequent at this point. But it is still not the very bottom of the cycle. This comes when I discover that, if I leave the smelly T-shirt in the bottom of a pannier for long enough, *the smell actually goes away.* And that gives my clothes a whole new lease on life.

Now, though, I was in a city where people might notice such things. There were hairdressers and leg waxers and eyebrow shapers. I had not seen any of these kinds of people for many weeks. It was time to do things depilatory.

The hair-washing girl took Kiwi friendliness over the top and up into outer space. Whereas, in most countries, the shampooer will ask you one or two questions about whether you'll be doing any shopping in town this afternoon and then shut up when you're monosyllabic, this one had stamina. With all the fortitude of her pioneer forebears, with that same determination that saw Sir Edmund Hillary conquer Everest and Sir Peter Blake bring home the America's Cup, this girl was not giving up.

"So, are you having a good weekend?" Hair-washing Girl quizzed me as she yanked my head back into the uncomfortable porcelain curve.

"Er, yes thanks," I replied, hoping this would do.

"What've you been up to?" Water sprayed, shampoo lathered.

"Um, this and that ..." For heaven's sakes, my head was extended back so far my throat was at full stretch. My vocal cords were about to ping. She didn't really expect me to *talk* in this position, did she?

"Did you go out last night?" Who was she, the police? Was someone murdered? Was I a suspect?

"Er, yes." Ever vigilant, I didn't give too much away.

"Great!" What? Was that it? Was that enough to keep her happy? It seemed as though she genuinely wanted to know if I had friends, or if I was sad, lonely, and desperate. It's a good thing she caught me today and not on a day after an evening spent all alone in my motel room watching reruns of *Coronation Street*. Phew. At least today I had the opportunity to look funky and cool.

"Got any plans for later on?" she bravely battled on. *And what's it got to do with you, you nosy cow?* I wanted to bellow. *Can't you just wash my hair and shut up?* But then she would have known that I was from London, so I didn't.

Wellington, as well as being a good place for having your hair cut and your legs waxed, is the cultural center of New Zealand. In addition to politicians, this is where the dancers, artists, and literati hang out. It's also home to Te Papa, which means "Our Place," New Zealand's most popular museum.

Te Papa has taken Kiwi ingenuity out of the garden shed, added several gallons of creativity, a few tons of fiberglass, and a couple of thousand tubs of brightly colored paint to become one of the premier attractions of the country. In the Time Warp rides, the auditorium divides into three separate roller-coaster cars and you bump and judder your way through the sea, explode in volcanic eruptions, and in one particularly dramatic moment get eaten by a shark.

Personally, though, I preferred the interactive sheep-shearing game. This is how it goes: You put two dollars in the slot, manfully seize the cuddly stuffed sheep by the forelegs with your left hand, and grasp the laser shearing tool in your right. Then you run the laser around the sheep's body as quickly as you can, following the direction of the arrows and numbers painted on the sheep. There is no room for creativity in this trade. It's not like hairdressing—sheep don't wander into the woolshed with a magazine clipping of Dolly and say, "I want my wool to look just like that"—which is lucky, really, because my attempts would have left any poor sheep looking like a moth-eaten old carpet. I really wasn't very good at it at all. "You shear like a townie," the scoring sheet rebuked me.

The townies I'd met were certainly very different from the shearers I'd been with a few days earlier; they were more into duds than dags. I walked some more, along the harbor front and up Mount Victoria, which affords remarkable views across the city. I walked to the cable car, rode up to the Botanical Gardens, then strolled around those. Coming back down into the city, I passed the Prime Minister's residence, a green, leafy compound that didn't seem to have a single security guard at the door—though, admittedly, Parliament was on holiday, so the Prime Minister would have been out of town.

New Zealand's Prime Minister Helen Clark is, as her name suggests, a woman. So are many other prominent politicians. The Leader of the Opposition was a woman until 2001. A third of MPs are female; many hold high posts. It's interesting: Could the prominence of women in positions of power be linked to a failure of men to flourish in the changing world?

Austin Mitchell, a British Labour Party MP, spent many years living in New Zealand as a university lecturer and television current affairs frontman and commentator. He argues in his recent book *Pavlova Paradise Revisited* that it is exactly the

New Zealand man's well-known liking for the bush and beer that has led to the increased influence of women. In the early days of colonialism, he says, society tried to be egalitarian, and it was hard for the male breadwinner, earning much the same as his neighbor, to make a difference to his family's standard of living. It was the wiles and management savvy of the purse-wielding women that dictated whether a family became rich or poor.

"That long experience made women the stronger characters compared to weaker, sport- and booze-obsessed males, hiding out in sheds, gardens, pubs and clubs while the women ran the homes like a small business, generating a dividend for men to waste."

Then along came the pill and legal abortion. Now that women could control their fertility, they could take their skills out of the home. Having cast off the apron and burned the diapers, they could begin to take over the world.

"The best indicator of the prospect to come is young people. The young male culture is defensive, escapist, even resentful. That of the young women is real and realistic as well as more serious and dedicated. The one looks well geared to progress, the other for regression. So perhaps it's time for the emancipation and radicalization of young males, but no doubt women will take proper care of that, as soon as they're in effective control," Mitchell concludes.

Oh dear, guys, it's not looking good.

Coming down past the Prime Minister's house, I walked through the parliament buildings, past the Beehive, a terrible monstrosity that some people claim to be the architectural symbol of New Zealand. The area was quiet now; the politicians were promulgating their views elsewhere.

Jeremy and Vinny were in town, back from the Hansen family's bach. They invited me over for a drink that evening. Their flat was on Cuba Street, strategically placed between the humming Cuba Mall and the activity of the harbor.

We talked about Te Papa, about the Prime Minister's accusations that the place was too pop; about its treatment of the Waitangi Treaty, where the visitors walk through a maze of pillars, each fitted with speakers from which different voices clamor with their different views. Jeremy told me I had missed a brilliant exhibition at Te Papa on one of the higher floors. He was right. I'd grown tired of Time Warps and interactive sheep-shearing and given up.

The next morning, a Sunday, the shops were closed, so I went back to Te Papa and spent a happy hour or so looking at the exhibition on Maori contemporary art. I then *ran* up Mount Victoria, along the dirt pathways through the woods, and was rewarded with spectacular views of the city from the top. As I jogged back down, I thought about the city men. With the men in Wellington, I'd talked about art and politics. I'd hung out with a bodybuilder who'd set up a support group. There wasn't a tank top in sight. The men in the cities were more sensitive souls than those in the boondocks, it seemed. It was in the cities, with their cosmopolitan, multicultural influence, that the environment was changing the fastest, and the men were more willing to mutate.

Wellington came alive on Monday morning. The Wellingtonians who couldn't manage a whole three weeks of closing down had returned from their vacations and were generating, if not quite a rush hour, certainly a collective stroll. I checked out of my hotel and headed to the ferry terminal. An hour or so later, I checked out of North Island altogether. I was heading south. New Zealand's North Island has more people—roughly three million to the South Island's one—and is the more significant nest of Maori culture, for the majority of Maori settled in the north, where the climate is warmer and closer to that of their native Polynesia. But the South Island has the wild West Coast and the monumental, snowcapped Southern Alps. It is the South Island that is home to the mists and waterfalls that enshroud the staggering granite rock formations of Fiordland and plays host to the endless, golden expanses of Otago. The South Island, people had told me, was a whole new world. If I'd liked the north, they said, I was going to *love* the south.

Gone South

AN OILY SLICK DRIBBLED menacingly down the ribbed metal gangplank.

"Come slide on me, Leatherpants," it beckoned, oozing and unctuous.

Riding onto the ferry had not been easy. The whole charade seemed to have been set up for cars and RVs, for vehicles with four nice, stable wheels and glove compartments in which to stash the paperwork. Boarding on a motorcycle was a whole different story.

First of all, I had to produce my ticket for a man at a little kiosk window. It was at this point that I realized I had locked my ticket in the top box on the back of the bike. A growing line of cars growled behind me as I turned off the engine. All their tickets, of course, were ready and waiting in the hot, eager hands of their passengers; at the merest tap of a little black button, their electric windows would whir and whiz and they would exchange their ticket for a boarding pass.

"Thank you," they would say, and, beaming smugly at the efficiency with which they had conducted this little operation, they'd put the car in gear and purr off toward the boat.

I kicked down the bike's stand, swung my leg over, and clunked in my cumbersome biker boots around to the back of the bike to retrieve my ticket. I gave it to Kiosk Man. He reciprocated by offering me a large green plastic disk, which apparently served as a boarding pass. I looked down at my hands. There were still only two of them.

In my left hand, I was grasping sundry bits of ferry-related paper, which made pulling in the clutch without dropping everything into an oily slick something of a challenge. My right hand was taken up with the throttle. There were no hands left for bright-green plastic disks. Panicking slightly by now at the line snaking out of sight behind me, I stuffed the whole lot down the inside of my jacket.

Clatter-clatter-rattle-bump. I juddered over the symphony of slippery ramps, greasy rods, and life-threatening divots that led up into the ferry's deck. A stout, tattooed man wearing a neon-yellow plastic vest directed me to a corner where a bevy of seasoned bikers in well-worn leathers were expertly tying and tugging on ropes. I quaked. The man in the yellow vest looked at me and shook his head, not so much with pity as with disdain. He sniffed witheringly at my squeaky-clean leathers, at my knee pads without so much as one stylish scrape, at the odd bits of paper protruding strangely from my chest. I responded with my best "I'm-so-helpless" smile. And then, letting out a disapproving "humph," the yellow-vested man yanked a handful of ropes from the railing above his head and tied my bike down himself. Clearly, I did not look the type to be trusted with complex matters such as knots and clips.

The ferry was a cacophony of children bawling, parents bellowing, and TV sets blaring. The PA crackled to life, adding to the din. For an extra fifteen dollars, said the disembodied voice that boomed from the megaphone on the wall, I could upgrade to Club Class, where no passenger under the age of eighteen was allowed and where the tea and coffee were free. I convinced myself that I would have spent at least ten dollars on coffee during the three-hour crossing anyway and went to join the grown-ups.

And so, in relative comfort, I crossed Cook Strait. After an hour or so the ferry cruised in among the rocky coves and outcrops of the Marlborough Sounds. With Arapawa Island to our right, and the bays and coves of the mainland to our left, the ferry wove its way through the narrow Tory Channel, into Queen Charlotte Sound, and toward Picton. Momentarily forgetting we were adults, we crowded excitedly to the tiny, scratched windows of our cabin to gawk at the sandy bays and jagged coves that provided our first glimpse of the scenic wonderland that is New Zealand's South Island.

I was met at the ferry port in Picton by Ian Fitzwater, who, together with his brother, John, owns Adventure New Zealand Motorcycle Tours, the company from which I had rented the bike. Although I'd picked the bike up at their depot in Auckland, Ian and John are based in Nelson—when they're not touring the country with groups of bikers, that is, for as well as renting out bikes they run guided motorcycling tours around New Zealand.

Ian appeared on a Harley so gleaming I could have eaten my lunch off its bodywork. He wore an easy smile, a worn brown-leather jacket, and jeans. On the back of his bike, his ten-year-old son rode pillion.

I'm not sure whether Ian strictly qualifies as a Kiwi bloke.

After all, he was born in Billericay in Essex and survived there for *six whole years* before he managed, with his family, to execute a successful escape. Once free from the constraints of garden gnomes and gatepost gargoyles, Ian worked hard at shedding his soft Essex ways.

"On the first day of school, our mum dressed John and me up in our best school clothes, like English kids," Ian later told me. When they got there, the New Zealand boys in their shorts, tank tops, and bare feet had laughed at them. From that day on, Ian and John decided they needed to toughen up. Every day they walked to and from school over the gravel roads in bare feet until their soles hardened enough to run around barefoot with the others.

"Where are your shoes?" their mother had asked, aghast, when they had arrived home without them.

"The kids in New Zealand don't wear shoes," Ian and John had replied with a newfound stoicism.

I was frankly apprehensive about having to ride with Ian. For all my attempts on the phone to sound as if I knew what I was doing, it was going to be a different matter when we were on the road. When Ian could actually see me crawling around bends like a leather-encrusted slug, he would understand instantly what kind of incompetent he had rented his precious bike to. There were telltale scrapes gouged into the plastic of the panniers following my early altercations with the asphalt up north. The top-box holder was held together with sturdy but unconventional fiberglass, thanks to Morris. There was little hope that Ian was not going to notice.

We rode into Picton and stopped for lunch.

"Ah," said Ian almost at once, raising an eyebrow at the poor, battered panniers, "you've fallen, then."

I tried to play it down. I focused hard on those incidents

before my luggage cull when the bike had tumbled when I'd tried to put it on its stand.

"Yes," I said. "I think I was carrying too much luggage to begin with, and the bike, well, you know, a few times it just kind of fell over all by itself. But then I got rid of most of my stuff and it's been much better ever since."

It's important, they say, always to accompany the delivery of bad news with an upbeat ending. Like: "Sorry, Bill, my executive bonus has slid five measly figures, so I'm having to economize. I'm afraid I've decided to let you go. Yes, I'm fully aware that you'll never find another job because you're over the age of twenty-five and you've got three gray hairs. Your family will from this day forward subsist on scraps gleaned from other people's garbage cans, and social exclusion will drive little Jimmy into a life of violent crime. But, hey, look on the bright side: To make up for things, I'm giving you a parting gift of this magnificent plastic paperweight *embossed with the company logo!*"

Or, in my case: "Yes, Ian, it would seem that your panniers have mysteriously trashed themselves, but there's no need to worry. Through great personal sacrifice, I have solved the problem. I have drummed up every ounce of courage and am attempting to live for the next couple of months without my designer denim jacket."

I think I fooled him. He didn't confiscate my bike—or, more accurately, his bike—anyway.

We rode from Picton on the scenic route over the narrow, winding coastal road to Havelock, the green-lipped-mussel capital of the world, and then inland and over to Nelson. Ian rode sympathetically slowly; after a few minutes, my nerves eased off and I began to rather enjoy myself. The main problem was keeping my eyes on the road, not the scenery.

"Be careful," Ian had warned. "On these roads you get tourists coming 'round the bends on the wrong side of the road 'cause they're so busy looking at the view they veer over to the right."

It was good to be riding with someone who knew these life-or-death survival techniques.

The next morning Ian took my bike in to his shop for a thorough servicing; then we sat down with maps, notepad, and coffee, and he imparted the secrets of motorcycling in South Island. I filled several pages of my notebook with gems of wisdom garnered from Ian's many months on the road.

"Don't take Highway Six between Wanaka and Queenstown; it's full of construction. Take the little yellow road via Arrowtown instead," he advised me. "On the West Coast, don't go straight down to Hokitika. Come off the main road at Greymouth, drop into Blackball, where you'll find some real characters at the pub known as the Blackball Hilton, and go around the back of Lake Brunner."

Then, when I'd written notes until my hand was sore, I took another piece of Ian's advice, climbed back on the newly serviced bike, and set off for Golden Bay, on the coast to the northwest of Nelson.

Golden Bay used to be called Murderers' Bay, until the brains at the Tourism Board decided it didn't sound sufficiently cozy. Personally, I think they should have kept the more gory name, partly because it sounds a lot more exciting, and partly because to rename it covers up the sanguinary events of a messy but significant date in New Zealand's history.

The date was August 18, 1642; five days earlier a Dutch seaman named Abel Tasman had spotted land. This, he thought, was the legendary "Great South Land"; its discovery would bring him wealth and fame. The native Maori sent out canoes to greet the strange white foreigners. They had something of a communication breakdown. Thinking that their guests had defied their ritual challenge, rather than just having failed to react through utter ignorance as was actually the case, the Maori switched the regular canoes for a war canoe. Tasman, not recognizing that the shape of this particular boat's prow denoted the hostile intentions of the paddlers within, sent one of his own boats to greet them. And then he stood and watched in horror as the Maori clubbed to death three of his men and took the body of one of them ashore, where they presumably ate him. Tasman's enthusiasm for this wondrous new land took a kamikaze nosedive, and he departed the turquoise waters as fast as his sails would carry him. It would be more than a hundred years before Europeans— this time led by Captain Cook—would "discover" New Zealand again.

Abel Tasman, however, has not been forgotten, as the national park that lies between Nelson and Golden Bay was named after him, and the coastal track is today one of New Zealand's most popular Great Walks. I rode around the edge of the national park now and wound my way up and over Takaka Hill. At last I seemed to be getting the hang of the tight little bends and going around them at a respectable speed. For the first time on roads such as these I wasn't having to pull over for cars to pass; they were pulling over for me. I started to take pleasure in the power and acceleration of my machine, leaning the bike one way then the other as I climbed higher and higher, trying not to look too hard at the sensational views for fear of flying away to the big bikers' paradise in the sky, then winding back down the other side until the road was low and flat, opening the throttle and roaring off into the distance.

Just beyond Takaka, I stopped at Pupu Springs. The water here was astonishingly clear. The water bubbled, creating a continually changing pattern rippling over the smooth stones and boulders on the pool bed deep below. The colors were extraordinary—electric blues and emerald greens over the yellows, browns, and purples of the rocks.

It was a hot day; I was warm in my leathers, and the water was inviting. Unfortunately, though, a swim was out of the question. These springs are, apparently, very sacred to the Maori, and the splashing about of putrescent tourist bodies, their rippling tires of flesh betraying the consumption of a carrot cake too many, upsets the resident taniwha—a mythological sea creature of the same kind as the one that had caused the government to pull the plug on its highway building project some months earlier.

In any case, I had no time for swimming. I had many more miles of road to burn before the day was through. I was heading to Farewell Spit, an almost two-hundred-mile round trip from Nelson. Farewell Spit is a renowned bird sanctuary, right at the northernmost tip of South Island. Just before the small township of Collingwood, the main highway ended, and I turned left onto the coast road. It was flat, straight, and deserted except for occasional minibuses ferrying visitors to the bird sanctuary. With my newfound familiarity with the throttle, I positively hurtled past them and cruised light and luggage-free alongside the ocean just yards away. Flocks of black swans bobbed on the still tidal flats. Cormorants and oystercatchers strutted and pecked.

At Puponga, the end of the road, I ate a sandwich in the

coffee shop. In the next room was a giant telescope; you had to put a coin in to make it work—but the room was humming with children fighting to take turns. I'd ridden all the way out here. It seemed a shame to go home without taking a look at the birds. I wandered into the tiny telescope room several times. I studied the wall charts that featured pictures of different kinds of swans. I fixed the children with a hard, grown-up stare, of the kind that frequently—and quite unreasonably—fools small people into thinking that your need is greater than theirs. Some while later, finally, the children were lured away by the bribe of ice cream, and the telescope was free. I inserted my coin in the slot with breathless anticipation, looked through the lens—and there, in the distance, were dozens of black swans.

They weren't really doing an awful lot. They were just, well, bobbing about on the water, really. After that wait, after all that buildup, I was determined to enjoy them—but, to be honest, there didn't seem all that much to be gripped by. What was it that had kept the children so amused? Had they seen something I hadn't? Was the sight of a bunch of swans sitting on the water doing nothing at all really very gripping? I felt mildly uneasy, plagued by a sense of spectator failure. And then I thought, Oh, forget it, left the telescope with some time to spare before my dollars ran dry, and climbed back on my bike for the long ride home.

On the way back, I stopped in the township of Takaka. It's known for its arty inhabitants, hippies, and herbalists. I stopped for a coffee in a funky café.

"Is that your bike outside?" a very hip-looking character with long blond dreadlocks asked me as I waited to pay. He cast his eye first over the bike and then over my leathers.

And then it dawned on me: My attitude had changed. I no

longer cringed when people mentioned the motorcycle, nervous that I couldn't talk bike. I no longer felt that I was a fraud, not a real biker, just a rather foolish woman posing in leathers. With a new sense of pride, I was suddenly starting to enjoy the bike and the attention it brought me.

"Yeah," I replied as coolly as I knew how. I sucked my tummy in and stood up a little taller and straighter in my leathers. "Yes, it is."

I sauntered outside as gracefully as my clunky motorcycling boots would allow, attempted to throw my leg over the bike without knocking it over onto the street, turned the key in the ignition, and, with a few more revs than were entirely necessary and a little toss of my helmeted head, shot off into the distance with a mighty roar.

It was only later that I discovered that image comes at a price. So concerned had I been with the way I looked, I hadn't noticed, when I took my helmet out of the top box, that I'd knocked my favorite sneaker onto the ground. Actually, it wasn't my favorite sneaker—I liked its mate equally—but the remaining shoe wasn't much good to me on its own. It wasn't until I was back in Nelson that I discovered the loss. Perhaps the tanned, dreadlocked character found it there as he gazed wistfully at my leather-clad form disappearing into the distance in a cloud of dust and is to this day touring the land, earnestly searching through woolsheds and slick city bars, clutching one slightly dirty Puma sneaker and trying it on the feet of all those women desperate to join his laid-back bohemian lifestyle. Or perhaps I can keep on dreaming. As I had already seen, the New Zealanders aren't big on shoes. Probably a green-fingered Takakan is using it to grow herbs in.

*   *   *

The next morning, I took the bike back to the shop so that the mechanics could fix a couple of new parts they'd had to order.

The shop was a little way out of town, and I had a few errands to run. I wanted to go to the post office to send a small package home and to the World of Wearable Art exhibition, which has become an annual catwalk fixture in New Zealand and whose costumes are on permanent display. I needed wheels to get there.

"Just give her the BMW to ride," Ian shouted to his son, who was also called Ian and who worked in the shop. Ian the Second passed me the keys and wheeled the bike around. I balked. What? I had to ride a whole different bike? I'd only just formed a relationship with the last one. What kind of two-timing polygamist did they take me for? Was it acceptable to be involved in a long-term relationship with a Suzuki but to sneak off with a BMW for a one-morning stand? And anyway, I might fall off. I climbed on and wobbled anxiously away, hoping the Suzuki wasn't looking.

The World of Wearable Art was wonderful. I particularly liked the bras. The "crystal candelabra" was made of glass with two candles on holders protruding from the mannequin's breasts; the "chicken breasts" comprised a bra sprouting vast yellow furry chickens; from another contraption emanated a pair of boobies. It was fabulously humorous, a joyous tongue-in-cheek takeoff on the strutting, emaciated vanity of the mainstream fashion world.

Back at the bike shop, my bike was ready. I had a fairly long ride today by my meager standards—about two hundred miles—and it was already midday. I had been planning to head over to the West Coast and then turn south, but Ian reckoned that the northern part of the coast was worth a stop for a couple of nights first. Given that he was the expert, I took his advice. The new plan, then, was to ride southwest out of town down to the spectacular Buller Gorge, then west over to the rather less spectacular town of Westport. From there, I'd follow the coast northeast up to Karamea. Of course, had I traveled as the crow flies, I would have had to ride a mere sixty miles, but the road doesn't go that way and I am not a crow. And, in any case, had I flown I would have missed the Buller Gorge and the café at Tauranga Bay.

The Buller Gorge was so pretty that I actually had to stop so that I could gawk at the view unimpeded by concerns about traffic hurtling around the bend on the wrong side of the road. I was beginning to see one of the major problems of riding a motorcycle in New Zealand: I had to battle constantly between getting a kick burning up every bend to the best of my—in my case, limited—ability, or going more slowly so I could take in the view. But like yesterday, the cars were no longer overtaking me. My motorcycling was definitely improving.

At Westport I took a detour around the headland to the seal colony and café at Tauranga Bay. The café is in a remote spot that is vying to be the most scenic location on earth. I had a coffee, then walked down to look at the seals sunning themselves on the rocks, then shuffling along, slow and slouching, and splashing into the churning waters that swirled around the crags where they dived and twirled with a new elegance.

The road out of Westport was long and flat. In one brief moment of courage and skill, I passed two cars at once. Admittedly, they were going very slowly—one was towing a camper and the other was towing a boat—but this was an achievement nonetheless.

"Take that," I called out with true, butt-kicking bravado as I zoomed past the first, "and that," as I hurtled past the second. I climbed the bendy pass over the aptly named Radiant Range and passed a number of sweating cyclists, wheezing and pink-faced with effort as they hammered down on their pedals. I remembered my own painful efforts to climb the Spanish Pyrenees a year earlier and felt quite smug at my change of status.

"Hey, guys, you should try a motor," I muttered as, with a broad and gloating grin, I whipped around the bend.

The last twelve miles were flat and straight as far as the eye could see. Just a few yards to my left, the waves of the West Coast crashed through the pale blue, early-evening light onto the driftwood-strewn beach. Rough-hewn rocks jutted out of the water, the silver-white waves lathering about them in foaming eddies. To my right, the green hills rose sharply, their dense bush canopy swathed in light mist. There was not a soul, not a creature in sight. It didn't seem like the kind of place to employ a policeman.

I wonder how fast I dare make this bike go? I thought, high on the fresh sea air, heady with the exhilaration of beauty and solitude. And then, with a quick check over my shoulder to make sure there was really nobody watching, I whispered a short prayer and opened the throttle.

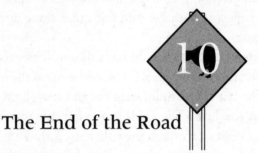

The End of the Road

KARAMEA IS THE LAST gasp, the final resort, the end of the line. At Karamea, quite literally, the road runs out. After Karamea, there's just track—and it's because of that track that most people come here at all.

Classified as one of New Zealand's Great Walks, the Heaphy Track is the only path that joins the wild West Coast to the calmer waters of Golden Bay to the north. Originally, back in the 1890s, the track was built so that farmers could move livestock between the two regions; nowadays, it's managed by the Department of Conservation, and hikers come from all over the world to walk the fifty miles over the tussock downs, through lush forests and down to the roaring beaches. The hikers, who generally start in the north and end their trip in Karamea, stay in specially constructed huts with bunk rooms and cooking facilities. In the early days, before Gore-Tex turned guys soft, things weren't so easy. Back then, men were *real* men, and wringing the necks of wekas (brown flightless birds) before boiling them up for tea, then bedding down for the night in a fetid bog, was all in a day's work.

Take this account from one Harry Washbourn, who carried out a survey of the land in 1883: "We had only one blanket each and that was always wet from being carried outside the swag to protect the food and, as soon as we had finished tea, each one took his blanket and turned in. At first, until our cold wet clothes and blanket got a bit warm, we thought going into a very cold bath would be warm and comfortable by comparison.... For a fortnight on this part of the journey, we were never dry day nor night, and we seemed none the worse for it."

So, if it never did Harry any harm, who are the modern-day tourists with their high-tech breathable waterproofs to complain?

I slowed down as I came into the township and rode down the long straight road. The buildings were spread out, a handful here, then a stretch of road before another cluster of one-story constructions: a gas station, a café, a general store. A little further down, on the corner of the intersection at the end of the road, was the Karamea Hotel. It was here that I had booked a room. It was a well-tended, cream weatherboard building with a freshly painted dome-shaped signboard declaring it to have been established back in 1876. Its window frames and door panels were painted brown; its roof was green. Hanging baskets dangled from the corrugated-iron porch; beneath the windows, pink flowers grew in the beds. Two doorways led within. Above the one on the left hung a small dark green plaque: "Restaurant." And above the right-hand doorway, another sign, large and yellow with red letters this time: "The Local."

Around the back of the pub, the landlord, Kevin Storer, had done up some rooms complete with luxuries such as bathrooms and TV sets. My French windows looked out across the hills. In the coin-operated laundry, the machines churned perpetually with the gear of those who had just emerged from the track. I parked my bike outside my room, unloaded my panniers, then wandered back over the garden, past the wooden bench tables, and through the doorway marked "The Local" where I ordered a pint of local beer and a plate of fish and chips.

The next morning, I planned to run for a couple of hours through the first stage of the Heaphy Track. Because the track officially starts a couple of miles away from the township, I put on my leathers over my running clothes and rode my bike out there. Arriving in the clearing at the end of the dirt road that designates the beginning of the track, I simply stashed my leathers and helmet in the panniers (which were conveniently empty since I'd tipped their contents in a pile on the floor of my room) and headed out in shorts, tank top, and running shoes.

The sky was overcast, with just occasional flecks of blue. I wobbled uncertainly over the long, swaying swing bridge at the entrance to the track; this was the first time I'd ventured onto one of New Zealand's bush bridges, and they pitch unnervingly for the newcomer. Back before the bridges were built, though, the men who surveyed and cut the track with their saws, picks, and axes had to ford this river.

From the bridge, I descended into a rich grove of nikau palms. For the first mile or so, I didn't run at all. I was too busy staring in wonder at the tall ceiling of palm branches and fronds, at the riot of vegetation at my feet, at the luxuriant, lavish, overwhelming sense of green. I was too occupied taking photographs—which now do the scene no justice—even to think about breaking into a jog. But after I'd polished off half a roll of film or so, I set off at last over the packed-earth path through the forest. And then, half an hour later, the green ended. The path broke out into the light, onto the coast itself.

Through the clouds the colors were delicate and muted. There were none of the electric cobalt skies and shimmering turquoise seas that I had seen in Nelson and Golden Bay; here the scenery shifted subtly between shades of misty-blue and gray. In contrast, where a shaft of light broke through and caught on the crest of a wave, the effect was brighter than white, almost lucent. The spuming water flashed and gleamed as it encircled rocks and then rolled down the boulder-strewn beach. The bays and coves wove in and out, away into the distance, each promontory enshrouded in an ever softer hue.

There were few people out here on the track. It was a glorious, remote spot. Occasionally, I would pass a hiker, laden with several days' supplies, shuffling in the opposite direction to me. This was the end of their walk; they had given up pretending to look happy as they lugged their packs, sleeping bags, and four days of trash to the finish line.

"Is it far to go?" a couple of gray-haired American men croaked. One was walking several yards in front of the other. Conversation had long since ceased. Every few paces, they stopped to rest. They looked as though they were about to breathe their last.

"Ah, it's probably only about another hour," I reckoned.

I had the misfortune to pass them on my return, a couple of hours later, as I ran back to where I had started.

"You were a little conservative with your hour," the leader of the two gasped, bitter and accusing. I muttered apologies and ran on. Just around the bend, I passed the last distance post of the track: Thirty minutes to the end, it declared. I ran a little faster.

I arrived at the end of the track, carrying only my camera, the remains of my water, and a long-sleeved running top. The pack-laden Americans were nowhere to be seen; others, though, were milling about, waiting for their ride into town, or simply lying on the grass, drinking in the last of the view.

Trying to look casual before my audience, I sauntered over to the bike, slithered into my leathers, pulled on my helmet, and roared off along the unsurfaced road in a cloud of dust. Frankly, I thought I looked pretty good. I felt quite the action heroine—and even managed to keep up the cool biker-chick image for several hundred yards. Then I felt a terrible itching just below my right eyebrow. A sand fly had found its way into my helmet and was tucking into lunch. I let out a little yelp, flung up my visor in a frenzy, and started slapping wildly at my head.

After all that running, I thought perhaps I deserved a little reward in the form of a chocolate brownie. I'd seen a big, enticing basket of them on the counter of the café I'd gone to that morning for my energy-enhancing prerun chocolate muffin.

"Nice bike," said a bloke in tank top and shorts as I clambered off it outside the cake shop.

"Nice leathers," said the cheerful, rotund woman in the café. "But you won't be able to fit into them for much longer if you keep coming in here twice a day." And she grinned knowingly. The great disadvantage of being in a town with just 640 inhabitants now became horribly clear: Big Cake Shop Lady was watching you. She knew exactly how many cakes each inhabitant ate in a day.

I went to the pub for a whitebait patty that evening. I sat on a high plastic stool at a faux-wood-coated Formica table in front of the large screen playing sports, at a safe distance from the two Americans I'd met earlier, who were drinking beer and playing cards in the corner. They must have been well into their third or fourth beer by now; their cheeks were rosy and their humor seemed much improved.

Three guys in rough working clothes were playing pool behind me. One, a big man in jeans and boots with unkempt hair, finished his turn and walked by my table on his way to the bar.

"Hey, you're with John's tour," he said, recognizing the Thunderbike T-shirt that Ian had given me from his shop in Nelson. John Fitzwater had been in Karamea with a tour the night before, but they'd left early that morning and I hadn't caught up with them.

I had a couple of beers with the man, whose name was Daniel, and his mates Gerie and James. I explained that I wasn't actually with John's tour but that I'd rented one of his bikes. Daniel was the most garrulous of the three friends. Gerie actually came from East Ham and, despite having moved out here eighteen years ago, still spoke in a broad London accent but with Kiwi vocabulary thrown in. Every inch of his arms was covered with twirling, entwining tattoos, in faded shades of red, green, and blue. James was the quietest of the trio. He seemed embarrassed that his friend had just started chatting to a random woman in the pub; he would have preferred to go back to the pool table with the boys.

Daniel, Gerie, and James were good customers at the Karamea Hotel, to the extent that a number of their fellow 637

Karameans had deemed it necessary for them to have alcohol counseling. So once a fortnight, a counselor from Westport would drive out to Karamea, courtesy of the taxpayer, and talk to the guys about taking control. The counselor, apparently, was a good bloke and the guys liked talking to him.

Now hold on a minute. Counseling? *Here?* So far, I had concluded, only the city boys had mutated to such a level as to actually seek the talking cure. Mary and Bill, the psychotherapists in Auckland, had plenty of business, and Aylmer in Wellington had his support group. But they were all urbanites, subject to wider influences. According to the principles of evolutionary theory, where there are more genes to choose from, mutation will be more rapid. Here in Karamea, though, there were only 640 people, and *still* the men were taking therapy. Karamea was slam-bang in the middle of the boondocks. It was the very end of the road. My theory that rural men mutated more slowly was, in one fell swoop, disproved.

This was the problem with science, I thought. Just as soon as you come up with a nice clear theory, some pesky bit of research or evidence comes along to undo all your hard work. I sighed, took a large and soothing gulp of beer, and changed the subject.

"So what do you do for a living in a town this small?" I asked Daniel.

"Aw, nothing much," he said.

Gerie gave the same answer. He loved Karamea: He could live how he liked, go fishing when he liked, work when he liked. He never bought meat or fish, just caught his own food in the river or the estuary and, when he felt like meat, swapped his fish for some venison that some other guy had shot, or a bit of pork.

"I could never go back. If I went back to London, all those

people in a hurry, all that dirt, I'd shrivel up and die, I reckon," Gerie said.

Life in Karamea sounded pleasant enough—but I still hadn't recovered from the indignity of being recognized in the café.

"The problem with a town this small," I said to Daniel, "is that the woman in the cake shop knew when I'd been in twice in one day. In the morning, I went in and had a chocolate muffin, and then in the afternoon, I went in for a brownie, and she commented that if I kept on going in there twice a day, I wouldn't be able to fit into my leathers for much longer."

"Ah yeah?" Daniel threw his head back and laughed. "That woman's my wife."

At this point, James chipped in. "Yeah, we saw you in the café this afternoon. You were wearing black leathers."

I was mildly embarrassed that my brownie-guzzling binge was such common knowledge. Not only had Big Cake Shop Lady been watching me; the rest of the township had too.

"But when you went in this morning, when you ate the chocolate muffin, you weren't wearing your leathers. You were wearing a white T-shirt." James's reticence was fast dissolving. All of a sudden, he seemed to be enjoying himself.

"*Was I?*" I was astonished that he could be so sure. Frantically, I cast my mind back. Yes, he was right: That morning I'd been wearing running shorts and a white tank top, ready for my run on the Heaphy Track. Good heavens, every man in the place had my daily calorie count tracked.

"You were sitting at the last table by the shelves," James carried on, as if I needed to be any more mortified.

At this point, two women walked in. One was in her fifties, round and smiling; the second was in her early twenties. She was no sylph either. They both grinned when they saw me.

"Recognize this lady?" asked Daniel, putting his arm around the elder of the pair.

"Ah, the woman from the café!"

"Aw yeah, she came in twice today," said Big Cake Shop Lady.

"So I don't suppose there's much crime going on in Karamea, then, given that you all know exactly what everyone else is doing," I remarked, trying hard to move on from the niggling, carping issue of cake-consumption.

"Well, not a lot. Occasionally there's a robbery from the tourists, or something, but they don't get very far. Even if you're driving fast, it's an hour from here to Westport, and by that time we've been on the phone. They just throw a tractor across the road in Little Wanganui [the next township down] and catch them."

I reckoned they didn't have much need for policemen.

"Well, there's one policeman," said James. "Lives just across the road."

"So his house doubles as the police station?"

"That's right."

"Does he have cells?"

There was some discussion as to whether he had one cell or two; the popular vote came down in favor of a couple.

"But they're no use anyway," Daniel concluded. "His wife's filled them up storing her stuff."

"Nah, if there's any trouble he can't put 'em there," said James. "He'd have to take 'em to Westport."

"So he has a cop car, right?" I asked.

"Yes," laughed James, "but that's no good either because the back's taken up with kiddie seats. And anyway, most of the time his wife uses the cop car to drive down to the shop, 'cause that's where she works."

The policeman himself, it transpired, could be found most of the time down the beach indulging in a spot of fishing.

The following morning, I rode out of town, back down the long, straight coast road and up over the winding pass to Westport. Then I continued down the rugged West Coast. My destination for the day was Punakaiki, about ninety miles straight down the highway.

"You really gotta take it easy," Daniel had insisted last night. "That road is so beautiful, down along the coast, and at this time of year the rata trees'll be out, eh. Just go slow and look at the view."

And so, after a leisurely breakfast in that same café, I sauntered out of town. I rode slowly. I worked hard at absorbing the spectacular views. I made a point of admiring the red blossoms of the rata trees. I was still there by lunchtime.

Punakaiki is not really a town, or a township. The word hamlet, even, might be excessive. Really it is just a handful of buildings—almost all of which are hotels—that have grown up to cater to the tourists that come to gawk at the "pancake rocks."

The rocks themselves are incredible. Their limestone formations pile up high out of the sea. To geologists, the weathering process that has created this natural phenomenon in the limestone is known as stylobedding. To the rest of us, the rocks seem to be layered like a stony stack of gargantuan pancakes. At high tide, the water surges into the caverns among them and blasts through the blowholes in violent geysers.

The weather was moody and overcast. Above the murky, dark-green ocean, the horizon created a barely discernible line against the sultry blue-gray of the sky. It started to spit with rain as I walked around the pathway lined by tall grasses. Then the clouds moved and parted. Just for a second, a chink of brilliant blue sky was revealed and a stream of light reflected off the crests of the waves that rolled up the sand of the next bay. The layered rocks in front of me were still dark gray and in shadow, but in the distance, the bays and dusky promontories beyond were lit in a hazy, blue light, and the white of the water gleamed bright.

It was a fabulous half hour. But half an hour was all it was. Now the rain started to come down harder and I was faced with the troublesome reality: There wasn't much else to do here. Yes, it's incredibly beautiful, but Punakaiki has no soul. It's not a "place." Personally, I don't get it. If I were an early settler, I'd have built a city here. But they didn't, and so nobody, other than the odd hotelier who is by now tired of tourists, actually *lives* here.

The rocks are spectacular, yes. But they don't move, or dance, or sing. And there's only so long you can gaze at a pile of stone before it's time to move on to the next activity. If passersby should find themselves with a further twenty minutes to kill, they could pass them quite happily with a plate of outstanding carrot cake in the café opposite the rocks. But after that, the best option would be to climb back into their camper and head off.

I had some lunch in the café. I looked at my watch; it was one-fifteen. I went for a walk following some signposts along a footpath and was slightly surprised to have to wade knee deep across a fast-moving river over slippery rocks. In England, taking a stroll along a signposted footpath doesn't generally involve fording a rushing torrent. The most strenuous activity might be to clamber over a stile, or to open and close a gate or two. It would be the kind of walk on which you could take your granny or a small child in a stroller. Here was another sign that in New Zealand—despite their tendency to counseling—they're made of sterner stuff. Septuagenarians here probably think nothing of ripping off their socks and leaping nimbly across foaming cataracts. An ingenious Kiwi bloke would just whip a roll of wire out of his pocket, and after a few minutes' twisting and twirling he would have transformed his child's stroller into a serviceable boat.

As for me, well, I stood and stared disbelievingly at the river for quite some time. I was convinced I must have gone the wrong way. The rest of the walk, after all, had been on a clearly marked path of packed soil, the width of a small road. But on the other side of the river I could just make out a signpost pointing up a steep path. This really did seem to be right. In the end, I became bored with standing on the riverbank looking confused, randomly selected a shallow section, and crossly stomped across.

Including the time I'd spent staring at the river, my walk took two hours. I returned to the pancake rocks to see the blowholes perform at high tide. I was not alone. Cars and tour buses lined the streets. Everyone was German or Japanese or American. It was becoming horribly clear that the population of Punakaiki, like the blowholes' performance, was tidal. They swarmed along the walkway, each one elbowing the next out of the way so that they could take the perfect photograph. Girlfriends, husbands, and toddlers with sauce-spattered T-shirts posed. And then, fifteen minutes later, that picturesque strip of coast was overwhelmed by the sound of ignitions firing, of car and bus engines spluttering back to life. Their incumbents ticked a sight off their checklist and headed away to the next. It was strange; here I was in an incredibly beautiful place, but I felt weary and lonely, restless and low. I was desperate to jump into the back of one of those cars and drive off, away from the rain clouds and this strangely depressing, uninviting handful of buildings.

The real problem was that I'd decided to stay that night in a backpackers' hostel. So far on this trip I'd limited myself to hotels, motels, pubs, and B&Bs. But I was beginning to feel guilty and extravagant, so I decided to give the cheaper option a chance. This was New Zealand, after all. The hostels here would be squeaky-clean, well-tended places. It was a mistake.

Probably it's a terrible personal failing, but I just don't like staying in backpackers' hostels. I used to like them well enough, back in the days when I really was a backpacker. But now I had upgraded to panniers, and this afforded me the delusion that I had in some way moved on. Staying in places I don't like has a strange effect on me. Just the knowledge that I have to sleep somewhere dank and cheerless instantly depresses my mood. Even if I'm in an immensely lovely spot, as I was today, the feeling of having no safe haven into which to retire for an hour or two to read or lie down, no safe, cocooning substitute for home, makes me feel immediately ill at ease. Even when I'm nowhere near the room, out looking at scenic rocks or poking about in some strange town, at moments when I'm not even *thinking* about the wretched room, still I feel this underlying unhappiness, a weight of discontent, an overwhelming desire to get out, to go anywhere but here.

Really, the backpackers' hostel at Punakaiki wasn't a bad place. I didn't even have to sleep on a bunk in a dorm; I had my own room. The facilities worked. The people were friendly. My room, trying to be cheery, was painted lurid yellow. In an attempt at decoration, somebody had glued seashells onto the frame of the mirror. More misguidedly, they had also covered the ceiling with those adhesive stars that glow in the dark.

But the squashed sand flies whose innards had been splayed all over the bright yellow walls by a previous inhabitant suggested just who was going to be providing whom with hospitality that night. The room smelled musty; the bedding was very slightly damp. The living area was full of people in sturdy boots whiling away the evening playing Scrabble—and finding it funny. They ate heated-up stuff that came out of cans. I'd been there for about five minutes when I started to wish I'd booked into the posh, expensive hotel with balconies and ocean views down the road. This room was costing me fifty dollars; it wasn't worth the very small saving.

I didn't have any cans of things to heat, so I went out into the rain, which by now was pounding, and found my way to Punakaiki's only pub. It was packed with tourists, so I had to eat standing up at the bar. Everything on the menu seemed to be battered or bread-crumbed and served with chips. I went for the fish and chips on the premise that the fish, at least, should be good. It was. Fortunately, I was befriended by an Australian couple. He was a journalist and told me of the time he interviewed a farmer on the border of Israel and Lebanon. When he took out his tripod to take a photograph, the farmer shouted and dived for cover: Apparently the soldiers on the other side would have thought the tripod was a missile launcher and would try to save their skins by being the first to fire. I thought of my own self-pitying misery in the backpackers' hostel. I felt entirely inadequate.

I bade the Australians good-bye and went for a walk down the amazing beach. The rain had stopped, though the sky was still overcast. The evening light was low and yellow, descending in shafts between the dark clouds and lighting the downward slope of each shimmering wave. I strolled along the sand, which was covered in driftwood and faultless, intact shells. In the distance, at the other end of the beach, I could see the lights from the classy beachfront hotel. The soft murmur of voices, laughter, the telltale clink of glasses echoed over the sand as the guests sat on their balconies and enjoyed a bottle of chilled New Zealand wine.

I returned to my musty, neon-yellow room. Gingerly, I went into the communal bathroom to wash. The cheap linoleum was bubbling up where it had come unstuck. An unidentifiable puddle had appeared on the floor. And then, to cap off the day, I dropped my toothbrush right into the middle of it.

It's Wet Out West

"IN ITS DAY HOKITIKA was one of the world's most fabulous mining towns. From native bush it developed in a matter of months to a booming gold city, almost entirely masculine, with a population of 35,000 diggers using it as their base and with ninety-nine hotels or saloons to serve their thirst and entertainment needs," wrote Leslie Hobbs in his book *The Wild West Coast*.

I found the book in an old glass-fronted cabinet of secondhand books in Hokitika's only bookstore. It was raining again. I had already visited the possum fur shop and the man who paints tiny, intricate kiwis in bright colors onto round stones gathered from the beach. I had been to the kiwi house and, when my eyes had adjusted to the darkness, seen three of those strange, nocturnal birds strutting about on their spindly, stiltlike legs and poking their long, nostril-tipped beaks in the soil of their windowpaned cages.

The book was faded and dog-eared, published back in

1959. I lay on the bed in my B&B—soft lacy quilts, a heap of pillows, a pristine en suite bathroom—and read about bygone days. Curiously, the last owner of the book had underscored two lines in it. The underlinings were wobbly and black, etched by a heavily wielded, soft-leaded pencil: "The hardest task facing any West Coaster is to spend any night anywhere without the whole community knowing where and with whom he spent it," that earlier reader had highlighted on page eighty-three. Then, sixty-three pages later: "The Coast is no place for a married businessman to be carrying on any sort of liaison with his typist."

I wondered what intrigue the reader before me had been embroiled in. Who had marked the book in this tantalizing way? Was it a philandering man, or a third party—a jealous girl, a disapproving relation—who had chosen this under-handed way to reveal that his discretion had failed?

Back then, as now, it had probably been raining. On the West Coast, it rains a lot. That morning, I had journeyed from Punakaiki through a downpour. The rain pummeled down; the roads were slick. Once, riding over the white lines painted on the road, my tires slid from under me. I managed to hold my balance, but I was tense and fearful. The rain was driving against my visor, the droplets running in wet channels down the plastic and obscuring my vision. With the damp, the visor steamed up; I had to open a crack at the bottom to let the air circulate. The rain drove through the chink so that water ran down my chin. It was a bad day for motorcycling.

It wasn't far to Hokitika, just over sixty miles. I had there-fore intended to take in some interesting diversions en route, to take a left turn inland at Greymouth as Ian in Nelson had recommended, and ride up along the Grey River to Blackball, a strange little mining village with a famously eccentric pub, and then to take the scenic route around the back of Lake Brunner and through Kumara, site of the West Coast's famous racecourse. But heavy mists, almost fog, engulfed the hills. Even the beach, yards away, was scarcely visible. My leathers were damp under my waterproofs; my gloves, unprotected, soon started to squelch. Diversions were canceled; I was taking the main road straight to shelter.

Twice, the road passed along single-carriage railway bridges. Here the road didn't bisect the track as most crossings do. For a hundred yards or so, the railway track was cut into the road, running in the same direction as the cars, trucks, and motorcycles.

The tracks were narrow, their deep, unfilled crevices lined with slippery, wet metal. I ventured forward, sickeningly aware of the logging truck that was hugging tight to my rear. One unfortunate twitch of the handlebars would send me onto the watery skin that coated the metal; my tire would slide and plunge into the deep crack down the side of the track. I would fall off the bike for sure—and on these wet roads, the truck behind seemed far too close. I felt as though I was riding the bike along a tightrope. Apparently on these stretches of road, if a train comes, you have to slam your car into reverse and get off the track. A motorcycle doesn't have reverse.

Fortunately, though, no trains came, so I never had to figure out a solution to that particular problem, and I arrived a short while later, safe if somewhat soggy, in Hokitika.

"Aw, don't worry, we're only meant to be getting showers today," my bed-and-breakfast hostess for the night, Frances, exclaimed with inexplicable cheer when finally I arrived dripping on her doorstep. A small puddle was beginning to form about my feet. The house within was spruce and comfortable, with freshly vacuumed carpets. I peeled off my outer layers on the doorstep for fear of dirtying the place; Frances took my wet waterproofs and leathers to dry in her laundry room.

"Just stay there a minute while I get a towel to wipe those," she said, eyeing the mud spattered all over my panniers and anxious, no doubt, not to allow them entry to the bedroom in such a state.

I suppose, strictly speaking, she was right about the showers. They were showers—they were just rather long ones. The first shower had started before I woke up and lasted until about one-thirty. There was then a brief respite, until the second shower kicked in at about a quarter to two. This shower was shorter (perhaps they were petering out, I hoped in vain) and lasted only until about four-thirty. Then there was a whole half hour with no rain; at five o'clock it started again and carried on for the rest of the evening.

Still, once I'd changed into dry clothes and had acquired from Brian, Frances's husband, a golfing umbrella to fend off the elements, I felt sufficiently strengthened to go out, to discover the kiwi house, the stone-painting man, and the bookstore.

Hokitika, like so many of New Zealand's towns, does not believe in building things high. You don't get elevators in New Zealand buildings. Many of the houses are built from weatherboard—strips of overlapping wooden planks—because when the early European settlers arrived here, wood was plentiful and cheap. The clay needed to make bricks, meanwhile, was scarce, and so most buildings were made from wood. Today, the weatherboard houses are interspersed with ones constructed from brick and concrete, but they still don't build them high. Towns with no more than a few thousand inhabitants seem to ooze across the countryside in a kind of low, creeping spread.

The streets of the larger towns tend to be straight and grid-shaped—after all, these towns were only built in the late 1800s and were planned as settlements—with the occasional war memorial standing gray and stony in the middle of a junction. Usually, the regularly crisscrossing streets have names that leave nobody in doubt where the towns' founding fathers' hearts lay. In Blenheim, near Picton where the interisland ferry comes in, parallel streets are named Alfred Street, then Charles, then Arthur, then George. In Invercargill, in the south, there's a Tay Street, followed by Forth, Tyne, Eye, and Tweed. Up in Tauranga, however, where I stayed several weeks ago with Morris and Fay, the town planners lacked even that level of inspiration and opted for First Avenue, Second Avenue, Third Avenue, and so on.

Hokitika is a typical kind of town. The roads are named after early pioneers or dignitaries—Revell, Sewell, Bealey, and Hall. They run perfectly parallel, intersected at equal distances by their perpendicular counterparts—Weld, Stafford, and Hampden.

As the rain eased slightly, I left the streets and walked down to the beach. The sand was heavy and pockmarked with rain. Dark, damp driftwood lay scattered across its breadth. A man walked with his dog, bounding with energy after a day cooped up indoors. Stones lay in heaps, not only the usual brown and white pebbles smoothed by the sea and sand but huge quantities of green stones as well. The high-quality greenstone, or jade, they use for carving is mined from deep within the rock face, but here on the beach lay thousands of smaller stones. When they are dry, their surface is white and chalky. But when it rains, when the stones become wet, they appear a dark, gleaming green. I strolled along gathering the smoothest, roundest specimens and tucked them into my pocket.

Today was a good day to be in Hokitika, despite the weather. It was one of the biggest days in the town's social calendar: It was the day of the Gold Nuggets race meeting at Kumara, where the champion wins a real gold nugget. The West Coast has a strong Irish heritage—many Irish congregated around this area in the late nineteenth century when they came in search of wealth on the goldfields. The result is that the traditional Irish loves—horses, gambling, drink, and dance—have always lain close to the West Coaster's heart, and never so much as at the annual Gold Nuggets meeting. Today, the population of Kumara swelled from 324 to around fifteen thousand. By evening Hokitika, the nearest town to the racecourse, was awash with racegoers determined to blow their winnings or drown their sorrows.

I had enormous difficulty finding a restaurant that would feed me without a reservation; in the end, the fourth place I tried allowed me to wait for a table outside under a veranda while the rain pelted down and the harassed staff, overcome by the sense of occasion, rushed around muddling orders. I sat under the porch and read my book, peering in every few minutes through the rivulets pouring down the misted windows at the families and friends living it up inside. After ten or fifteen minutes of this, I caught the waitress's eye: She clapped her hand over her mouth—clearly she had forgotten about me entirely—and cleared a table that had been vacated a little while earlier. The service was slow, but the steak— fresh from the rump of a West Coast cow—was extraordinarily tender. It was the kind of food you'd pay a fortune for in a city restaurant, but here in Hokitika it cost only a few dollars.

After dinner, I went out for a couple of beers with Michael and Rose, two South Africans who were also staying with Brian and Frances that night. Hokitika was heaving. In the bar of the Southland Hotel, a strange-looking duo had been hired to provide live entertainment for the evening. The two long-haired guitarists wore sheepskin vests; they looked as if they'd been recently discovered in somebody's attic and hauled out, blinking in the light. They made little eye contact either with each other or with the audience but just strummed and plucked a dizzy array of Irish folk tunes.

The bar was packed. We elbowed our way through and found a couple of square inches of faded, beer-stained carpet on which to stand and drink our Monteiths, brewed in Greymouth just up the coast. From there, we watched as the checked-shirted West Coasters poured the local ale down their throats and threw their bodies about on the pub's circa-1970s patterned carpet in a range of extraordinary Highland-fling-meets-Top-of-the-Pops dance moves that can rarely have been witnessed outside New Zealand's rural communities. These people flourished under an apparently blissful disregard for conventional movement, for anything remotely rhythmic or recognizable. Some wildly stamped and twirled, bucked and romped, their limbs akimbo, defying the regular rules of coordination. Others went for the angrier punk-rock effect, their heads frenetically banging and hair flying. All the while, the sheepskin-coated guitarists impassively played on with skippy little ditties and jaunty Irish jigs.

Michael, Rose, and I stood and stared, dumbstruck.

"Oh my goodness," said Rose.

"This is astonishing," said Michael.

I started to laugh. The people were so totally enjoying themselves, so delightfully unconcerned about what they looked like, so entirely removed from the self-conscious demands of the outside world, that it was a joy to be among them. Here there was none of the big-city chic; fashion counted for naught.

Perhaps it was something they put in the beer: I grabbed the nearest plaid-clad, long-haired man and joined him in a galloping, hurling, whirling caper.

Hokitika's Revell Street, where we were now, was no stranger to revelry. Back during the gold rush, this street was jam-packed with hotels where the diggers spent liberally. Arguably, the men in those days took a little more trouble over their appearance than the checked-shirted, sheepskin-clad boys of today. Back in the 1860s there was a definite fashion sense, a recognized dress code, almost a uniform. When the diggers came to town, they took off their work clothes and dressed up. They would have been a colorful sight. In addition to their white or cream moleskin trousers, knee-length Wellington boots, and gray Crimean shirts, the diggers would tie wide crimson cummerbunds around their waists. The outfit would be topped off with a high felt wideawake hat, dented on top like a cowboy's.

The women, too, disregarded the practical dress most of us would think suitable for hiking down the muddy tracks of a rainy goldfield town—for, despite its riches, Hokitika was in those days a rough, rat-infested place. Instead, they persisted in wearing the voluminous full-length skirts and crinolines that had become fashionable in England in the 1850s.

"Why don't you wear an ordinary dress when working?" a mistress is said to have asked a girl who was scrubbing her floor wearing a silk dress.

"*All* my dresses are of silk," the girl apparently replied.

It was all to do with appearances, with flaunting the wealth that many of the diggers found in these early days of the gold rush. The town would have been teeming with men high on the riches they had literally dug out of the ground, men who had no thought for the day the gold might run out, who were determined to reap the rewards of their backbreaking work. To show off their success, to demonstrate their disregard for money, miners used to light their pipes with banknotes.

"At one famous supper party in Hokitika to celebrate the results of months of hard work on a difficult claim, the lucky miners served up a supper of champagne and ham sandwiches, with minced up five-pound notes in the sandwiches with the ham," reported Leslie Hobbs.

It was the local custom that none of the bars in Hokitika's ninety-nine hotels gave change: A miner would hand over a note and carry on drinking, or buying drinks for others, until the money ran out. The party would roar on throughout the night. There were never enough beds to go around, so patrons would sleep on the floor—and pay for their place there. If they were really in favor with the landlord, they might be given a spot on the billiard table, though they would rarely manage much sleep as the games would go on all hours. The dancing halls imported girls from Australia to entertain a town whose population was almost entirely male. The girls were paid a percentage of the money their escorts spent at the bar. In order to entice the men to spend, they would therefore come up with ever more inventive ruses, throwing "birthday parties" as often as once a month and inviting all their male acquaintances to attend. But even given the amount these men drank, the gold towns saw little drunkenness.

"Hokitika was a much more sober town than Ballarat or Bendigo in their heyday, and was a positive Sunday School beside the fabulous San Francisco. . . . The West Coaster who can drink without showing signs of intoxication, as very many of them can and do, is highly regarded. The man who drinks a lot and gets drunk is regarded there in much the same way as, in other parts of New Zealand, a man is regarded who is in ill-health—not quite as strong as his fellow," wrote Hobbs.

As Michael, Rose, and I walked home after our wild night of drinking and dancing, a gray-bearded character stumbled off the curb, the beer from the can he clutched slopping over the sides and onto his blotched trousers. He hiccuped, then burped loudly. By West Coast standards, this man was very unwell.

The next morning, the rain lashed down unabated.

"Ah, well, it might clear up in an hour or two," remarked Frances jauntily as she surveyed the leaden skies.

Yes, right, and kiwis might fly, I thought to myself.

I had been hoping to make up for lost ground yesterday and take a day trip to Blackball. Brian reckoned it was a good place to go.

"Once a year they have a festival there," he told me. "They call it the Blackballzup. They have a pub crawl where you actually have to crawl between the town's two pubs. They have gum-boot and cow-pat throwing competitions. And there's a coal-shoveling competition. And of course they have horse-plopping."

My interest was instantly aroused. What on earth was horse-plopping?

"Well, what they do," Brian continued, "is they take a paddock and they divide it up into sections of about a square yard. Everyone bets on a section, and then they let a horse out into the paddock. Whoever has money on the section where the horse 'plops' first is the winner."

It sounded like a fascinating place, ripe with extraordinary characters. I *really* wanted to go. But I also wanted to wait for the rain to stop. I read for a while, then, armed once more with Brian's golfing umbrella, I wandered the streets. I had some lunch and came back to the guesthouse. The rain was still hammering down. Even Frances with her boundless optimism had given up calling it a shower.

"Oh well, if it doesn't stop by three o'clock I think I'll just go anyway," I told Brian and Frances, who were taking a ten-minute break from the vacuuming and drinking a cup of tea. I went back to my room and read some more.

A little while later there was a knock at my door. It was Frances.

"We really wouldn't feel comfortable letting you go out on a motorcycle in this weather," she said. "And Brian's got to go to Shantytown to deliver some brochures this afternoon. Blackball's not much further. He'd be happy to take you up there in the car."

So the afternoon turned into a history lesson. Brian was a keen local historian; he was on the committee of the local Historic Places Trust. We drove to Shantytown, a replica gold-mining village built for tourists. We rode on the little red train, clambered up the muddy bank, and looked at tiny, dripping corrugated-iron huts like those the diggers used to live in. And then, train ride completed and brochures delivered, we drove on to Blackball.

Blackball was once a small center for gold-mining, but it's coal that made the township prosper. In its boom years, in the late 1800s and the beginning of the twentieth century, Blackball was apparently a bustling town, the shopping center of the Grey Valley. There were two grocers, two bakeries, a butcher's, a fishmonger's, a candy shop, and a fish-and-chips shop. There was a dress shop, a men's outfitters, and a dry-goods store.

There were two bookshops and a post office, a billiards saloon, and a picture hall that showed movies four nights a week. Blackball was happening.

It isn't anymore.

Nowadays there's just the general store, the salami factory, and a couple of pubs. The houses are dilapidated. Their paint is peeling, their gardens are overgrown. In the grassy driveways stand rusting old cars—a decrepit, pale-blue Triumph 2500, a brown Ford Cortina—that surely must have wheezed their last many years ago.

"So what do the people who live here now do for a living?" I asked Brian.

"Not a lot, I suppose, most of them," he replied, and went on to comment that many of them had a good line in growing illegal weeds on their property.

We went into the infamous Blackball Hilton. "Blackball ... The Centre of the Universe—the part where nothing moves," proclaimed the T-shirts sold at the bar. Life in Blackball, then, was not changing fast. The gene pool, for sure, must have been tiny.

The pub has been standing, under various names, since 1910 but really gained notoriety a few years ago when the Hilton International chain of hotels found out about it. It instructed its lawyers to issue a legal demand that this run-down weatherboard hotel, stuck up in the hills in a remote part of New Zealand, change its name. At first the proprietors assumed it was a hoax. It seemed unbelievable that a company of such standing as the Hilton International could really be concerning itself with them. But the Hilton chain stuck to its guns, and the placard nailed to the hotel's wooden veranda now reads: "Formerly THE BLACKBALL HILTON." West Coasters are not known to be fond of suit-swaggering authority.

Blackball, in particular, has a reputation for its refusal to comply. The township used to be a hotbed of trade unionism. Later, the New Zealand Communist Party made its base here, such was the small town's socialist reputation.

It all started in 1908, when Blackball's coal miners were one of the first groups in the country to break the law by going on strike. Their demand was an increase in their lunch break from fifteen to thirty minutes. The newly formed trade union was taken to court, where the judge ruled against them—after adjourning the court for eighty minutes for lunch. A fine of seventy-five pounds was imposed, but the union had no money. Refusing to give up, the court sent bailiffs to individual miners' homes, where they confiscated any salable possessions and put them up for auction.

In the days that led up to the auction, Blackball boxers roamed the streets with their gloves on. Nobody bid—except for one man, himself a miner, who bought the whole lot for twelve shillings and sixpence. He promptly returned his purchases to their original owners.

Every inch of the walls of the Blackball Hilton's bar seems to be covered with reminders of the township's militant past: photographs of striking miners, trade union banners, letters, and newspaper clippings. It's a highly characterful, ramshackle old place, almost swamped by the piles of paraphernalia that are dedicated to making a talking point of this defunct mining town.

Brian and I poked around the bar, looked at the photographs, and read the letter from the Hilton International's lawyers, now framed and hanging on the wall. Stepping over the piles of children's toys that littered the floor, we leafed through scrapbooks of newspaper cuttings about the town and browsed through the stacks of photo albums. We looked at the soap they were selling, piled up in a basket on a bar, apparently made from goat's milk right here in Blackball. We flicked through the souvenir menu, which offered, among other thrills, the opportunity to go and shoot possums with Bob after dark.

"And the horse-plopping?" I asked Brian with some eagerness. It probably says something terrible about my psyche, this infantile delight I take in toilet humor, but I thought the horse-plopping sounded terrific. I was desperate to join in. I had joyful visions of myself in a state of high excitement on the edges of the paddock, betting slip in hand, studying with neurotic anticipation every flick of the horse's tail.

"He's walking toward my square now … go on, go on … yes, yes, *yes*! He's twitching his tail … go on, you old nag, a bit further to the left … yes, that's my square, yes, he's stopping.… *OH NO!* He's walked through my square without plopping!"

How long would it go on for? This was the first time I'd given the matter of horse excrement a great deal of thought, and I realized I had no idea how many times a day a horse relieves itself. The fun could last for hours. Maybe they mix a bucket of bran into the chosen horse's morning oats to speed up proceedings.

It was admirable, really, the talent these people had for celebrating the more basic facets of life. Who needs to spend money on a hat to go to the races, who needs to bother driving to the dogs, when you can just shut a horse in a field and enjoy a fun-packed day out betting on its bowel movements?

"Aw," said Brian ruefully, "they don't have horse-plopping every day. It's just once a year at the Blackballzup Festival. And that's in June."

I fought hard to contain my disappointment and vowed that, one year in June, I would return.

There were only a couple of people in the bar—it was the middle of the afternoon, after all—but they were not conventional types. One man had long black dreadlocked hair hanging heavily from the top of his head; the back and sides were shaved. He was wearing thick black-and-white-striped tights underneath ragged khaki shorts, together with an array of torn sweatshirts and tank tops, which were not layered in the logical order—and all this on one person. His garb perfectly mirrored the scene of eccentric chaos in the bar area. I had no idea how to fit this strange character into any theory about the transformation of modern Kiwi man. This one seemed to be from another planet altogether, his mutations not tiny genetic shifts but a total departure from the human race.

I felt slightly ill at ease. For sure, it was an interesting place. But it was slightly too hip and grungy. Even with my jeans and T-shirt shouting of weeks on the road, I felt outlandishly clean, stultifyingly conventional. In my window boxes I grow cherry tomatoes, not dope. Even on my travels, I wash my hair every now and then. This was not my kind of a place.

Brian and I each drank a very law-abiding lemonade, then wandered upstairs to check out the guest rooms. There didn't seem to be anyone staying that night, as all the doors were open, the rooms empty, the beds uncrumpled. Each room was painted a different color, every one so lurid you would have to close your eyes and go to sleep just to shut it out. I wondered what kind of substance the person who had painted them must have smoked or swallowed. And, curiosity satisfied, I returned with Brian to the lacy white pillows and gleaming en suite bathroom of his house in Hokitika.

The Terrible Tale of Ferg

"UNATTENDED CHILDREN WILL BE sold as slaves," announced the laminated sheet of paper stuck to the wall of the Bushman's Centre.

The Bushman's Centre is in Pukekura. The township, if one can in all honesty call it that, has a population of two. It sits astride Highway 6, the road that runs down the West Coast, about thirty miles south of Hokitika. On one side of the road is the Bushman's Centre, on the other the Puke (pronounced to rhyme with bookie) Pub. Both are owned by Pukekura's sole inhabitants, an ex-bushman called Peter Salter and his partner, Justine Giddy.

The pub started life in the late 1800s on the banks of the Waitaha River, a few miles to the north. But then the new highway came to the coast and it didn't run past the pub.

Well, if the cars won't come to the pub, thought the publican of the day, we'd better move the pub to the cars.

And so he started. In New Zealand, the concept of home

removals frequently takes on a whole new meaning. Because the houses are usually wooden, it is often perfectly feasible to hook the building onto a trailer and, quite literally, move house. The problem was that in those days, a law forbade licensed premises to be moved by more than one mile a year. So each year the publican edged the pub, little bit by little bit, toward its intended location.

"They were originally planning to move it further," Brian had explained to me the night before, "but after a few years they just got fed up with shifting it. So they left it where it is now."

Later a timber mill was built on an adjoining piece of land. The tiny township of Pukekura was born. The mill closed in the mid-1980s; then Peter came along and built the Bushman's Centre. Having been a bushman himself, he created this place to educate the passing trade about the ways in which local people used to make a living from the forests. Later he bought the pub as well. Now he owns the town.

I parked the bike outside. Thankfully, it had stopped raining. A giant model sand fly hung from a pole jutting from the apex of the center's roof; outside, in a paddock, a stag grazed. For a moment he raised his head and his remarkable lush velvet antlers and stared at me, proud and steady. There was a breathtaking poise in this creature. He held his muscular neck high, showing off those prolific, branching, and perfectly curved antlers. I gazed back.

The heads of less fortunate deer than the stag outside were now looming from the wall alongside boards recounting the history of the deer industry. I pushed through a little gate into the darkness of the possum house. There was a squeak, and a furry thing landed on my head. I squeaked back. It was a joke, a booby trap. I gave a tremulous little laugh and continued, peering through the glass at the small furry creatures with their beady black eyes and bare pink noses.

Possums, I had to conclude, are not an attractive species. There's something about their vacant, moist eyes and nasty pointy noses that made me recoil. Somehow, they're not small enough for those attributes to be cute: Possums are about the size of cats. My loathing might have just been the result of indoctrination, though, for in New Zealand possums are regarded as a plague.

Possums were brought to New Zealand from Australia in 1837. The colonialists who were in the process of settling the land thought it would be a nice idea to create a fur industry in this country that had no indigenous mammals. The possums, blissfully unaware of the murderous intentions of their benefactors, were delighted. Gone were the dingoes and bush fires that consumed them in their native land. Here was a country rich in foliage and food, with no natural predators. The possum population ate and ate, and multiplied and multiplied. And multiplied. And ate.

Today, there are about seventy million of these critters in New Zealand. The Department of Conservation estimates that, between them, they eat seven million tons of native foliage in a year. For creatures that eat so much, though, they're picky about their food—they tend only to eat the new shoots. In some areas they have devoured entire canopies of rata, titoki, kowhai, and kohekohe. As if that weren't antisocial enough, their voracious appetites deprive native birds, such as the kiwi, of food. They disturb nests and occasionally even forgo their vegetarian diet to eat eggs and chicks. Possums, concluded the conservationists, may have nice cuddly coats, but for the environment they are bad, bad, bad. And so, in 1947, they introduced a program to eradicate them. It didn't work.

The Puke Pub, across the road from the Bushman's Centre, is doing its bit to help, though. Giving the old man-as-hunter ethos a modern, fuel-injected twist, the pub serves possum roadkill—or so it says. "Roadkill of the Day: You kill it, we'll grill it" heads the list of delicacies on the menu. Then there's "Guess that Mess," which apparently consists of possum, pita bread, salad, and hot sauce, and "Shovel-flipped Roadside Pizza." Toppings include possum, cheese, mushrooms, tomatoes, olives, and fruit. I really wanted to sample some of the dishes, but I was there on a bad day. I pushed open the door to the pub to be met by Justine, looking anxious. She was just on her way out, to go to the funeral of a man in Franz Josef who had been run down and killed by a tourist last week. The locals were understandably distressed.

Justine apologized profusely for her lack of hospitality and said that I really should have been there last night when they had a whole group of people staying—the pub also has guest rooms. As if to prove her point, she waved her hand over at the piles of dirty plates, replete with puddles of tomato ketchup, and empty pint glasses with dregs of beer.

I felt slightly sad. I wanted to join in, to pour a pint of beer down my throat in the company of the fantastically interesting, stimulating, and immensely good-looking folk that had been here yesterday. It's always like that. The minute I know I've missed a party I automatically assume it was the most exciting event since the invention of beer, when that first primitive farmer left some grain in the rain, then left it a while longer until it went bad and then—and this is the bit that's hard to get your head around—thought, mmmm, moldy rained-on grain that's been sitting there for weeks. Think I'll lick it up.

The old pub seemed like a welcoming place, with its wooden

bar and comfy chairs, a fine spot for a party. But I'd clearly come on the wrong day for sampling the possum menu. Next time I'm passing this way, I'll stay the night and raise the population of this bizarre little place to three, for one night at least.

I was heading to Franz Josef myself. Franz Josef, like so many of these tiny South Island townships that have grown up around a single attraction—in this case the glacier—is really just a huddle of buildings along the main road. Most of these were dedicated to the passing tourist trade: information outlets, booking offices for scenic trips, souvenir shops, and cafés. The residential houses—low-rise weatherboard, some newer brick buildings—trailed out along the highway from the main central cluster.

On the outskirts of these, about twenty minutes' walk from the center of the township, was Holly Homestead, a quaint old colonial house where I had booked a room. Its weatherboard was painted pale yellow, its window frames and balcony colonnade pure, wholesome white. The garden was perfectly tended; the vines up the side of the house crept just where intended. Inside, the wooden staircase was old enough to have developed a deep, characterful patina. The house dated back to the 1920s. It was, I thought as I roared anarchically down the pristine driveway on my bike, just the kind of place those early immigrants envisaged for themselves when they set out on their long boat ride to "paradise." It was just the kind of house in which to bring up a squeaky-clean family, where small rosy-cheeked Kiwi boys could run about in their knickerbockers, breathing the fresh mountain air and growing into lithe, fit Kiwi men.

By the time this house was built, the crews of the late 1800s—the gold miners and their ilk—had died out or moved on. Changing times led some even to remove their genes from the pool altogether: "No work, No friends, No money, Nowhere to go," wrote one old crewman in his suicide note.

By the 1920s, the emigrant ethos had entirely changed. New Zealanders now were clean and green; they placed an emphasis on purity and hard work. The crusade for moral harmony was rampaging through the land. From the 1890s onward, New Zealand's censors banned books considered too racy for paradisiacal reading, including the works of Balzac and Zola.

"Cinemas, which mushroomed from 1910, were described in 1916 as a 'curse to the community' and linked to venereal disease and smoking," writes historian James Belich in *Paradise Reforged*.

Dancing was denounced by a writer in the feminist publication *White Ribbon* because it sent "blood powerfully to the pelvis." Prostitutes were to blame for most of society's ills.

"Avaricious money-making harlots ... are at liberty to contaminate the nation from end to end. One cannot wonder at the number of young people wearing glasses, artificial teeth and other evidence of constitutional weakness when these female vultures are able to fatten and become wealthy," wrote Wellington's Superintendent of Police.

It seemed impossible that such aberrant sinners could have come anywhere near Holly Homestead. The place was glistening, quaint, and picturesque. I sat down in the kitchen with Bernie, the proprietress, a petite woman with curly gray hair and a genuine concern that her guests should enjoy themselves. Through the windows towered the majestic, snow-capped peaks of the Southern Alps. Bernie made tea, offered biscuits, and talked me through her prodigious collection of brochures.

"You can take a guided walk up the glacier," she said, riffling through and showing me the relevant glossy piece of paper. "Or you can take a scenic flight."

"Ah yes," I said. "I've already been in touch with the guys who do the helicopter flights, so hopefully they're going to take me up there in the morning." When I'd been in Nelson, Ian had given me their number and recommended I give them a call.

"And you can go heli-hiking on the glacier. Or you can go ice-climbing." She showed me a picture of a happy-looking couple huddling in an icy hole. They seemed to be enjoying themselves, if their radiant expressions were anything to go by, but, on the other hand, perhaps their faces had frozen into that position.

"Or, if you're interested in fishing, there are the fishing tours," Bernie carried on. I was, of course, wildly enthused by fishing since my heart-stoppingly exhilarating foray on Lake Taupo. In my more pensive moments, I had even toyed with the idea of giving up writing books for a living and retraining as a professional angler instead, but I was only in Franz Josef for one night and I wasn't sure I had time for fishing as well as flying about in helicopters and participating in all the other fun this township had to offer.

"Or there's the glowworms," said Bernie, brandishing a picture of grinning folk in anoraks having a fine time in a brown, gloomy cave.

I was politely silent. "And there's loads of lovely bush walks. Or," said Bernie, with a note of triumph in her voice now, "there's the kayaking trip to Lake Mapourika. They have a sunset tour. You could probably get on that trip tonight."

And so I wandered down the road, along the carefully maintained walkway into the center of the tiny township, and booked a place on a sunset kayaking tour with a man called Wayne from Ferg's Kayaks.

We were a small group of five—and we were the only people on the lake. It was remarkably quiet, astonishingly still. The silence was punctuated only by the resonant calls of bellbirds and tuis echoing across the water and the gentle slosh of paddles dipping in and out.

Wayne guided us across the lake and up a tiny tributary, where the willowy reeds and fluted rushes splayed out and leaned over, their sharp tips skimming the water; overhanging branches of trees forced us to duck beneath them. As we kayaked along this narrow stream, each one leaving a gap of several minutes after the person in front, the water was utterly smooth, totally flawless. Not a ripple disturbed the glassy surface as the tip of the kayak carved through. The sense of still, the silence, was mesmerizing and, in the evening light, the water became a perfect mirror. The pale-blue sky was smeared with streaky white clouds; under them lay the heavier, blotchy gray remnants of the rain clouds of the last few days. Upon the surface of the lake, their colors shone back with a deeper intensity. The blue of the sky became almost electric, the shafts of sunlight catching on the white clouds luminescent. The reflection was faultless.

We paddled back across the lake to the spot where we'd left the minibus. The sun was starting to set now. The sky was turning moody shades of pink behind the clouds; before them loomed the snowcapped mountains and the infinitely slowly moving glacier ice. The water, reflecting the sunset, took on myriad shades of rippling purple and blue in the kayaks' triangular wake.

I chatted to Wayne.

"So who's Ferg?" I asked.

The story that followed was a sad one. Anyone reading this book in public might like to skip the following paragraph for fear of weeping in front of strangers.

The Terrible Tale of Ferg

Once upon a time, when Wayne and his buddy were starting up their kayaking business, they found a lone little duckling down at the lake. He was a depressed, distressed little duck because he had lost his mother and his brothers and sisters and had been left all alone in the vast expanses of still, dark water. Wayne looked all around, trying to find the little duckling's family, but they were nowhere to be seen. So Wayne adopted the duckling and called him Ferg, after the New Zealand Olympic kayaking champion Ian Ferguson. Every day, Wayne would forage for tasty insects to delight Ferg's ducky palate, and whenever he went kayaking on the lake, he'd take Ferg along for a swim. Ferg grew up to be a happy, healthy little duckling. And then, one day, tragedy struck. The dog ate Ferg.

The End

"Oh no," I said when Wayne had finished relating this desperate story. "What a tragic tale!"

"Yeah, it was tragic, eh," said Wayne. "We'd named the bloody business after him."

*   *   *

I was up early the following morning, ate my breakfast while gazing at the mountains, and checked out of Holly Homestead in time to be in town by eight-thirty, for that was when Helicopter Line had offered to take me for an aerial view of the glacier.

I squeezed into the cabin next to Gerry, the pilot. He looked as though he was in his fifties and wore a neatly pressed pale-blue shirt over dark trousers, dark sunglasses, and a faded navy baseball cap. He beamed continuously with infectious good cheer, and his trimmed, dark mustache smiled with him.

Gerry seemed to have covered pretty much every aspect of piloting in the twenty-nine years he'd been making a living from flying helicopters. He'd dropped scientists into Antarctica and explorers into the Burmese jungle; he'd flown in high-speed police chases and transported venison hunters. He'd operated in search-and-rescue missions for climbers lost on the mountains—and now "as a bit of a hobby" he was taking tourists up the glaciers.

The glacier was an awesome sight. The view from down below, from the township, had been slightly disappointing. The river of ice that snaked down the mountainside valley had looked, in the distance, like the grubby, days-old snow you see on city streets; the boulders of moraine—the rock carried by the glacial ice—appeared as gray specks and streaks across the white. From far away, they looked like the spewed-out gravel of the snowplows.

From the helicopter it was a different story. I squeezed in with four others; it was a tight fit. Two of us sat in the front. I was nearest to Gerry and had to suck in every muscle to stop my errant body parts obstructing his controls. Wearing aviators' headsets so we could listen to Gerry's instructions and commentary, we climbed high over the mountains, between the peaks. As we rose higher and higher, the thrumming of the helicopter blades drowning out all sound, the view of the mountaintops became clear. The peaks rose and dipped far into the distance, the more immediate ones covered in white velvet, the more distant ones progressively deeper, hazier shapes of blue silhouetted against the sky. Up here, most of the rock was still covered, even in midsummer, with a thick blanket of ice and snow. The weather was clear; the morning sky was a uniform cobalt-blue with just the occasional streak of high, white cloud. The early-morning sun cast dusky blue-gray shadows from the gently undulating mounds of snow that softened the rocks' sharp angles.

We landed on the snow, beneath which the glacial ice stretches to a staggering five hundred feet deep. It was surprisingly warm up here; I was wearing my motorcycling leathers, ready for the day ahead, but others were walking around comfortably in jeans and T-shirts. Yet, even beneath the warm sunshine, the surface of the ice stayed crisp and easy to walk on. Then we climbed back into the helicopter and followed the wide crevasse through which the Franz Josef glacier flowed infinitesimally slowly. Here, at these higher levels, the ice had frozen into tremendous cliffs and crevasses, and icefall had created spectacular piles of boulders. It was vast, bright, and white, an astonishing landscape of ice formations.

Back on the ground, I climbed on my bike to continue my journey south. Haast, my destination for today, was my last stop on the West Coast. After that, the road would snake inland following the Haast River before descending to Wanaka and the great playground of Queenstown.

I set out from Franz Josef and up over the Fox hills, a series of tight, steep little bends.

"A friend of mine had a nasty accident riding his motor-cycle over those hills," Wayne had told me last night as we kayaked on Lake Mapourika. "He was riding 'round the bend when there was an earthquake. It threw him from his bike."

An earthquake threw him from his bike? I was loudly incredulous—and quietly alarmed.

"Yeah. It was genuine as well. The insurance company looked into it and agreed they had to pay up," said Wayne.

It was proving to be a dangerous place, New Zealand. They give the impression that it's all clean, green, and super-safe—there are no snakes that can finish you off with one snap of their poison-tipped fangs as there are in Australia, there are no salivating rabid dogs as there are in France, there are no mad cows lurking behind clusters of clover and waiting to turn your brain to goo—but the landscape is a different mat-ter. All this tectonic shifting meant that the very ground on which I stood was fraught with hazards. Up north in Rotorua, one misplaced foot and I could have met a sticky, steamy demise in a pool of boiling mud. Or here, in the foothills of the Southern Alps, the earth could at any moment shudder and judder and hurl me from my bike.

I rode with extra care and kept a neurotic watch for un-toward seismic grunts. Coming safely down the other side of the hills, the road straightened out into a thin avenue lined by towering trees. My mind began to wander from the troubling subject of earthquakes and onto the men I'd met in the last day or two. It seemed that, here on the West Coast, plenty of the men had kept their traditional Kiwi male attributes, but they were now channeling them into a twenty-first-century industry: tourism. Peter from the Bushman's Centre had obviously shot his fair share of deer but had now given that up and opened a tourist venue. The notice that threatened to sell children as slaves had, admittedly, betrayed something of Peter's inner feelings toward the smaller members of his species and suggested he might have been happier out there all alone in the bush with just pink-nosed possums for company, but it was into the lucrative tourism industry that he was nonetheless plowing his energy.

Wayne was similar, in a way. That whole business of adopting pet ducklings cast a bit of a shadow over his bloke credentials, but he was nevertheless a fit, outdoors type. A hundred years ago, he'd have been sawing planks to build a house just like Holly Homestead. He'd have shorn his own sheep and raised a fresh-faced pioneer family; today he was using these same attributes to rear small ducks and take tourists kayaking on the lake.

Gerry the pilot had done his share of hunting, of transporting shooters through the bush. But now he, too, was using those skills to ferry tourists up the glacier. These men showed many of the attributes of their forebears but had changed their ways to put their skills to a modern-day use.

As I ruminated, I passed a signpost to a "Blue Pool." A few cars had pulled over and parked in the turnout. I was in no hurry to arrive in Haast, so I stopped beside them and walked through the trees following the direction of the arrow.

The path wound through dense, majestic woods. At the other side of the forest, steps led up to a swing bridge that crossed a river of vivid, lurid blue. It was a ramshackle construction of planks and bits of wire that swung vertiginously as I edged gingerly across, knowing full well that the bridge must be safe, that thousands had crossed it before me, but unable, somehow, to coordinate my walking with this unfamiliar rocking. On the far bank of the river, a path led downward to the Blue Pool.

The pool was remarkable, even after the incredible glacial scenery of that morning and the coastal views of previous days. Its water was a deep turquoise green and astonishingly clear. You could see the rock wall on the edge of the pool just as sharply beneath the waterline as above it. It was like looking through a turquoise-colored sheet of glass. Even on the pool's bed, each pebble was perfectly in focus.

Back on the bike, I continued through the forests, crossing countless tiny one-way bridges under which flowed rivers in otherworldly sapphire blue and extraordinary shades of milky turquoise. Unlike the Blue Pool, this water is opaque; its coloring comes from the silt that descends from the glaciers. In the summer, when the ice melts and the rock is more energetically eroded, these rivers range from whitish gray to bright green. In the winter, when the silt no longer falls as the glacier is frozen, the rivers are crystal clear. Then, after a couple of hours, the road once more joined the rugged, windswept coastline of the Tasman Sea for the final twenty miles into Haast.

Haast is a tiny settlement. It has just three hundred inhabitants. The township itself is nothing spectacular. It consists of a handful of characterless, boxy little buildings constructed without much thought for aesthetics. I checked into my motel, which was comfortable if unimaginatively shaped, and booked a place on a jetboat trip down the river later that afternoon.

The jetboat trip started a little way out of town, on the banks of the Waiatoto River. I had a couple of hours to spare and somebody had told me that at the township of Jackson

Bay, further down the coast beyond the Waiatoto River, there was a pie cart from which a woman dished up some of the best fish and chips in New Zealand. It was lunchtime. I was hungry. I went there.

Jackson Bay must be one of the remotest communities in the whole of New Zealand. It is thirty miles even from Haast, along a tiny minor road. The fish-and-chips cart was not hard to find in such a small place. It was parked on the beachfront among the tall untended grasses that grew in front of the shallow, sandy beach. A wooden jetty jutted out into the sea, the only visible evidence that fishermen make a living around here. In the background, beyond the still waters of the bay, the Southern Alps created a snowcapped horizon.

Following the smell of frying, I walked up the steps of the pie cart, as New Zealanders call these campers that dispense food. One end of the vehicle was given over to a makeshift-looking kitchen, the other to diner-style benches and tables. Outside the pie cart was parked a police car, and there at the first table, by a window looking out onto the turquoise sea and the white-tipped mountains beyond, sat the policeman, writing reports.

"Great spot for an office," I commented.

"Yeah, well, there's nowhere else around here to do the paperwork," he said. He was on loan for three weeks as the only policeman in Haast. He didn't seem to think much of it and said he was greatly looking forward to returning to normal duties in Greymouth.

I bade good-bye and good luck to the lonely policeman and went to sit on the beach to eat my fish and chips and take in the view across the ocean to the mountains beyond. I sat on a grassy mound just above the sand and unwrapped the paper package: big, fat, potatoey chips, battered fish without a drop of excess oil, fresh from the sea that morning. Their smell was tantalizing. They were gloriously, deliciously fresh—and terrifyingly, blisteringly hot. They'd been scooped from the bubbling oil just seconds ago. And so I was stuck with that agonizing dilemma—do I use every shred of willpower to wait five minutes, ignoring the anguished cries of my stomach, stoically enduring the shrieks of my salivating tongue? Or do I just gobble the lot and burn the roof of my mouth? I took the latter option. And then, the last delicious chip devoured and my mouth just beginning to blister, I clambered back onto my bike and headed back up the road to the banks of the Waiatoto River, where I was to meet my jetboating companions.

Jetboats were invented by a New Zealander called Bill Hamilton. He never trained as an engineer and used unorthodox methodology but is hailed as a fine example of a man with Kiwi ingenuity. He wanted to be able to take a boat up the shallow Canterbury rivers, where the water ran only a few inches deep. His first models in the 1950s were slow. Today's offshoots are not, and provide a backbone to that other industry of Kiwi inventiveness, adventure tourism.

But what made this trip a success was not the speed of the boat, or the spectacular scenery of the blue, glacial river whose edges were scattered with driftwood and whose waters swirled white around vast boulders resting on the riverbed, but the remarkable knowledge of Roger, our guide. He told us about glacier formation and tectonic plates. He explained all about the local breed of kiwi that can climb from sea level to alpine heights, a remarkable feat for a bird that can't fly and hobbles around inelegantly on its thin, sticklike legs. He talked about the problems of stoats and possums who eat the kiwi eggs, the controversy the consequent poisoning campaigns have sparked, and told us that attempts to tag the kiwis had had to be abandoned after one of the birds died of a heart attack induced by the stress. It was probably the first recorded case of stress on South Island.

That night I ate three vast slabs of filet steak. They don't skimp on portions in this part of the world. Nor are they even remotely pretentious. When I ordered a glass of pinot noir with my beef, the waitress asked, "This one?" pointing at its entry on the menu. "It's just that I have trouble with those French words."

I liked this woman. I admired her utter lack of airs and graces, her straightforward nature. Why on earth should she bother with ridiculous French words? Why has the wine world been taken over by names that no normal-thinking person can pronounce? Wouldn't it be nice if restaurants would give up trying to humiliate us and just number the wretched things so we could order a bottle of "number seventeen" and be done with it?

I finished my food and sat back, content with the comfortable sensation of a full stomach. New Zealand really was turning out to be a wonderful place, I thought. Yes, the landscape was incredible and diverse, but it wasn't just that. It was really the people that made it. I started to regret having been so mean when they tried to be nice up north. Maybe I'd mellowed a little in the last few weeks, because now I was really enjoying their down-to-earth friendliness, the total lack of conceit, and the genuine welcome I received everywhere I went. New Zealand is a long way from home, but I was beginning to understand why people moved here.

There was a brilliant sunset that night. The sharp, dark line of the hills lay silhouetted against luminous fiery orange layered beneath deep, vibrant crimson and, above, a pale purplish blue. Clouds streaked across the sky, their upper parts dark and gray, their lower edges tinged and glowing with the rich colors of the setting sun.

The next morning's ride inland from Haast to Wanaka was the best yet. As my confidence increased, and the weather stayed bright and clear, every day I took new leaps toward motor-cycling competency. At last, after a couple of months' riding, I was beginning to consider that this trip might not have been the most foolhardy decision of my life so far. For the first time, it was beginning to look possible, indeed probable, that I might survive intact. As my ability grew, I was beginning to really enjoy the speed, the sensation of the bike's leaning around the bends, the continual shifting of weight as I went around and around the tight mountain ascents, and the smells and sights of the almost fantastical scenery.

Today, as I dropped down from the winding roads of Haast Pass, I arrived at a pair of huge, glimmering lakes. First came Lake Wanaka on the right-hand side of the road; then I rounded a bend and Lake Hawea lay to the left. The weather was perfect: Cloudless blue skies showed off the snowy moun-tains and deep-blue waters shimmering in the sunlight at their best. The road wound in easy, carefree bends along the lakeside for miles. Around the water a thin, bright strip of sand dipped in and out, outlining tiny promontories and coves. The shallower water at the edge of the lake appeared a pale blue; then, as the bed of the lake dropped off and the water became deeper, there was a discernible line as the color shifted to a richer hue.

Again and again I stopped just to gaze at the view.

"Just look at that," I murmured in awe as I stood and stared.

"Ahhh," sighed the bike with what sounded to my ears like wondrous gratification—though it could just have been the engine settling.

After about the fifth stop, I began to fear that I'd never arrive at all. I had to steel myself to continue with the ride, to finish my journey to Wanaka.

I rode into the lakeside town, where Kiwi vacationers celebrated summer. They lounged around on the grass at the water's edge and ate ice cream, and sat in cafés drinking the super-strong coffee with which the Kiwis have so recently fallen in love. They messed about on boats. There were very few foreigners here. They were all in Queenstown, thirty miles to the south. I checked into my motel, wandered down to the lake, and found that all my noble intentions featuring bush walks and mountain-bike trips had mysteriously evaporated. I found myself strangely drawn to the magazine stand and the liquor store, settled down comfortably on the grass with a magazine and a couple of cold beers, and watched the Kiwis play. As the sun went down, I was drawn unhealthily to real estate agents' windows, where I learned that I could exchange my ex-council two-bedroom flat in London for a five-bedroom, three-bathroom mansion in Wanaka, with two decks and extensive gardens, and I'd still have fifty thousand pounds change for a boat, a sporty convertible, and a kitchen renovation.

Top Gun

"BETTER THAN SEX" IS one of those bizarre comments people write in the customer-feedback ledger when they've just free-fallen from a plane at twelve thousand feet or dived at dizzying speed through their first bungee jump.

Those people must have had some really terrible sex.

Let me put the record straight: Falling very fast through the air is not better than sex. It's not even better than bad sex. With bad sex, at least you can give up halfway through and say, "Never mind, let's just have a beer and watch TV instead."

When you're dropping toward the ground at God knows how many miles an hour, your mouth stretched to its fullest capacity in a silent scream, your eyeballs bulging from the sheer terror of it all, you can't give up. From mid-plummet, there's no backing out. There's no beer. There's no TV. There's not even a duvet under which to hide your wilting enthusiasm.

I have learned from past mistakes that I do not remotely enjoy leaping out of planes or off bridges, whatever kind of elastic or parachute I'm strapped to. I have tried it several times and the outcome has always been the same. Up until the moment when I can actually look over the edge and see just how ridiculously far away the ground is, I'm fine, rational, calm. I can easily reassure myself that the operator's safety record is impeccable. I'm fully confident that I have nothing to fear. Then I peer out and see with my own eyes that it's a very, very long way down. My knees go weak, I have trouble breathing, I am taken over by an irrational, uncontrolled, shaking, gibbering fear. And so I have concluded: Hurling myself off high things isn't for me. I'm not intending to try it ever again.

For this reason, I didn't for a moment entertain the idea of bungee-jumping in Queenstown when I arrived there the next day. But despite my refusal to participate, I thought I should at least put in a few minutes on the spectator platform at the Kawarau bungee, because it's a historic place. This is the site of A. J. Hackett's first commercial operation—the first bungee jump in the world. It's a sacred site of Kiwi ingenuity, of pioneer inventiveness at its most ludicrous and lucrative.

Except that Hackett didn't exactly invent it. What the Kiwis don't tell you is that he was inspired by a small island in the Pacific where they have been doing this, in a more primitive form, for generations. And if those bungee-jumpers in Queenstown thought they were brave, they should see what the island folk do.

On Vanuatu's southernmost Pentecost Island, from April to June each year, the people build high wooden towers from which the island's menfolk "land-dive" in a religious fertility rite. Leaping from the timber constructions, they plummet headfirst with a stretchy vine tied around their ankles: Their hair is supposed to scrape the ground and fertilize it to ensure a successful yam harvest. Unfortunately, the vines are not as reliable as Hackett's bungee cords, and the Vanuatuan safety record is not quite so good. But at least the islanders' diving has a purpose. To fertilize the land, to ensure food for your fellow villagers, is really very useful. To pay good money just so you can jump off a bridge with a piece of elastic tied around your ankles is not.

And this, really, sums up the problem with Queenstown. It is dedicated to nothing other than the pursuit of adrenaline. With only one real industry in the place—adventure tourism—and almost all of the town's eight thousand inhabitants involved in providing it, Queenstown has a strange character. It's not really like being in New Zealand at all, for New Zealanders are in a minority here. They find the pace too hectic—and the prices quite unbelievable—and so they stay away, choosing other, more laid-back resorts for their vacations. In Queenstown, the people are American, Japanese, Danish, Korean, Canadian, and British. It's a tiny, action-packed global melting pot, a place where people of all colors, all creeds, all shades of suntan and burn come together for a few days to scare themselves silly and party themselves to oblivion. The buildings that vie for space along Queenstown's street fronts all sell one of Queenstown's two commodities: adrenaline or alcohol. It's fun, fun, fun, but it's not much like the rest of New Zealand.

Still, there's no better place for seeing just how ingenious a Kiwi can be when there are tourist dollars up for grabs. Ever since A. J. Hackett's bungee started hauling in the cash, New Zealanders in this part of the world have been looking for ways to out-invent each other. You can do crazy things all over New Zealand—zorbing in Rotorua consists of rolling down a hill inside a gigantic plastic ball, then there's boogie-boarding down the sand dunes in Northland, to name just two—but Queenstown is the Mecca. It's here that foreigners flock in their millions to be thrilled by the vast outdoor amusement park. The men I'd met in the last week or so—Wayne and Gerry in Franz Josef, Roger in Haast—may have adapted their good Kiwi genes to the tourism industry, but that was nothing compared to the way Kiwi ingenuity had exploded in Queenstown.

Kiwi ingenuity, originally, was of some use. To be able to perform postpartum surgery on a sheep using just a piece of old wire was handy, though possibly unpleasant for the sheep. In Queenstown, though, inventiveness has mutated beyond its early practical form. Here, they just invent things for the sake of it.

Adrenaline, too, once had a practical purpose. Kiwi blokes of yore used it to increase their chances of success when tussling with wild pigs. In Queenstown today, it's just a recreational drug.

There's not just bungee; now there's rocket bungee too. There's "the biggest swing in the world" over a canyon—you free-fall for two hundred feet at up to ninety miles per hour before the swing starts to rise up the other side of the arc. There are countless different varieties of jetboating, all purporting to be the most mind-blowing ride of your life. There's river-surfing, white-water rafting, skydiving, heli-mountain-biking, a luge, moonlight horse trekking, and more, more, more. If you went on all the rides in Queenstown, you'd be there for months, and you'd have set yourself back many thousands of dollars.

I searched the streets, where every doorway offered a new form of terror, looking not for the scariest, not the most dangerous, but the most ingenious, ludicrous, crazy activity I could find. And then I saw it. Fly By Wire.

Fly By Wire advertises itself as "the nearest you'll get to fly-ing a fighter jet." The victim lies on his tummy in a contraption that looks like rocket-meets-deadly-missile. A cable winches him high up the hillside until the nose of the plane points downward and out across the valley. Then the poor soul, by this point scared witless, releases the winch, zooms across the valley to the next hillside, where he loops and turns back again at speeds of up to one hundred miles an hour. It looked very silly. Entirely ridiculous. Totally insane. I walked through the door and handed over my cash.

It wasn't until I was lying suspended halfway up the hill-side, tied down by a series of straps onto the base of the "jet," that I began to wonder if this had been such a great idea. I didn't feel much like a fighter-jet pilot, dangling impotently with my feet in the air and the blood rushing to my head. The red plastic goggles I was wearing over my sunglasses didn't ex-actly scream of shock and awe. Down on the ground, a nice man called Justin, transformed at that distance to little more than a speck, was leaping around waving his hands in the air. This was the signal that I was to grab both levers on the handle-bars and pull them with all my might: the left-hand one would release the tow cable, the piece of wire that had dragged me up to this uncomfortable and inelegant starting point and the only thing holding me from plummeting at unspeakable speeds across the valley. The right-hand lever was the throttle. I wasn't to twitch it gingerly, Justin had said. I wasn't to pull it halfway; that would spoil the fun. I was to grab both levers and clench them in one hard, brave, all-or-nothing yank. I was to squeeze the very life out of those levers. Down on the ground, it had seemed a feasible thing to do. From up here, the wisdom of such an action was cast into some doubt.

Oh, bloody hell. Justin was still waving. His arms were probably getting tired by now. His waving seemed to be becoming increasingly frantic as I procrastinated, dangling upside down from my cable, my hands resting gently on the levers, not quite daring to go. I was starting to get dizzy. This really wasn't a good position to be suspended in. What on earth was I doing up here anyway? I closed my eyes, pulled on the levers, and shot out across the valley.

In the event, I only managed to get my "jet" to fly at a disappointing seventy-five miles an hour, which would be pretty lousy if you needed to avoid an enemy missile in a hurry. Proper fighter jets fly at twenty times that speed. It wasn't even very scary after the initial terror had passed; in fact, it was a lot of fun. But as I grew used to it and started to glare at the speedometer, willing the machine to go faster and faster, I couldn't help but think: My motorcycle can do much better than this.

Fly By Wire was a laugh, it was ingenious, but it didn't petrify me. The adrenaline rush wasn't sufficient. So, like an addict in need of a fix, I went in search of more.

The Shotover Jet is the most famous jetboat of them all: This is the only company allowed to use the famous Shotover Canyon, just outside Queenstown. The ride down the narrow channel of green water winding between vast, rugged boulders is the stuff of a teenage boy's action-packed dreams. I booked it.

The boat was driven by a blond, suntanned man. We hared off at speed, avoided the boulders by a hairbreadth, spun around in 360-degree turn after turn. We dodged logs and rocks; we spun some more. We were drenched by the spray. It was fun. And, yes, the canyon was very pretty. But, again, it didn't compare to my bike. My bike went infinitely faster, required heaps more skill, and was much, much more dangerous. Riding through the Shotover Canyon in a jetboat had none of the thrill of careering through the bush of South Island and suddenly coming out onto the wild, rugged beaches of the West Coast, where a salty spray filled the air. It couldn't compare to leaning around the tight, climbing bends of Takaka Hill and descending to the amazing beaches of Golden Bay, or winding for miles around the vast blue lakes north of Wanaka. And so, the next day, I gave up on the thrills of Queenstown, climbed back into my leathers, back onto my bike, and took a ride up the banks of Lake Wakatipu to Glenorchy.

Glenorchy is only thirty-one miles from Queenstown, and a whole world away. But the real trip lies in the journey, for the road along the lakeside was the most perfectly winding and scenic road I'd ridden on yet. First, I just hummed gently along the shores of the lake, enjoying the mountains rising majestically on the other side, admiring the greens and blues of the water, thinking it might be quite nice to sip a cold beer on one of those boats bobbing on the lake. Then the road became more interesting as it started to rise. The bends became more frequent, and then, just as I came out of one particularly tight bend . . .

"Oh my God!" I actually shouted out. There was the most spectacular view. From that height at the top of the hill, the blue of the water seemed more vital, and perfectly silhouetted mountains stole center stage. It was breathtaking. Frankly, it was a little dangerous. I should think the traffic police have spent years trying to block that view out.

Glenorchy is a charming if very, very small place, featuring little more than a pub and a man selling possum pelts from a garden shed. From there, the road continues north to Paradise.

Paradise is nothing more than a handful of buildings, though the settlers who named it presumably thought it was rather nice—nicer than Croydon, or wherever it was they'd come from, anyway. Given that this might be my only chance to go to Paradise, I thought I'd better pay the place a visit.

It's a long, rough ride to Paradise. The paved road held out for the first five miles, then it turned to gravel. I chugged on, somewhat slower, over lumps and bumps, through clouds of dust. The track became packed dirt as it wound through bush, then it took a turn for the worse. The gravel became thicker and deeper. Streams of water flowed across the road. I plowed on through. Then the gravel ran out and became boulders. I prayed to arrive in Paradise soon—it could surely only be around the next corner. Or the next? Or, maybe . . . the next?

At one point I passed a house. Could *that* place be Paradise? But it was only a building. It wasn't by any stretch of the imagination a settlement. Paradise *had* to be better than that. Surely it was something more. I struggled on and on.

What if that house really was Paradise? I started to wonder. What if I actually did get to Paradise but, when I arrived, failed to recognize it? What kind of allegory for life could that be?

But the track had carried on past the house, and Paradise was supposed to be at the end of the road.

I'm sorry to say I never made it to Paradise. I was worried that, in trying to get there, I might fall off my bike and take the quick route directly to hell. And, on a more prosaic, earthly level, the bike's gas gauge was hovering unhappily in the little red box that indicates imminent perdition.

"Screw this," said the bike. It was turning out to have quite a way with words. "Paradise is bound to be overrated. And in any case, I'm hungry. I saw a classy little Mobil gas station back in Glenorchy. There was, um, quite a cute little one twenty-five parked outside. I wouldn't mind, well, you know, stopping there for a quick drink."

"Oh, all right then," I reluctantly conceded.

Turning my back on Paradise was no easy task—not least because of the challenge of U-turning between the boulders—but turn I did. I was sad not to have experienced whatever heavenly delights the tiny settlement might have had to offer, but the bike, at least, was happy.

Bachelor Pads

IT WASN'T UNTIL I reached Mossburn and turned right onto the main Te Anau highway that I really lost control of the bike. The forecasters had predicted rain; the first drops had fallen as I rode out of Queenstown. But then the weather had cleared, and sheltered by the hills I had wound easily in and out of the bends of the road that followed the eastern shore of Lake Wakatipu. The Remarkables—a mountain range—looked remarkable to my left, and the clear blue waters stretched out to my right. I was warm and dry and seemed to be keeping ahead of the bad weather front. I thought I was going to get away with it. I was far too smug.

I rode further south, leaving behind the green and blue landscapes of the lakelands. I was in real *Lord of the Rings* country now; it was sparse and striking. The hills here were lower than the mountains further north and the horizon more distant. The mounds of brown and golden scrub rose and fell across great, uninhabited spaces. This was Southland, the southernmost province of New Zealand and the one most loud and proud of its traditional masculinity. If I couldn't find an original Kiwi bloke here, one with all his traditional qualities intact, the mutation theory would be indisputably proved.

The stereotype of the "Southern Man" as a beer-drinking, sheep-mustering country dweller has become nothing short of an ideology in the last few years, following the success of a marketing campaign from Speight's beer, which is based in Dunedin. Even Dunedin International Airport now features a life-size bronze statue of the Southern Man on his horse. The Speight's commercials take the unsophisticated country bumpkin and, with stunning photographic sequences of Southland, turn him into a super-masculine demigod who says, "Good on yer, mate," and, of course, drinks nothing but Speight's. His hands are made for clutching beer glasses and shearing tools, his stomach is designed for holding beer and red meat, his legs are meant for running all day over hills—oh yes, and walking to the bar to fetch another jug of Speight's. You get the picture.

But in order to find out whether this mythical creature, the Southern Man, existed for real, I had to arrive at my destination in one piece. As I progressed further south, the weather deteriorated. My safe arrival suddenly seemed far from assured.

The problem was, I was staying ahead of the wet weather, but the front that brought rain was preceded by winds. To begin with, they were light gusts and easily manageable. Then, at Five Rivers, I turned off the main highway, taking a shortcut along a minor road to Mossburn. The road was straight and flat through fields and forest. There were no hills to shield me here, and the wind whipped across the plains to my right. To my left, the trees of the forest were dancing dervishes, their branches swirling about in a frenzy. By now I was clutching the handlebars with a white-knuckled death grip in my desperation to keep the bike steady. I told myself that I'd soon be at Mossburn, where my sharp change of direction onto the main highway would surely take me out of the worst of the wind. I was wrong.

At Mossburn the wind, instead of dying out, became very much worse. I slowed right down to about thirty-five miles an hour, but even at this speed I could scarcely control the bike. I was being blown so fiercely from the right that I had to lean the bike over to a forty-five-degree angle. Laden with luggage, it was perilously unstable. But the wind was gusting and, every now and then, it would whip around and blow me from the left, forcing me to quickly throw all my weight to the other side. My bike was tall, its riding position upright. I was sitting on top of it like a weathervane, flung around in all directions. I veered across the lane and back again, desperately trying to keep the bike between the white lines to avoid being hurled into the ditch or, worse yet, into the steady stream of oncoming traffic.

The miles slowly, slowly ticked by. Behind me, the cars and RVs lined up. I passed a handful of houses at a place called The Key. After leaving that small settlement, things became still worse. I should just have rung the doorbell of one of those houses, I concluded too late. I had to stop, I had to abandon my journey—but there was nowhere, just field after endless brown field, not even a house at which to bang on the door and seek refuge.

Perhaps I should just stop here on the edge of the road and sit in a field for a while, I mused. Perhaps the wind might die down after a couple of hours.

But I had to accept that on the other hand it might not and

that, perhaps, I'd find myself spending the night all alone in a desolate field in the middle of nowhere. It was not an attractive option.

I did arrive in the end, of course. As I passed the chipper little sign at the entrance to the town that announced "Welcome to Te Anau!" my relief was such that tears welled in my eyes. As I came into the town, the speed limit dropped to thirty miles per hour, and the buildings and trees shielded me from the worst of the wind. My quaking began to subside as I rode around the edge of the lake, then turned right up the main street, a wide road with a central island. There, on the left, was my hotel—warm, safe, and dry, and complete with a parking lot where I could abandon the bike for as long as I liked. I checked in, went to my room, and changed my clothes and shoes. And then I went back out in the street, cosseted in the knowledge that, for the time being at least, I could rely for transport on my own two, very stable legs.

Te Anau is the gateway to Fiordland, home to the world-renowned Milford Sound. I had been intending to ride out to Milford the following morning. The road is supposed to be one of the most scenic in New Zealand. But in addition to its beauty, Fiordland is known for its wet weather. It was still squally. The terror of the day's ride had not yet subsided, and the mere thought of climbing back on the bike after my brush with calamity filled me with a deep, sick fear. I left the bike to sit out in the rain in the hotel parking lot.

As punishment for my cowardice, I had to haul my traumatized body out of bed at five-fifteen the next day. Instead of exploring Milford by Suzuki, I'd booked a place on a kayaking trip. In an attempt to be on the sound before the coachloads of tourists arrived and piled onto their steamers, our minibus was leaving Te Anau at a quarter to six.

I dragged myself out of bed, pulled on a few clothes, gathered a little food, my camera, some insect repellent, and, in a moment of boundless optimism, put a bottle of sunscreen into my rucksack, and went and sat on the cold, dark steps of the hotel to wait for the kayakers. The rain had stopped, but the streets were wet beneath the dim streetlights. There wasn't a soul to be seen. Behind me, in the hotel lot, my motorcycle sat in a puddle. I turned my back on it. I didn't really want to dwell on the fact that I was supposed to be taking a motorcycle tour and that, when you go on such adventures, you're really not meant to opt for the bus.

A short while later, a van drew up with a man named Tex at the wheel; we collected a handful of others from various hotels and hostels.

"Christ, was it you we saw on a motorcycle riding into town yesterday? Were you wearing a yellow rain jacket?" asked one couple.

"Oh, sorry," I apologized. "I must have held you up. I was going really slowly."

"Not at all," said the guy. "It looked terrible. I was just glad it wasn't me riding that thing."

I agreed that it had been truly awful and felt marginally less pathetic.

It was a couple of hours' drive to Milford. Waterfalls thundered down the sheer rock faces at the side of the road. The granite soared high, a vast backdrop of dark, foreboding gray.

Before the building of the road, Milford Sound was a desperately remote community, accessible only from the Milford Track, which runs from the northern tip of Lake Te Anau, or from the sea. In the end, the building of the road was made possible by the cheap labor of men who could find no other work during the depression years of the 1930s. Their life in this remote, flood-besieged, and avalanche-ravaged land was immensely hard. Many died. The Homer Tunnel, which runs for almost a mile through the mountainside, was hacked out through the rock by hand. It took nearly twenty years to complete.

The Milford Road is still threatened by frequent avalanches today. Now, of course, there's a monitoring system, and when there's a high risk of avalanche, the powers that be close the road. The 170 people who live in Milford Sound are given about twenty minutes to pack their bags and leave town, or they have to wait until the road reopens.

To be honest, it wouldn't be all that bad to be stuck there for a few days, or even a week, particularly if the tourist buses couldn't get through. Yes, it's too much talked about, there are too many buses, and lots of visitors sniff and say they are disappointed. Maybe they didn't get out of bed early enough.

We were in our kayaks and on the water by eight o'clock. The early-morning rain had cleared and now left stunning mists hanging over the vast, tree-covered mounds of glacier-carved rock that surrounded the fjord. It was almost impossible, sitting in our tiny yellow kayaks, to conceive of the huge space that engulfed us. Because the hills were so enormous, the waterfalls that thundered down them for many miles looked like long, skinny thunderbolts drawn onto the rock face with a fine white pencil.

Tex had taken a second group out on the water; I was now with a guide called Bev. Bev had a big personality and a crop of platinum-blond hair. He was a self-confessed Southern Man. He and Tex lived with the rest of the kayaking fraternity in a tight-packed conglomeration of rusting, run-down caravans on the lakeside.

"How far away d'you reckon that waterfall is?" asked Bev,

pointing to a particularly spectacular cascade that was foaming down the granite face on the other side of the fjord. It looked quite close—a mile perhaps? But even that seemed too much.

"Nope," said Bev. "That waterfall is almost *six* miles away from where we are now."

Tex and his group on the other side of the fjord had diminished into tiny yellow specks, yet the rocks beyond them seemed close. Any normal sense of scale was totally destroyed here, such was the vastness and grandeur of the deep glacial valleys and ice-gouged ledges.

We paddled across the still, murky-blue waters. We were surrounded by utter silence. In the distance, the cliffs soared up out from the water, the clouds still hanging about their peaks. Every now and then, the sun would peep through a crack in the cloud where blue sky broke through.

As we paddled over to the other side of the fjord, about thirty dusky dolphins arced in and out of the water before us. Some played alone, others dipped and dived in small groups. As I sat still in my kayak, one group dived down an arm's length away and, with perfect synchronicity, swam five abreast beneath me. A few minutes later another, single dolphin swam under my kayak, then broke up through the water so close I could almost touch it. It curved in a perfect arc, let out a playful snort through its blowhole, and then dipped back down and swam gracefully away.

We continued to paddle down the edge of the fjord, where a couple of whiskered fur seals chilled out on the rocks and wallowed in the shallows.

"Only the male seals actually come into the fjord," Bev said. "The females stay out at sea. This is a real bachelor pad."

He went on to explain that there was a colony of female

seals nearby, but that seals aren't big on sharing: One dominant male gets all the women to himself. So the other males
come down here, lie around, and beef themselves up until they
reckon they're virile enough to take on the head honcho and
assume his place in the harem.

"Yeah, they're pretty sexually frustrated, these guys," Bev
said sympathetically. "That's why they just lie around like
this."

Something, certainly, seemed to have sapped the seals' spirit.
Occasionally one of them would stir just enough to rub its
head or tummy with a flipper. It looked just like a man lying
on the sofa the morning after several beers too many. The only
thing missing was the remote control.

Bev shook his head sorrowfully. He seemed to empathize a
little too closely with the seals. I wondered whether any analogy
could be drawn between Bev and his kayaking fraternity, living in that huddle of RVs on the water's edge, and the sexually
deprived male seals wallowing nearby on the rocks, and wondered how *they* were planning to perpetuate their genes living
in this tiny all-male community. Still, Bev and Tex seemed to
have a lot more energy than the seals, so maybe things weren't
so bad.

We made our way back to base, past a face of rock that lay
bare except for a recent, new growth of ferns and mosses.

"There was a tree avalanche here two or three years ago,"
Bev told us. Only a few of the trees that grow up these impene-
trable granite fronts manage to root themselves in the rock's
tiny cracks. The rest of the trees tie their roots around each
other. When one tree falls, then, it pulls great swaths of forest
down with it. The roar as hundreds of mature trees tumble off
the rock face and disappear into the cold, dark depths of the
fjord can apparently be heard for many miles around.

Bev's trip back into town incorporated some unusual stops. We didn't just drive through the Homer Tunnel; we parked in a turnout just before it and climbed up onto the tunnel's roof, where we stood and waved, grinning, at surprised bus passengers and car drivers. Bev sat on the edge and dangled his legs. Some drivers stopped their cars and blinked, tentatively edging forward, clearly terrified that this southern lunatic might come to a sticky end on their windshields.

Bev pointed out the saddle just above the tunnel between the two peaks.

"You see that saddle there?" he asked. "That's where the postman used to ride to in the days before they built the road. He'd ride up there on his horse, to the very top, and then he'd *throw*"—Bev hurled his body in a demonstrative heaving action—"the mail as far as he could. Then a Milford man would clamber up this hillside here to fetch it."

At another turnout, Bev pulled over so that we could see kea on the side of the road. A kea is a muddy-green, alpine parrot. It's the only parrot, in fact, that nests in the snow. During the second half of the nineteenth century, much of the kea's natural habitat was destroyed by settlers who torched the lush mountain grasslands to improve their grazing pastures. In doing this, those early farmers diminished much of the food—fruit, seeds, and leaves—that the kea depended on to build up their winter fat reserves. Looking for an alternative food source, the kea turned to eating the fat from dead sheep carcasses or even feeding on live sheep: They would peck through their backs and eat the fat around their kidneys.

Kea were labeled "sheep killers," and the government paid bounty hunters to cull them. Between the 1860s and 1970, when the birds were granted partial protection by the government, it is estimated that 150,000 kea were killed. Today, there are estimated only to be between one and five thousand of them living in the wild.

Even with numbers so low, kea are easy to see, because they like to loiter about areas inhabited by humans—our trash is great kea junk food, the parrot equivalent of a night out in the bars followed by a steak and fries. The results are similar. The trouble comes almost always from groups of young males; locals call them "hoon groups." Fueled with high-energy food from the dump, they hit town like a group of marauding young vandals, pecking out the rubber from around car windshields and even pulling out nails at construction sites. They also have a line in tearing apart motorcycle seats and in picking up tourists' cameras, flying off with them until they're hovering over a particularly hard, unforgiving piece of rock, and then dropping them to smash to pieces below.

"I reckon New Zealanders should give up calling ourselves after the kiwi," commented Bev. "It's pretty boring—just a brown, flightless bird. I think we should call ourselves keas instead."

"Why's that?" I asked.

" 'Cause they're cheeky, inquisitive, and always in trouble."

Our final stop was simply a roll in the roadside grass. Bev turned off the engine, locked the van, ran exuberantly into the long sheaves—and promptly lay down and took a nap. We all stood around, bemused, then shrugged, lay down, and joined him in sleeping off the rigors of the morning.

I had been intending to leave the rains of Fiordland and continue my journey south the next day, but the woman in the tourism office told me I couldn't leave without at least a one-day walk on the world-renowned Milford Track.

The Milford Track is known as one of the most scenic walks in the world. It's also one of the wettest. It rains for about two hundred days a year around here, reaching levels of more than twenty feet. When you consider that England's famously damp Lake District receives a meager six feet of rain annually, you begin to realize just how wet Fiordland is.

The next morning, at a very leisurely nine-fifteen, I met Chris from Trips 'n' Tramps and an assortment of five or six fellow hikers. Chris's smile lines beamed through his suntan; his blue eyes burst with enthusiasm and delight. He had started work, years back, as a hut warden, both looking after the hikers' huts and maintaining the track itself.

"I remember walking down here, five days out of high school, with a pack on my back on my way to my first day at work." He grinned as we set out down the bush path. "I thought I was the luckiest guy in the world to have a job working out here."

He lived in the warden's hut with his friend Ewan. Both men were more than six feet tall; their hut was only six feet long. After several uncomfortable nights of cramped sleeping, Chris returned to the hut one day to find Ewan hard at work sawing the end off their quarters.

"Just fixing an extension on, mate," Ewan explained, demonstrating the problem-solving abilities that his pioneer forefathers had passed down to him in their genes.

Chris's enthusiasm for the track didn't seem to have died over the years. He knew every shrub and tree, every birdcall, along the way. We'd be hiking along, nattering, when suddenly he would stop.

"Look, just there," he would whisper with excited urgency, pointing at two rare yellowheads perched on a branch a few yards away. He picked out for us a fantail with four chicks, then two parakeets in a tree right by the track, so close we could see clearly their amazing bright-green and yellow plumage. The forest was filled with birdsong—bellbirds, the mimicking tuis, and the high-pitched babble of parakeets.

Crouching down, Chris found a tiny orchid, just a few inches high, by the side of the path and explained how it lured insects and trapped them inside its hooded head. He showed us an eight-hundred-year-old beech tree and considered with wonderment that this very tree had seen the Maori pass when, in years gone by, they used this route to walk to Milford Sound, where they collected greenstone, known to the rest of the world as jade. Later, the early European settlers would have trekked past this tree too. One of the men who built the track, Donald Sutherland, settled in Milford Sound with his wife. The only way they could have revisited civilization, and the only way their guests could have reached the comfort of their eighteen-room house in Milford Sound, would have been to walk along the track. The men in their wool suits, the women lifting the hems of their skirts through the floods and thick mud, would have trodden the very same path that the tourists in their protective Gore-Tex hike along today.

Before we headed home, we stopped for tea at Clinton Hut, where the hikers who walk the whole track over four days spend their first night. This place was not just a hut: It had four buildings—two bunk rooms, sleeping a total of forty people, a toilet block, and the main living–dining–cooking hut. The compound was larger than some of the townships around here. The main hut was not the dark, dingy cavern I had anticipated: It was all clean wood and chrome, with rows of gleaming gas burners, sinks, and aluminum work surfaces. I liked it there. I could easily envisage myself spending the night in such a place—though I had to accept that it might have been marginally less attractive at night after a rainy day, when forty damp, malodorous hikers had hung their wet socks and gear from the metal drying racks bolted to the ceiling. There's no electricity out here in the bush, of course.

"Sometimes, for a laugh, we used to screw an electric socket into the wall. You'd be amazed how many people tried to plug stuff in. Some had even carried hair dryers all the way out here," said Chris of his warden days. "But there's still nothing you can do about the snoring," he went on. One night some years back he had stayed in one of the other Great Walks huts. A fellow inhabitant had proved to be a particularly resonant snorer.

"All through the night, you could hear 'eeeewww' through the air, then *thump*. In the morning every last boot in the place was lying 'round his bunk. But he just slept right through it. Never woke up at all."

We took the ferry back across Lake Te Anau, to where we'd parked the minibus. We sat on the floor of the upper deck, sheltered by a metal overhang, and clutched cups of weak powdered coffee that were handed out free downstairs. As we faced backward, toward the track, the hills receded into panoramic vistas above the water, slate-gray beneath the cloud, and Chris recounted tales of Kiwi blokes of bygone days, who had made their living in the Fiordland bush.

"There was this one guy who was a pretty runty shot," he said. "In fact, I think they used to call him Runty."

He was talking now of "bulldogging," a form of deer-hunting dreamed up by men eager to make money from the new venison farming industry that sprouted in the 1970s and '80s. The deer had to be captured alive so they could be sold to the farms, where they would, hopefully, breed. To ensnare them, "bull-doggers" would balance precariously on the skids of low-flying helicopters, shoot nets over the deer, then with breathtaking bravado (or utter folly, depending on your point of view) leap onto the back of the entangled animal and attempt to pinion it to the ground.

"So this bloke Runty," Chris went on, "he managed to jump out of the chopper and got the hind in the net, but then the hind fell over backward as she was trying to get away and rolled on top of him. His feet got caught up in the net, and they started cartwheeling downhill. The deer would crash over Runty, then Runty would be pulled back over her. They were heading toward a cliff edge—but the pilot, with incredible bravery, managed to fly the chopper down to just below the drop, and as they fell off the cliff he hooked the helicopter's skid into the net and lowered Runty and the deer to safety." Runty survived the adventure with cuts and abrasions; the deer, in the end, wasn't so lucky.

Had Runty perished alongside his prey, I wondered, would he have qualified for a Darwin Award? Surely he and his fellow bulldoggers, rather than being hailed as hearty heroes, should instead be awarded one of those posthumous honors that are given out to those who meet their end through such staggering acts of foolishness that their demise—and therefore the removal of their genes from the pool—is considered to be of benefit to humanity. I'd started off my trip, all those weeks ago, thinking that the demise of the macho Kiwi man was an evolutionary catastrophe—but now I was starting to wonder. I had begun to understand that mutation was a necessary tool for survival. And now I considered the fact that the loss of some of those original Kiwi blokes might not be such a bad thing after all. Perhaps that was why nobody was creating much fuss.

That night was a big night in Te Anau: There was live music

in town. Chris and a couple of others were going. Meet us down there, they said, "there" being Redcliffs, which universal opinion seemed to designate the most happening bar and restaurant in town. Given that Te Anau is a very small town, the live music (one man and his guitar) was a much talked of event.

I wandered down to Redcliffs at about ten o'clock to find that I already had friends in the place: a British couple who'd been kayaking the day before and a couple of hikers who'd been on the track today. This is the great thing about small New Zealand towns. I'd been here two days and already I felt as though I belonged. I had traveled halfway across the globe, I was in a room I'd never seen before, but I recognized people. In some instances, I could even remember their names. I felt warm, cozy, and swathed in the company of friends—which was strange, really, as in truth I didn't know these people at all.

Trying hard to blot out from my mind the horrible reality—that I had to climb back on the bike tomorrow and wend my way out along that windy, exposed road—I had a Speight's, and then another. The man on the guitar turned to Cat Stevens cover versions; the beer flowed some more. Just moments seemed to pass—and then it was one-thirty a.m. and I had indulged enough to think that tomorrow might be ugly even if there was no wind. I tore myself away and skipped far too merrily back to my hotel.

Don't Mention the Marmite

"THE FORECAST IS FOR heavy rain and snow," said the girl at reception with a wholly inappropriate smile when I went to pay my bill.

Snow? For heaven's sake, it was the very height of summer.

"That's it," I said crossly. "If it starts to snow I'm just getting off the bike and stopping."

The hotel manager emerged from his office behind reception.

"Huh, I thought you bikers were supposed to be tough," he said.

"Not me," I replied.

I think that the bike was pleased to be back on the road, to be rescued from its puddle-plagued purgatory in the parking lot, but in this it was all alone. I'd been fearful for the last three days about riding out on that exposed stretch of road that had terrorized me on the way to Te Anau. The forecast wasn't helping. The strange thing was that, outside in the street, there was blue sky and a light breeze. This is the problem with this part of the world. There can be bright sunshine in the morning and snow in the afternoon, even in midsummer. Floods can sneak up on you in minutes and wash you away. Divert your attention for an instant, and you can be buried alive by an avalanche. It's a dangerous place, New Zealand. Maybe that's why the people grew tough.

The ride into Lumsden was sunny, with a light tailwind. The sun shone on the golden tussock, which rolled like waves in the wind. The flax swayed and twirled, creating a play of light as the sun glinted off its spiky leaves.

I had only planned to pass through Lumsden to visit Adrienne and Chris, distant relatives of friends of my parents, on my way down to Bluff and Stewart Island. But the poor weather forecast—which though unpredictable in these parts nonetheless sounded unpromising—had put me off the ride to Bluff, the notoriously rough crossing over the Foveaux Strait, and the prospect of being holed up in the rain on Stewart Island for days to come. I changed my schedule once again and stayed the night in Lumsden.

Chris was the local vicar in these parts; a few years ago he and Adrienne took part in a six-month exchange with a vicar in Wiltshire. As a result of their time in England, they were great connoisseurs of English cuisine.

"In England," Adrienne pronounced soon after my arrival, somewhat accusingly I thought, "you can't buy Tim Tams" (which, for the record, are a chocolate sandwich cookie).

Chris looked up. He had a serious expression on his face. "Or hokey-pokey ice cream," he said.

"Or Marmite!" Adrienne countered. She was becoming a little more excitable now. The charges were building up in a resonant crescendo. I wanted to butt in and point out that, in fact, we do have Marmite in England, but I couldn't find a polite way of breaking the news. Adrienne had clearly been much deprived during her time in Britain and, although some years had passed since, the effects of living for months with such restrictions had imprinted long-lasting bitterness on her psyche.

Then, with some flamboyance, she flung open the kitchen drawer and, wielding a small, straight object with a blade, she let fly her final charge: "*Or proper potato peelers!*"

She waved the object, which was indeed a potato peeler, around in the air for proof.

"You see," said Adrienne, "in New Zealand, our potato peelers are like this! But yours are different! *They don't work! We Kiwis can't peel potatoes with them!*"

It was a difficult situation, a moment of horrible cultural collision. An International Incident was looming. An overwrought woman was slightly out of control with a bladed object. Worse, she was standing only a yard or so away from me. I was no longer wearing my super-armored Dainese motorcycling leathers. I was going to have to think on my feet, and fast. It was a tense situation, and one that required diplomacy, discretion, political agility, nimble eloquence.

"Er," I said.

The problem was that the potato peeler Adrienne was brandishing looked remarkably like the potato peelers I'd been using in England for years. I didn't like to disagree with her too strongly—after all, these people were being immensely kind, putting me up for the night, and had offered to spend their valuable time showing me around the area. Also, the kitchen drawer was still open, and there was no telling what cache of weaponry lay lurking within.

On the other hand, how could I not stand up for my potato-eating heritage and let this terrible accusation go uncorrected? I was in a dilemma indeed.

"Um, I think we have various kinds of potato peelers, actually," I mumbled, embarrassed. "We have the ones with the blade across the top, the ones with the blade down the side, the ones where the blade is fixed, and the one where the blade swivels, like that one you've got."

That seemed to do it. She put the potato peeler back in the drawer and agreed reluctantly that maybe she'd just been to the wrong shop. I felt rather pleased with myself: Who knows, perhaps I have a future in diplomacy, after all. Or hostage negotiation, perhaps? You want world peace? Look no further. Here is the woman who defused the crisis known to history as Potato Peelergate.

Back in the real world, Chris's parish stretches nearly forty miles from the tiny township of Waikaia west almost out to Te Anau, and north up the valley to Kingston. To drive from one end of the parish to the other in the car takes almost two hours. Chris spends a lot of time in his car.

As a result, Chris and Adrienne know some interesting people, and, once we'd gotten over the difficult subject of kitchen utensils, they very kindly drove me for many miles over gravel roads to visit Stan and Bev. A sheep-and-cattle farmer, Stan took tinkering in sheds to a whole new level: He was building an *airplane* in his. He was a large, taciturn man, age about sixty. He took us to see the work in progress.

Stan may be a MESS (Man Experiencing Shed Syndrome), but his shed was immaculate. A wing of the airplane-to-be stood on a stand in the middle of the room. On the workbench lay the immensely complicated plans and a doorstop of a manual with astonishing, squiggly diagrams and symbols that meant absolutely nothing to me. I was vastly impressed. Stan was in the process of finishing off the wing that stood on display. Endless rows of rivets were paraded along its length, even and perfectly spaced. He had just sealed the gas tank.

"What would you have done if you'd put it all together and then realized you'd done something wrong inside?" asked Chris.

"Aw, I had a pretty good check first to make sure it was all okay," laughed Stan wryly.

I asked him, rather more incredulously, just *why* he was building an airplane in his shed. Fixing the washing machine, yes, I can understand that. Changing the oil in the car, fair enough. But building an airplane? Why exactly would anyone do that?

"So I can fly it," said Stan.

The sun gods were angry with Southland. The next day when I set off on my bike, the midsummer temperatures reached a high of fifty degrees, but that didn't take into account the icy gales that were howling fresh from the Antarctic. It was only an hour's ride to Invercargill from Lumsden. It was just as well I didn't have to freeze on that motorcycle seat for any longer. I was wearing all the clothes I could fit under my leathers plus my bright yellow rain jacket to keep out the wind, but still, after fifteen minutes my fingers were aching and numb with the cold.

On the outskirts of Invercargill, a couple in a car pulled over to where I had stopped by the roadside to look at the map. The woman leaned out the passenger window.

"If you have learner plates on a motorcycle, are you allowed to carry a passenger?" she asked.

"Er, well, I don't know what the laws are here, because I got my license in England . . . in England you couldn't . . . but here, I don't know."

"Oh!" said the woman. "Sorry, I thought you were a policeman!"

I was going to have to seriously consider changing that rain jacket for one that was a less lurid color.

"Actually, seeing as you've stopped, could you tell me the way to the Ascot Park Motel?" I asked.

"Follow us!" They grinned and led me all the way to reception.

I had to drink several cups of hot tea to warm up when I arrived at my motel. When my fingers were once more agile enough to dial phone numbers, I called Gordi, way up north in balmy Auckland.

"Where are you?" he asked.

"Invercargill," I said.

He laughed and laughed and laughed.

That is the problem with Invercargill. It is so highly unfashionable, even by New Zealand's unexacting standards, that it just makes people snigger. Being soft-hearted—or perhaps cursed with the British tendency to back the underdog—I felt a little bit sorry for the town and was determined to find something good to say about it. And so, wearing a ridiculous number of layers—running tights under my jeans, polypropylene T-shirt, thermal long-sleeved top, fleece, sweater, and, yes, even the neon-yellow rain jacket—I ventured into town.

To be honest, it was hard to like the place while a perishing wind made my ears ache. My motel was a forty-minute walk away from the town center, something I had failed to figure out before I booked it. Even with all my clothes, one vital item was missing from my wardrobe: In packing to come to New

Zealand in the height of summer, I had carelessly omitted to bring a fleecy hat with earflaps. I began to get a headache from the gale howling down my ears. Then the rain set in. This was no measly drizzle; it was a full-force blast of watery diagonal icicles. And then, just when it seemed as though it could get no worse, the rain turned to hail. This was summer in Invercargill.

Invercargill is not the center of the universe. I do not recommend that you drop everything and go there for a two-week vacation. Judging from the front page of the regional paper, the *Southland Times*, not much happens here.

"A cell phone was held for ransom in Invercargill last night," the newspaper's front page announced with a gravitas that in other countries would be reserved for hijackings and mass murder. "The cell phone was lost earlier in the day by an Invercargill man and another man demanded a reward for its safe return."

The ransom in question was a mere twenty-five dollars. The phone's owner called the police, who sent *two units* to the scene! In the end, the owner of the cell phone wasn't required to pay up. This being New Zealand, "an amicable settlement was reached by both parties."

Still, how can you hate a place where such an event is received with such horror that it hits the headlines? When the rain stops, Invercargill even has a certain charm. Faded, well, maybe. But because it has such a terrible reputation for being dull and hick, if you do actually make the effort to come here, the people are very friendly. Total strangers guide you to the reception desk of your hotel. And the great advantage of a town in which nobody much wants to live or invest is that back in the 1960s nobody pulled down the grand old buildings and replaced them with groovy gray concrete. So Invercargill, of all New Zealand's cities, is one of those that best retains its original character. The buildings on the main street are actually very attractive, elegant turn-of-the-century brick. And— yes, I'm grasping at straws here—it has a very nice park indeed, which would be pleasant to walk in should you happen to visit on a day when hailstones are not being hurled from the sky in a manner that leaves you wondering whether God is in training for the discus event at the next Olympics. Invercargill is not fashionable; the clothes in the main-street stores are dowdy and, all right, I even saw a couple of people wearing checked shirts. But even in Invercargill, you can get great coffee.

I took refuge in a café and read the paper. It was a particularly good issue.

"Southern blokes are reeling at news that one in seven of their mates could be wearing girls' knickers" opened the lead story on the front page of the *Southland Times*. Taking up most of the front page was a photograph of a man leaning against a sheep pen, wearing a thick red-and-black-checked shirt, green gum boots, and a pair of frilly French panties.

The story ran that an Auckland mail-order underwear company had commissioned a survey which revealed that 14.6 percent of Kiwi men admitted to buying women's lingerie for themselves.

"I've met big, hairy truck drivers with beautifully painted nails, who are dressed in more beautiful lingerie than I have," an Invercargill-based adult entertainer was reported as telling the paper. "Heaps of real blokes down here wear women's underwear, just heaps. But no one will admit it, will they?"

The mayor of Invercargill, Tim Shadbolt, refused to believe that good Southern men would do such a thing. "I can guarantee most of that fourteen percent came from Ponsonby or

Parnell or the leafy suburbs of Auckland," he was reported as saying. "We're just not like that down here."

"You'd be struggling to find many Southland blokes who wear women's lingerie, because down here we know what it means to be a man," said another interviewee.

The greatest attraction of Invercargill, though, is not its coffee, nor yet its panty-clad men, as they have so far failed to reveal themselves. The real draw is Henry. Second only to the truck drivers with toenail polish, Henry is said to be Invercargill's most stimulating resident. He's a 120-year-old tuatara—a lizard whose ancestry dates back 225 million years. I was eager to meet him.

The problem with Henry, I found when I arrived at the "tuataratorium" at Southland Museum, is that he isn't exactly an exhibitionist. I stood and stared at him for some while: He didn't move a muscle. He didn't even appear to blink. It was as though he and the other tuataras were playing a game of dead possum—or, in this case, dead tuataras. On the other hand, he might have been asleep with his eyes open, because it was the middle of the day and tuataras are nocturnal creatures. Measuring in at about a foot and a half long, he had dry, reptilian skin that hung in loose folds around his neck. Along the top of his head and back lay a row of spines ("tuatara" is Maori for spiny back), but even these looked flaccid and pointedly unaroused.

One man, Lindsay Hazley, has dedicated much of his life to trying to breed tuataras here. Looking at Henry today, it seemed as though encouraging these creatures to do anything at all might be an uphill struggle. A male tuatara, furthermore, doesn't have a penis to keep him interested: He has to content himself with climbing on top of the female and entwining his tail around hers so that their holes touch. Apparently this can last for up to an hour—and that's after the courting process, which involves the male strutting around in circles with his throat puffed out and his spines erect. This all looked as though it might be a bit much for Henry. But one of the adult males around here is certainly up to something, as the museum has a flourishing breeding program. The only real problem is naming the babies: You can't tell a tuatara's sex until it reaches the age of twelve.

Outside, it was still hailing large globs of ice. Tomorrow I was heading to Stewart Island, where I was planning to spend a couple of days wallowing in the great outdoors, observing birds in the bush and generally communing with nature. Nature was not playing the game. On Invercargill's main street, I found an outdoor-gear shop.

"That's it," I muttered crossly. "I've had enough of being cold and wet. I'm giving up on summer."

And, wielding my credit card like a weapon against the weather, I went in and bought boots, merino-wool thermals, and a fleecy hat with earflaps.

The next morning, I rode down to Bluff, the Land's End of New Zealand, where it was raining. I checked in for the ferry an hour or so ahead of time and, as it was lunchtime, asked the woman at the desk if there was anywhere to eat in Bluff.

"On a *Saturday*?" she exclaimed, grasping the counter with both hands in a manner that suggested, were she to let go, she might just topple over from astonishment.

I felt slightly ill at ease. I didn't like to tell her that, with horrible gluttony, I actually eat all seven days of the week.

The woman frowned, thought a little, and then said that if I drove down the road to Stirling Point I would find a couple of cafés.

Stirling Point is the very end of the road. I sat in a café

overlooking the signpost that declared Cape Reinga, New Zealand's northern tip, to be 871 miles away, London 11,781. I watched the cars swing around in the little parking lot, the people emerging from within stopping only to take photos of themselves in the rain in front of the signpost, and then drive off again. Other than the café, Bluff was very definitely closed.

The Ford Cortina
Capital of the World

"THERE ARE TWO WAYS of getting here," they say on Stewart Island. "An hour of seasickness, or twenty minutes of sheer bloody terror."

The Foveaux Strait, the stretch of water between mainland South Island and Stewart Island, is choppy at the best of times. The alternative to crossing by boat is to fly from Invercargill; the flight, too, is renowned for being a little bit lively. People with delicate stomachs avoid going to Stewart Island solely on account of the horror of getting there. Stories abound of crossings that were, in island language, "a wee bit rough." On days like these the ferry leaves the water, flying off the crest of the swell before crashing back down. The white-knuckled passengers apparently vomit so copiously that the boat crew can scarcely keep up as they move through the cabin gathering overflowing seasickness bags and handing their green-faced contributors fresh ones. Today was not a rough day, but still the boat lurched and rolled across the swell. My constitution, I'm proud to say, held firm.

Stewart Island, in any case, is worth a little queasiness. It's a wonderful place, a world away from Bluff and Invercargill across the strait. The island has only a few hundred inhabitants, and nearly all of them live in Oban, Stewart Island's only township. Oban must be the Ford Cortina capital of the world. Its three or four streets were littered with them, and each boasted an array of rust, dents, and all the other forms of corrosion that one would expect to batter a car by the seaside over the course of thirty years. There were Cortina two-door sedans and Cortina wagons, resplendent in 1970s colors with twenty-first-century embellishments: muddy brown, rust and cream, battered baby blue. The ferry from Bluff doesn't bring cars over, so this is not a place for automotive poseurs. In any case, a car here doesn't need to be reliable. There are only a few miles of road. If the wheels fall off, you can always walk home. And then, great joy, you can spend a few delightful hours holed up in your shed sticking them back on again.

The vast majority of Stewart Island is bush, for though it only has a couple of very short roads, it has 466 miles of coastline. With fewer predators here than on the mainland, rare birds stand a better chance of survival, so if you want to see a kiwi in the wild, Stewart Island is the best place to try your luck. The relative prosperity of the kiwis here isn't only due to the lack of predators, though. Another major reason is that the Stewart Island kiwi has adapted to its changing habitat in a more effective way than its northern cousins.

For kiwis, the great problem of the modern world has nothing to do with machines making their masculinity redundant. The biggest threat for the kiwi is the stoat, which eats huge numbers of kiwi eggs and chicks. (Stoats were introduced to New Zealand by European settlers in the late 1800s so that they would eat the rocketing rabbit population that had been introduced for hunting—it's all a bit like that song, "There Was an Old Woman Who Swallowed a Fly.") Kiwi eggs on North and South Island are incubated solely by the male. When he waddles off to feed, in come the wily stoats and gobble up the eggs. On Stewart Island, the kiwi has evolved differently. Not only are there fewer stoats in the first place, but also the male and female birds share the incubation. While one parent goes off to feed, the other looks after the egg. This way, a greater number of chicks actually hatch. The equal division of domestic labor, then, was mastered down here in the remote bush of Stewart Island well before men up north started changing diapers and becoming acquainted with the washing machine. The erosion of traditional roles according to gender is not just a human phenomenon.

Experts reckon that there are about twenty thousand kiwis on Stewart Island, but they're still almost impossible for the uninitiated to spot. They're nocturnal, notoriously shy, and colored an inconvenient shade of brown that blends rather well with the undergrowth. They're antisocial, feeding separately and with only one family per patch. As if that doesn't make them difficult enough to see, they spend most of their waking hours with their long beaks buried in the mud as they forage about for grubs. Sometimes they get so enthusiastic about rooting out a deeply wriggling worm that they head-butt the ground, on occasion so hard that their feet leave the floor.

To find them, you have to go out at night, and you have to take a guide. And so, at nine o'clock on my first evening on Stewart Island, I met up with an islander called Philip, a middle-aged couple from Buckinghamshire, a man from Gloucestershire, a Melbourne businessman taking a weekend off en route home from Christchurch, and three Melbournites in their early twenties. We piled onto Philip's boat and, a while later, arrived at Ocean Beach on Stewart Island's west coast.

Philip was clearly determined that the kiwis shouldn't see him. He was wearing gum boots and a camouflage jacket. It seemed an excessive precaution—after all, it was dark—but I had to concede that I didn't know a lot about kiwis. Perhaps they had very good eyesight.

Philip gathered us to the front of the boat to brief us on the mission ahead. He handed out flashlights and told us to point them at all times toward the ground. We were to turn them off when told to do so. We were to be quiet. We were to stick closely together and walk in single file. We were strictly to obey his instructions.

We all nodded enthusiastically and practiced turning our flashlights on and off. And then, when Philip deemed us ready for action, we silently tiptoed off the boat and into the forest.

Up and down the paths we crept. Masters of subterfuge, we kept our flashlights pointed at the ground and shuffled along in single file. Twigs cracked, leaves crackled, boots lumbered loud.

"Watch out, there's a log," hissed the man from Buckinghamshire.

The girl from Melbourne had an attack of coughing.

"My flashlight battery's died," complained her friend.

We prowled up and down the trails some more. We found no sign of life. I began to worry that the problem might lie in my yellow rain jacket. My fellow kiwi-spotters weren't much better in their array of pink, red, and blue anoraks. The poor kiwis had probably taken fright and run away, blinking and hiding their heads under their stubby little wings. Perhaps we all should have dressed in camouflage. Maybe we could have painted our faces with that green-and-brown face paint while we were at it. That might have been fun—

"You stay here! Don't move!" Philip cut into my reverie in a very stern voice. "Turn off your flashlights!"

We stumbled to a halt and huddled in a tight circle on the path.

"Do you think he saw something?" whispered the business-man from Melbourne with great urgency.

"I'm not quite sure," I replied.

We stood stock-still on the wooded pathway in the pitch darkness, anxious that if we so much as stretched a cramping leg we might cause a twig to crackle and blow our cover. For several minutes we stayed like that. Philip, it seemed, had pulled off a very stealthy vanishing act. As for the kiwis, they had clearly gone to ground.

Then there was a faint rustle of leaves and Philip furtively reappeared from behind a tree.

"Did you find anything?" we whispered feverishly.

"No," he said.

We had been sneaking about in the woods for an hour or so when we heard the loud, chirruping call of a kiwi. The ex-citement was too much.

"Gosh, was that a kiwi?" I piped up, momentarily forgetting that I was supposed to keep quiet.

"Yes. Now ssshhh. Follow me!" Philip instructed.

We bumbled along a little further. Dredging up every dram of our detective abilities, we shone our flashlights at the path and squinted purposefully, searching for fresh tracks. There was nothing. We came out on the beach on the other side of the island.

"You stay here!" commanded Philip once more, and he stalked off into the night once more.

There was a hurried crunching of leaves as he abruptly returned.

"Right," he said. "There's a kiwi down on the beach. Follow me. *Quietly*."

We really, really wanted to be quiet. We had been traipsing around the woods for a couple of hours now. It was past midnight and I think, secretly, we were all quite keen to spot a kiwi, get back on the boat, and go home to bed. We summoned up all our powers of stealth and tiptoed, quietly, quietly, down onto the sand. When we were all gathered, standing in our silent huddle once more, Philip slowly raised his extinguished flashlight, pointed it at a clump of twigs, and then, as we watched with bated breath, he turned it on. I just caught a glimpse of something round and brown and then, *pad, pad, crunch*, the kiwi strutted off into the bush.

"Who saw it? Did *anyone* see it?" Philip demanded despairingly.

I was the only one to have spotted the fast-disappearing feathery bottom.

"You're too slow!" Philip exclaimed with frustration, momentarily forgetting the importance of silence and subterfuge in this highly covert operation. "You're slow as . . . as . . . as *molasses*!"

Much chastised, we tiptoed more quickly back up the track, hoping the kiwi would pop out on the path at the top. It didn't. Philip crept off to the beach again—and hurried back. It had returned.

"Now come on, *quickly* and quietly," he hissed crossly.

We tried hard to obey. Whispering and shuffling, eager not to upset Philip any further, we hobbled ineptly down the pathway, over the rattling twigs and crackling leaves, onto the sand.

This time we were rewarded for our speed. There on the edge of the beach, beneath the shrubs where the bush meets the sand, a female kiwi fed. She was a lovely young lady by kiwi standards—her big, round, plump bottom stuck up in the air while she nosed around for grubs. The man from Gloucestershire lent me his binoculars, which granted me a wonderful view of her big feathery behind.

After a long, untroubled sleep—you don't get woken up by car alarms going off in Oban—I put on all my thermals, boots, and rain jacket. I ate a leisurely breakfast in one of Oban's two cafés, took a gentle putter around its streets, and then walked over the hill to the bay from where the water taxis depart for the bird sanctuary of Ulva Island.

The weather today qualified as "a wee bit rough." The wind was roaring, the sea choppy and frothy with white. I wandered down to the jetty, unsure as to whether I'd find a water taxi willing to take me across in this weather. But sure enough, within a few minutes, a small boat appeared, pitching and rolling in a terrifying manner over the great crashing breakers. It literally seemed to have to power up the sides of the waves, which looked taller than it was, before plummeting down the other side, keeling precariously as it dropped.

"What are the chances of getting over to Ulva Island?" I asked Ken, the driver, dubiously.

"Depends how long you want to stay," he replied. "I'm going over now, then collecting some people to bring them back at three. That's it. I'm not going again. I wouldn't go at all if I didn't have to collect that bunch."

Ken didn't seem too happy with the weather, but the people getting off the boat assured me that the ten-minute crossing had been a lot of fun. I clambered aboard.

The lurching of the boat didn't seem as bad from inside as it had looking at it being thrown around from dry land. Still, I found myself unintentionally forming a contingency plan.

If this thing goes over, I figured to myself, as long as the motor cuts out immediately so I don't have any parts of my body sliced off, I should be able to get out of here. I would definitely have to lose the boots in order to swim, though. That would be a pity, given that they're brand-new, but I could probably get the money back on the insurance.... I'd probably have trouble untying the double knot once the laces got wet and I was submerged in the water, though, maybe even trapped under the boat.... Maybe I should untie them now to make for an easier escape.

I hoped that Ken could swim. I reckoned that on my own I'd stand a pretty good chance of survival. Having to life-save Ken, who was a sturdy specimen, would add complications.

We made it over with no major mishap. The rain held off and I spent two wonderful hours exploring. Ulva was created as a bird sanctuary back in 1922; they have managed to eradicate rats from the island, which now suffers from fewer predators than almost any other part of New Zealand. The result is that, as soon as you step off the boat, you're overwhelmed by the birds. Even I, who only became a bird-watcher a few hours ago, couldn't miss them. Red- and yellow-crested parakeets flitted from tree to tree around my head; I was so busy looking up at them that I almost tripped over a weka—a brown, flightless bird—that was pecking around on the path at my feet. A black-and-white Stewart Island robin sat on a branch just an arm's length away from me and posed dreamily for a photo. No binoculars or zoom lenses were needed here, though such was my overexuberance in snapping it that the photo came out blurred. Up high in the branches a kukupa—a huge New Zealand wood pigeon—cooed and then dived down across the path to a tree on the other side. Hearing a scratching, rustling noise, I peered through the branches of a tree to see a kaka, a type of parrot, stripping its bark and munching on the insects underneath. Another red-crested parakeet simply sat in the path as I tramped along; dozens of tuis and fantails flitted between the boughs.

Creeping through the bush, my ears straining for sound, I was even beginning to learn to identify a bird by its song: The call of a yellow-eyed penguin, I learned, sounds like the scream of a murder victim to untrained ears. A parakeet sounds like a car that won't start on a cold, rainy morning. A tui can sound like pretty much anything, as it is a masterful copycat: Tuis have been known to mimic not only the other birds in the bush but also cell phones and the whir of a camera film winding on.

My pace slowed; I listened more intently. There was no doubt about it: I was taking on the characteristics of a bird-watcher. Was this a good thing? I wondered. Or would it mean that I had to buy a new anorak and some heavy-framed glasses when I got back home? Would I perhaps have to abandon the fishing idea and take up a whole new career as a geography teacher? It was quite alarming, really, what many weeks of solitude on the road can do to a person. I had started out normal, healthy, and sociable. Then I'd started talking to my bike. And now I was tiptoeing around woods, wishing I'd invested in a pair of binoculars and getting in a tizzy at the sight of anything with feathers. Where would it end? Bus trips with octogenarians to rainy marshlands? Corned-beef sandwiches and thermoses of tea? In-depth conversations about brands of binoculars and incontinence pads?

I arrived back at the pier with a good twenty minutes to spare. Ken hadn't seemed to be enjoying his day very much, and I didn't want to miss the boat. The group he had arranged to pick up was a crowd of Americans with their guide, Ron. The crossing was even more rousing than the outbound trip.

"It's much more fun than Queenstown," I remarked as the boat plummeted vertiginously down from the crest of the umpteenth wave.

"It's killed more people than Queenstown too," said Ron grimly.

We talked some more. Somehow the conversation moved to alcohol, the New Zealanders' fondness for a tipple, and the joyful incident of my ID check in the Auckland supermarket. I told them how delighted I had been to be questioned at the age of thirty-two.

Back on land, I wandered up to the Fernery, a charming craft shop perched on the hillside above Oban and owned by Elspeth, a friend of Chris and Adrienne in Lumsden. I'd phoned her that morning and arranged to go up and have a cup of coffee when I got back from Ulva Island. I pushed open the shop door and asked for Elspeth; she was up at the house, the woman in the shop said, and then she phoned her to tell her I was here.

A few minutes later, a woman walked through the back door.

"Yes, you definitely look younger than thirty-two," she said, and laughed at my bewilderment. It turned out that Ron on the boat was the same person as Ron her husband. It's a small community on Stewart Island.

We sat in armchairs in their house filled with books, by floor-to-ceiling windows that looked out over bush and sea. Elspeth and Ron talked about the changes they'd seen on the island in the twenty-three years since they moved here. Back then, there was no public electricity. Everyone had their own generator, and heating came from coal burners. Now the electricity comes from a central generator, but it's three to four times more expensive than the electricity on the mainland. The people's principal source of income is moving from fishing to tourism: Many of the fishermen made good money from crayfish, then from paua (abalone) diving, but then they exhausted the resources. The problem with tourism is that the season's so short. Most people on the island reckon to make the majority of their annual income between December and the end of March. They work long hours: It gets dark late here, and the tourists don't realize the time. And when the tourists stay up late, those catering to their needs work late as well.

And so everyone on Stewart Island is tired. This year had been disappointingly quiet so far, so the islanders had anxiety to add to their tiredness. I'd overheard the girl working in the coffee shop complaining earlier that day about the way she had to work from dawn 'til dusk seven days a week.

"We moved over here for the lifestyle," she grumbled, "but all we do is work. I can't help but think that we could move to London and earn three times as much, and even there we'd get two days off a week."

Meanwhile, people are coming in from overseas and buying up the land at prices that seem staggering to the islanders; the

American girl who owns the coffee shop had just sold a piece of property for three hundred thousand New Zealand dollars, an inconceivable coup for most people living here.

"But I suppose we could have been buying up land and selling it too if we'd thought about it." Elspeth shrugged.

Stewart Island certainly seemed to be changing, and the people down here, men and women, were having some trouble adjusting to the demands of the new order. It wasn't just Elspeth and the woman in the coffee shop; Ken in his water taxi hadn't seemed exactly over the moon about his new role ferrying tourists, and Philip last night had seemed, in the nicest possible way, to find us positively irritating.

I told Elspeth and Ron about my kiwi-spotting experience and how poor Philip had become exasperated with the clod-hopping, bumbling tourists in his charge. Ron and Elspeth knew Philip well. Elspeth threw her head back and laughed.

"Ron, did you hear that?" she called into the next room. "Philip told them they were slow as molasses!" And she laughed some more. I never quite figured out whether it was Philip or the bumbling tourists, or perhaps the uneasy combination of both, that filled her with so much mirth.

I went to the pub after supper. The men here didn't seem to have let the change in their world, the island's shift from fishing to tourism, affect their ways. They were just guys drinking beer in a pub.

I started chatting to a man wearing an all-in-one jumpsuit with the words "Foveaux Express" emblazoned across it. His name was Friday. He worked on the ferry.

"So were a lot of people sick today?" I asked.

"Aw yeah, fair number of them weren't too good. It's the way they change color that always gets me. First off, there's loads of noise, then it all goes quiet. And then they start to change color. I don't like it when they're sick; I just want them to have a good time here. I say to them, 'Listen, I'm the biggest chicken in the world. And if this ferry wasn't safe, I wouldn't be on it.'"

Friday explained to me how the ferry driver charts the course, how he doesn't take the most direct route but the easiest one so that the boat doesn't battle the elements all the way. I asked him how often the ferry had to be canceled because of the weather.

"Aw, it's only actually canceled about six times a year. And then it's not because it's not safe, it's just because the passengers can't handle it."

He went on to tell me about the times he'd been on the ferry when only the back few yards of the boat had been in contact with the water, such was the ferocity of the waves. He showed me a photograph on the pub wall of the boat leaving Bluff on a particularly rough day, at a violent angle out of the water.

Friday's friend Jim worked in the only garage on Stewart Island.

"So, all those Ford Cortinas," I asked him. "Don't they need to pass some kind of roadworthiness test?"

"Aw, the warrant of fitness, yeah," said Jim. "Costs 'em a couple of pints usually, eh! But there's only seven miles of road on the island, so the distance any car on the mainland drives in a month would take ten years here."

Friday asked me where I was heading next. I told him I was going to Miller's Flat, a tiny township in central Otago. Friday knew the place well; he used to go to the rodeo there. One night, the pub he was drinking in was raided by the police for serving after hours. The landlord said, "Hey, Friday, you'd better get out of here or we'll all get busted."

"Nah, leave it to me," said Friday, and headed for the piano. He picked up one end, his mate grabbed the other, and they were just heading across the pub, carrying the piano between them, when the police came in.

"What're you doing with that piano?" asked the boys in blue.

"Ah, we're the band, just packing up," said Friday.

"Friday," said the landlord when the police had gone on their way, "you can drink here whenever you like. That's the best excuse I've ever heard."

The conversation settled into joke-telling. The first came from Friday.

"We're driving along the road past where there's a nuthouse, and there's a man sitting in the bus shelter in his pajamas. I ask him, 'Does this road go to Christchurch?' He thinks for a while and then says, 'Well, I don't know. But if it does, it must go at night, 'cause it's always here in the morning.' "

Jim countered: "The police catch a man doing 125 miles per hour in his car. They pull him over and say, 'You'd better have a pretty good excuse.' 'Yeah, well,' says the man, 'just yesterday my wife ran off with a cop who looked a bit like you. I thought you might be him bringing her back.' "

Another man, Kevin, showed me magic tricks. He extinguished a cigarette in my sweater and squeezed water out of my watch. He was a shy man, who seemed to need a couple of pints of Speight's and the encouragement of good friends before he would demonstrate his astonishing aptitude for sleight of hand. He could make a fortune off the island.

"So," I said, "what's this I read in the paper about Southern men wearing women's panties?"

There was sudden silence, an uncomfortable shuffling of feet. Then Jim started to unbuckle his belt and headed south toward his fly.

"C'mon, everyone," he yelled at the assembled crowd of men. "Let's see who's the one in seven."

It was time for me to leave.

Building Castles
in the Clouds

I WAS SECRETLY PLEASED when the smug English lady puked.

On the pier, in the cold early morning, I had looked un-enthusiastically at the ominous gray sea. A small huddle of anorak-clad folk heading back with me to the mainland on this morning's ferry had pursed their lips and eyed the unwelcoming water. We'd piled our luggage into rectangular containers and then watched as they'd been winched onto the small, lurching boat. The English lady, a stalwart type, had exuded confidence—*she* had some funny elastic wristbands with knobbly bits that worked a pressure point. They'd never let her down in ten years.

Until today. I, on the other hand, held out—but only just. Within five minutes I was overcome by that miserable, stomach-churning feeling that is accompanied not by full-scale projectile vomiting but by a failure to find any joy in the proceedings. I closed my eyes and tried to sleep. The boat leapt off the crest of a wave, plummeted down onto the water below, and lurched up the next watery incline. My stomach gurgled, unhappy at the way its contents were being energetically spun.

Thank God I hardly ate any breakfast, I thought to myself. The breakfast buffet had looked tempting, but the hotel restaurant had windows that looked out onto the sea, and the white-tipped waves had suggested that a full fry-up with a choppy-sea chaser might not be the best way to start the day.

Finally, we arrived back in Bluff, but even after reaching dry land I felt queasy for the rest of the morning. Stewart Island was wonderful, but next time I'll fly from Invercargill and brace myself for the twenty minutes of sheer terror.

Riding up to Gore, the midsummer weather rained and blew some more. By the time I reached the town, about sixty miles to the northwest of Bluff, it had settled into a steady downpour.

In a bid to escape the rain, if only for half an hour or so, I visited the Hokonui Moonshine museum in Gore. Hokonui Moonshine was a kind of bootleg whiskey made by the Scots who settled in these hills. (Their heritage lives on to this day in the slightly rolled "r" noticeable in southerners' speech.) Southland was one of the areas that suffered—or benefited, depending on your viewpoint—most from the crusade against the demon drink in the early twentieth century. Prohibition lasted here for fifty-one years, and even now alcohol can't be bought in supermarkets.

The temperance movement was all part of the crusade for moral harmony that swept New Zealand in the early 1900s. New Zealand was supposed to be a land free from perversity and sin. It was God's Own Country, according to Dick Seddon,

Prime Minister from 1893 to 1905—and New Zealanders would never forget the phrase. Seddon's government introduced old-age pensions to New Zealand in 1898, but a man's pension could be stopped if he was found in the pub. Good Kiwi blokes were to abstain from booze, forgo women, forget the wild ways of the crews, of the whalers and the diggers. If they wanted to survive in paradise, they had to weave from their manliness a new moral fiber.

It was interesting to see, in this museum, how a few hardy folk had held out against the law, and even more so to consider the attitudes that had given rise to prohibition in the first place. The temperance movement sprang from an intriguing era, from a world where people honestly believed, for a time, that they could create Utopia, could forge a new society on the other side of the world populated by noble stock that would breed out drunkenness, laziness, and corruption. The Kiwi bloke, these earnest folk believed, would be an honest, hardworking family man. The ideal had not proved as easy to achieve as they had hoped.

I rode out of Gore and through the hills in which those hardy whiskey-distilling Scots settled. The landscape, strangely for a place twelve thousand miles away, is not unlike Scotland—rolling, craggy hills that, once upon a time, were covered by native bush and birds until first the Maori, then the European settlers, cleared them. But Scottish roads are not flanked by flax. Rows of tall spiky leaves cradled chocolate-brown stamens and created an avenue down the long, straight road out of Gore.

I was heading northward now, to Miller's Flat in central Otago. Just outside the village, up a rough gravel track, live Kyle and Marion. Kyle is a novelist that my agent had put me in touch with; his wife, Marion, makes teapots that are in hot demand in the shops and galleries from Dunedin to Auckland and beyond.

Kyle built their house himself; all the crockery inside was made by Marion—which leads to an interesting point. If they were New Zealanders, no doubt Kyle and Marion would glow with smug pioneer pride and smile about their good Kiwi practicality. The problem is that they're not. Marion is German and Kyle is Australian.

"All this Kiwi ingenuity stuff really annoys me," said Kyle. "It's just so ridiculous. If a New Zealander makes something, they call it Kiwi ingenuity. If someone from somewhere else does exactly the same thing, nobody takes any notice."

He might have had a point. After all, this was the man who had designed his own composting toilet, and if that's not ingenious, I don't know what is.

I have to admit, the first time I needed to pay that smallest of rooms a visit, I was filled with consternation.

"Er, where's the bathroom?" I asked, as you do when you're in a house you've never visited before. I hadn't realized that the main sewerage didn't reach this far. I wasn't anticipating that I would need a whole ream of instructions before I was let loose on the facilities.

This was a lavatory designed for sitting-down performances only, Kyle explained. Liquid waste went strictly down the funnel in the front, and was washed away with a sprinkling of water from one of Marion's pottery jugs that was sitting by the side of the toilet. The other kind went down a second hole, at the back, and into a pit. This had to be followed down by a scoop of peaty-looking soil from a wooden box that also sat at the side of the toilet.

As Kyle explained these arrangements to me, my heart sank.

Oh, Christ. How long do I have to stay in this house, with these peculiar people and their complicated toilet arrangements? I wondered inwardly. I had a vision of a stinking latrine, a hut buzzing with fat flies heady on their latest feast of excrement.

But here is the remarkable thing: That bathroom was sweeter-smelling than most sewer-connected bathrooms I've been to. The only smell was a faint, really quite pleasant aroma of soil. Down in the pit, apparently, worms were at work processing everything, breaking it down and making it pure. And then, once every couple of years, Kyle would shovel it out onto the garden. Apparently it was dry and odorless, just like the compost you buy in expensive plastic bags from chic urban garden centers. It's a small matter, I know, but I was completely entranced by that lavatory and have ruined many people's dinner by telling them all about it ever since.

Kyle and Marion's house was in an idyllic spot; their veranda looked down onto the poplar trees that lined the banks of their own personal creek. Around the house were fruit trees, and in the greenhouse were lettuces, cucumbers, and tomatoes. At mealtimes, Kyle would go out and wander among the trees and bushes and return some minutes later with his arms full of ingredients.

I stayed a couple of nights with Kyle and Marion, just chilling out in that remote, paradisiacal place. Summer had, thank goodness, returned to South Island. I took Marion on the back of my bike as my first-ever pillion passenger: She needed to take her car to the garage for service, and it would have been a long walk back. It was a nervous experience for both of us, and for Kyle, who was left pacing anxiously at home, but we

lived. I went fishing in the river with Kyle. We caught nothing, and both of us squirmed when we had to pierce the wildly
wriggling worms with the hooks.

I left Kyle and Marion's in bright sunshine. At last, the
weather was warm once more, and I was left wondering quite
why I was hauling around a fleecy hat and merino-wool thermals in my luggage. I was heading today to Dunedin but was
taking the scenic route, traveling first north to St. Bathans,
then across through Ranfurly before riding south over the
Rock and Pillar range to the city.

I rode through the peach and apricot orchards, whose trees
were heavy with fruit ripening in the sun. By the roadside,
stalls were set up with vast wooden barrels full of cherries and
peaches. Then the road wound up through golden hills while
the remarkable turquoise line of the Clutha River twisted ever
further below. The clear skies brought alive the yellow grasses,
the browns and grays of the rock, and the vibrant blue of the
river. As I continued northward toward St. Bathans, rocky
hills gradually rose on the horizon. Beneath them stretched
expanses of yellow and green plain on which sheep grazed.
From time to time, I would meet a mass of them being mus-
tered along the endless strip of narrow blacktop that carved
the plain in two. For hours, it seemed as though I were riding
through the middle of a Graeme Sydney painting—which is
not surprising, really, as St. Bathans is where Sydney lives, and
these are the landscapes that many of his paintings depict.

I stopped at St. Bathans and ate a sandwich in the Vulcan
Hotel. The hotel is an old, single-story, bleakly rectangular
building, but its sandy mud-brick exterior and block-gray
painted lettering are full of faded character. Back in the days
of the Otago gold rush, there were around a dozen pubs here
to provide grog and girls to the diggers; the Vulcan is the sole

survivor. Given that only five people now live in St. Bathans, the bartender was not exactly rushed off her feet. As I sat and ate my sandwich, two more tourists came in and drank lemonade, then left again. The hotel has guest rooms for anyone who wants to spend the night here—though some, perhaps, might be put off by the ghost.

There are various stories about the ghost at the Vulcan. Some say that it's the spirit of a miner who was murdered here. Others say that it's a former dancing girl coming back to creak her way across the floor. Whoever it is, the ghost seems to like its spirits—consecutive landlords tell tales of gin bottles exploding at the bar.

Across the road from the pub, I walked down a short, grassy path to the Blue Lake—yet another stretch of seemingly supernaturally blue water towered over by jagged, almost lunar, white cliffs. The cliffs were cut away by decades of sluicing and water-channeling during gold-mining days. The gold here lay under about two hundred feet of soil. The most efficient way to disperse this top layer was to blast it away with jets of water that were channeled down from the hills. Building the races through which the water ran was a huge undertaking, though. In this dry land the channels needed to run for hundreds of miles in order to collect enough water to be effective. By the time the water reached the rock containing the gold, its jet was so strong that, if a miner carelessly stood in front of the nozzle, the force of the water could slice him in two.

I left St. Bathans and rode through the flat, grassy plains to Ranfurly. And then, in the middle of nowhere, on the fence running along the long, straight highway, somebody had tied dozens of pairs of old shoes. They were all styles and sizes, from old sneakers to black patent-leather high heels. There was even a giant pair of fluffy-bunny slippers. Apparently, people come along to this fence with their old shoes and trade them in for a different pair. In New Zealand, they call it ingenuity. Elsewhere, they'd call it ridiculous.

I turned off Highway 85 at Kyeburn and rode down through the Rock and Pillar hills. The low evening sun cast long shadows of craggy, dark-gray schist rock across the yellow scrub. The occasional harrier hawk glided effortlessly between the hills, through the deep-blue sky. The road was deserted. For a while it wound through the hills, then straightened out. I pulled the throttle in a little more, then nudged it further again.

"C'mon, you chicken," a hawk seemed to squawk as it skimmed and soared overhead.

I rode faster, the adrenaline starting to surge now as the wind rushed against me. I glanced down at the speedometer ... it still only read eighty-seven miles an hour.

"C'mon, you coward," I cackled to myself and, grinning like a madwoman, turned the throttle some more.

"Go, girl!" the bike seemed to roar.

I pulled the throttle a little more toward me, edging the speed a fraction higher. And then, when the speedometer nudged onto ninety miles an hour, I decided that was enough. The bike, of course, would have liked to go much, much faster, but I was a driveling defeatist and I was already far enough over the speed limit to invite serious disapproval should a policeman happen to pop out from under a rock.

Past Middlemarch, the landscape changed and became greener; the hills became rounder grassy hillocks. Then the road dipped down out of the hills and the flat agricultural plain below became divided into bright-green rectangles of crops. Poplar trees swayed in the breeze. The scenery became flatter—drab suburbs, down-at-heel hotels, gas stations. From these outskirts, the road picked up cars, vans, trucks. Its lanes divided as the volume of traffic increased and swept me up in its flow toward the city.

Dunedin was a strange shade of orange the following morning. The sky was dark yet lurid, almost as though the sun was setting at ten a.m. This time I was certain I could tell what was going to happen next. Within the next two hours, for sure, there was going to be a terrific storm.

I was wrong again. By lunchtime, there were blue skies and scattered clouds.

I was beginning to understand why nobody seemed to take the remotest interest in the weather forecast around here. It was because it was impossible to predict, even a couple of hours in advance. For weeks, I'd been avidly reading the weather reports and asking people for their meteorological predictions, and taken their failure to be interested in the forecast as cool, laid-back Kiwi nonchalance.

In Britain, if you ask a random passerby what the weather's likely to do this afternoon, their entire face breaks out into beams of joy. They immediately strike their "weather-prediction pose," usually with the head slightly askew facing up toward the sky, eyes half squinting to indicate deep thought, lips pursed, ready for the Great Pronouncement. Then they nod their heads with sagacity. "Looks like rain," they say. Throughout this charade, the British Weather Wannabe has made a good show of reading the subtle nuances of breeze and cloud. In reality, of course, he has no earthly idea about the clouds, beyond the fact that they're kind of gray and solid-looking, and is just repeating what that blond woman said on daytime TV half an hour earlier.

In New Zealand, it's different. Nobody seems to know or care what the weather is going to do. Up until today I had assumed this was because they had more pressing things to do than listen to weather reports. I had thought that they were all too busy fishing for trout, shooting goats, and being nice to each other to have time for such petty concerns. Only now did I realize that nobody gives a hoot what the weathermen say because they know that they don't have a hope of getting it right. In the course of a day, the weather could go from bright sunshine to driving rain and winds to snow. The weather here is so changeable, so unpredictable from hour to hour, that the newspapers might as well not bother printing the forecast at all. They would probably be far better advised to give the space to a nice, lucrative ad instead.

Dunedin was originally settled by Scottish emigrants in the mid-nineteenth century. It's meant to look like Edinburgh. In fact, Dunedin is the Celtic word for Edinburgh. There is a Princes Street and a George Street, a Castle Street and a Frederick Street. There's a Moray Place. The only problem is that none of these streets, so faithfully named, is in anything like the same place, relatively, as its position in Edinburgh, so Scots visiting Dunedin, or indeed Dunedin folk visiting Scotland, tend to get in a bit of a muddle.

Apparently there was some confusion among the town planners themselves. Dunedin was intended to be a kind of prefabricated church settlement: The first 344 inhabitants arrived on two ships within three weeks of each other. The city had been designed and mapped out back in Edinburgh. Unfortunately, the town planners had not taken into account the fact that Dunedin has hills. When the roads were built, some of them turned out to be ludicrously steep.

As a result of all this planning, though, Dunedin has a collection of Victorian and Edwardian buildings that you don't see in other New Zealand cities. During semesters, the city is swamped by its student population; it was now summer vacation, but the city's youth culture still defined it. The students may not have been here in person, but their heritage shouted loud in the endless bars and cafés, clothes shops selling funky-going-on-grungy gear, and the most fantastic range of cheap Asian restaurants I've seen anywhere, including in Asia. This alone would be enough to sell a city to me. Squeezed in along one street were sushi bars, Korean restaurants, little joints with Formica tables selling dim sum and noodles. There was a great vegetarian Indian, and a Cambodian place from which emanated gastronomically exciting smells. Best of all, none of the meals cost more than ten New Zealand dollars—around six U.S. dollars. I ate and ate. And then, fortified by a steaming bowl of udon noodles with vegetables, I climbed back on my bike and rode out along the Otago Peninsula to Larnach Castle.

Larnach is New Zealand's only castle. What is impressive is not the castle itself but the fact that, on this spot high up on a hill, seven miles from Dunedin, somebody actually chose to build such a thing. Admittedly, it has astonishing views over the Otago Peninsula and the ocean beyond. But most people on seeing a pretty view might take a photograph, or stop for a picnic at most. Not so William Larnach. He had to build a castle. Oh dear, William! New Zealand may be a long, long way from the Old World, but did nobody think to tell him that building castles went out of fashion several hundred years ago?

Larnach Castle is a fine example of Kiwi ingenuity going on Kiwi lunacy. The urge to build a castle may also have something to do with that other Kiwi fixation, the need to do everything big. Except that Larnach Castle is not big. In fact, it is rather small. It's really no more than a six-bedroom house with a ballroom attached. It does, however, have very good turrets.

It also has lions and eagles sculpted in stone by four carvers brought especially to New Zealand for the purpose. Larnach appointed Italian craftsmen to make the ceilings. Also from Italy came red, white, and black marble, as well as two marble baths (one of which has since been removed from the castle and is now used as a cattle trough on a nearby farm). Twenty tons of plate glass were used in the double-glazed windows; the doors and paneling were made from cedar, mahogany, oak, and ebony. Even in the stables, the floor was covered in Marseilles cobbles, and the ironwork between the stalls was ornamented with acorn finials cast by a Glasgow foundry.

The materials were brought by ship to Port Chalmers, on the opposite side of Otago Harbour. They then had to be punted across the water and transported in ox-drawn sleds up the steep road that led to the castle.

Larnach designed a crest for his new abode—a very grumpy-looking cat with the motto "Sans peur." Linguistic puns aside, this pretty much summed Larnach up. Like an exaggerated stereotype of the good Kiwi pioneer, Larnach was fearless, going on mad. He could not have contemplated such an undertaking otherwise. He was also frequently bad-tempered, especially in his later years, following a life tinged with sadness. His first wife, Eliza, died at age thirty-eight; Larnach then married her half-sister, Mary Alleyne, who died herself a few years later. Being married to Larnach was apparently not good for one's health. Furthermore, his second marriage clearly irritated wife number one: Her spirit is said still to haunt the castle. Since it has been open to the public, several visitors have asserted that someone or something has touched them on the back of the neck as they walked past the doorway to her bedroom.

Larnach married again, for the third time, but his flamboyant life became too much for him. There were family scandals to keep under wraps—his father hanged a man in his yard in Australia, and it became known that his grand family history was a creation of his overactive imagination. His children were failing to bow to his bombastic decrees. His business dealings were in trouble. His position as a Member of Parliament had lost its appeal. And so, in 1898, William Larnach locked himself in a committee room in one of Wellington's parliament buildings and shot himself. His will was unsigned; his family was torn apart by the subsequent fighting and sold the castle.

In the following years, the castle was used as a vacation retreat for nuns, then a mental hospital for shell-shocked soldiers. When the current incumbents, the Barker family, bought the place in 1967 it was dilapidated; the ballroom had been used to pen sheep. Told by all around them that they must be mad—as indeed, perhaps, they were—they renovated it to its present state. They reckon that Larnach himself still hangs around the place. When a play about his colorful life and financial ruin was staged in the castle ballroom a few years back, a terrible storm blew up from nowhere. The smoke from the fires blew back down the chimneys. Doors slammed and the room in which the play was being performed became cold. And then, at the point in the story when Larnach shot himself, a bolt of lightning sent a blinding white flash across the stage.

There were clear blue skies as I continued my ride back down the hill and along the Otago Peninsula Road. This narrow highway winds right on the water's edge with scarcely a grass shoulder between the road and the sea. An ambulance screeched past. Where exactly was I supposed to pull over? The slightest deviation would have taken me into the water.

A short while later, I arrived at Taiaroa Head, where a colony of royal albatrosses lives. These birds are huge. Their heads and bodies are pure white; their black wings span nine feet across, allowing them to swoop and fly at speeds of up to seventy miles per hour. As we stood in the viewing room, couples outside shared the incubation of their egg and preened each other lovingly with their long, curving orange beaks, which seem to grin when they're opened. (Albatrosses mate for life, though divorce and a return to the singles scene are not unheard of.) Meanwhile, the young male albatrosses soared and glided, flying around our heads just for the sheer fun of it, showing off their athletic prowess. Sometimes they don't look so good, though. As soon as the chicks first fly, eight months after hatching, they go straight out to sea and stay there for three years. They don't come back to land for the whole of that time: Their only resting place is on water. When they return to the colony as adolescents with a bunch of pickup lines tucked under their wing, they've never landed on solid ground before—and their first attempts can be pretty clumsy. Crash landings and multiple forward rolls are commonplace.

It was at the Royal Albatross Centre that I met Amanda. I was sitting watching the albatross video, waiting for my turn to visit the viewing room.

"Are you riding a motorcycle?" she asked, spotting my leathers. I turned around. There was a woman sitting a couple of rows behind me, wearing a leather jacket and jeans. "Are you the one that's writing a book?"

Amanda, it turned out, had stayed at Holly Homestead in Franz Josef shortly after I'd been there, and Bernie had told her all about me. She, too, was riding a motorcycle solo around New Zealand. Even more coincidentally, she lived just a couple of miles away from me in London. I reckoned she must be a pretty hardened biker. I confessed to only having passed my test in September.

"I passed mine in October." She grinned. "I'm the slowest motorcyclist in the whole of New Zealand."

"No, you can't possibly be. Because I am."

But she had one-upmanship on this one. One evening, early in her odyssey, she had met a woman who had been following her in the car that day.

"I didn't know that motorcycles *could* go that slow," the woman had laughed at her.

We agreed that the woman should rot in four-wheeled hell and that her skin should shrivel into a thousand wrinkles from the adverse effects of in-car air-conditioning. We discussed the vital issue of how to keep your hair looking remotely presentable after a day squashed under a helmet. We talked about our terrors of the first days, the rain, the wind, the best routes we'd ridden.

"So have you adjusted your chain yet?" Amanda asked.

"And what exactly is your top speed so far?" I countered.

So I was not alone. I was not the craziest person in the universe, the only one foolish enough to take off to the other side of the globe on a motorcycling tour having only just passed my test. No, I was not the maddest one around. There were two of us.

The next morning, I rode out of Dunedin. I was on my way to Lake Tekapo, a township built on the shores of an extraordinary turquoise-blue lake beneath the eastern flank of the

Southern Alps. Tomorrow I was going to climb into the mountains, but today I had a little detour to enjoy first. For around an hour, I rode up the coast, then stopped at Moeraki to look at the boulders.

A lot of people seem to miss these giant stones that just sit here on the beach. Nobody talks about them much. There's no neon-flashing signpost, no glitzy tourist hotels or buses spewing visitors. There's just a café overlooking the beach and a handful of people strolling along the sand. I'd only come here because, all those weeks ago in Nelson, I'd made a note that Ian had recommended a pit stop here. It's a shame more people don't break their journeys here for half an hour or so, because the Moeraki boulders are sensational in a very still, stony, gray kind of way. They are huge. Some were as tall as I was. And more astonishing still, they have been slowly forming here on this very spot for *sixty million years*.

Geologically speaking, they have apparently formed because their stony substance—carbonate of lime, silica, alumina, and peroxide of iron—has been attracted to and consolidated by a central core of lime crystals. To be honest, the scientific facts didn't mean a lot to me. But I was nothing short of blown over by the idea that these stones that I was walking among and freely touching came into being at about the same time as the first primates—the Kiwi bloke's very, very distant ancestors, the precursors to monkeys even, began to evolve after the death of the dinosaurs. And, here in New Zealand, just above Dunedin, they're just sitting there on the beach, some scattered, some lined up, as though a bunch of giants has been enjoying a leisurely game of bowling.

The Only Way Is Up

CLOSE MY EYES, AND I could have been transported to a war zone—which would have been disappointing in the extreme. The sporadic bursts of staccato rattling and crackling sounded to my inexperienced ears just like the machine-gun fire that blasts out of my television set every now and then.

"What's the noise?" I asked Roy, my guide, suspiciously. I looked around for homicidal bandits peering out from behind boulders.

"Ah, that's just rockfall," he said, and smiled.

We'd been climbing for a few hours now. I'd met Roy at eight o'clock that morning in a garage behind the office of Alpine Recreation in Lake Tekapo township. The two other members of our group, Sam and Paulette, were already there. Sam and Paulette were in their early twenties. They were Canadian but had been living for the last year in Korea, where they were teaching English. We'd introduced ourselves and sorted out our gear. We'd been given snow gaiters, crampons, and ice axes, and we'd set off in the van for the mountains. We were going to spend the next three days climbing on the Mount Cook range, over Ball Pass.

Roy was in his late forties, with longish, graying hair and the kind of lean physique that you would expect of a man who has been to the summit of Mount Cook seventeen times. He had guided walkers over this Ball Pass route so many times that he knew every plant.

"Don't pull on that daisy!" he called out in horror as I scrambled up one steep rocky section, grabbing the well-rooted alpine plant for support. "I like that daisy. It's been growing there for years."

His clothing covered just about every part of his body: He spent so much time high in the mountains, where the snow reflects New Zealand's highly damaging sun rays, that he needed to wear a cap with a skirt that came down beneath his collar and a remarkable-looking nose shield in addition to his long-sleeved white shirt and bright-blue fleece trousers. When Roy wasn't guiding—sometimes here, sometimes taking groups up Mount Tasman from the West Coast or, in the spring, ski guiding in Europe—he lived in Christchurch. He was a relaxed, easygoing person—you need to be if you spend your life guiding tourists up mountains—with a quiet, dry sense of humor.

We climbed higher, pulling ourselves up steep slopes covered in scrub and clambering over boulders. Beneath us, the wide, still river of dark-gray glacial moraine grew ever more distant. There's no trail up here; it's a route rather than a path and so, unless you are an experienced mountaineer, you need to take a guide. I was climbing more quickly than Sam and Paulette. Every now and then Roy would stop to help them over more difficult parts.

"You go ahead," he said to me. "Just follow the path."

I glanced around, then looked back at Roy. All I could see was an endless haphazard arrangement of boulders and rocks. There was no path.

"Or, alternatively, you could just wait there and I'll lead the way," said Roy.

As we climbed higher, the rattling of rockfall was replaced by the thundering booming of avalanches. I had expected it to be quiet up here, all alone in the mountains. Instead, it was a veritable cacophony of hurtling rock and collapsing crusts of snow. We stopped for a rest on a small plateau. White powder tumbled in the distance, like a light drizzle of talcum powder running down a tiny waterfall.

"So how much snow do you reckon is falling in that one?" I asked Roy.

He shrugged. "Aw, about a thousand tons."

A thousand tons sounded rather a lot. It was extraordinary that such a tiny trickle of powder over there on the opposite face could constitute quite so much snow—and make such an incredible, deafening din as it fell. If a thousand tons of snow fell on your head, I didn't suppose the outcome would be all that rosy. Shouldn't we have some kind of contingency plan? Or would we just be dead so fast that it wouldn't be worth it?

I racked my brains for the very tiny collection of survival techniques that I've garnered over the years and—ah yes— now I remembered. If you get dumped on by an avalanche, you are supposed to pee. Apparently, when you're lying there buried in snow, you can't tell which way is up, so you have to pee in your pants. Whichever way the pee dribbles is down, toward the center of the earth, so to get out you dig in the opposite direction.

It struck me now, though, that this survival technique is

supremely flawed for two good reasons. One: In the process of being buried by an avalanche, you would probably be so frightened you'd pee anyway, and then when it came to finding out which way up you were dangling you wouldn't have anything left. And second, even if you managed to exercise supreme bladder control while the snow pummeled down on your head, doesn't this theory overlook the fact that when you're wearing clothes, your urine would just ooze into the fabric and not flow anywhere at all? Wouldn't it get stuck in your underwear? Instead of finding out which way up you were buried, surely you'd just end up a nasty, soggy mess.

I dwelled on these difficult issues and considered that this quiet stroll in the hills was turning out to be more of an adventure than I had bargained for. After all, how did Roy know that a thousand tons of snow wasn't going to fall on *us*? I could tell from the narrowed eyes and suspicious expressions on Sam's and Paulette's faces that they were suffering similar doubts. There was a weighty silence. Then another BOOM, BOOM, DUM-DUM-DUM-DUM-DUM. I noticed that Paulette was biting her lower lip. Sam looked bemused and blinked.

"Er, so, um," he said finally. "How do you know that an avalanche isn't going to fall on us?"

"Nah. We're on the wrong bit of the mountain," said Roy. And that was the end of that.

After six hours of climbing, we arrived at the Caroline Hut, where we were to spend the next two nights. It's a private hut owned by Alpine Recreation. The great advantage of staying here was that, once a season, the company flies a helicopter up here and dumps several months' supplies of nonperishable food. This means that when you arrive here after a hard day's walking, you can have a glass of wine and a bar of chocolate.

Actually you could have several: There were entire boxes full of Cadbury's chocolate bars. Under the bed in the guide's room was a vineyard's worth of wine boxes. It also means that the only food you need to carry up here is fresh produce.

The hut itself was rudimentary but comfortable. Constructed from sheets of pale-green corrugated metal, there was a main room with eight bunks, a table with benches, and a cooking area. There was a second, smaller room with two bunks for guides. In the floor by the doorway, a hatch led down to a storeroom, where the limitless chocolate was kept alongside more prosaic supplies such as pasta and rice. Outside the door was a water tank and, a safe distance away, over a rocky path, two cubicles with latrine toilets. To be honest, the smell in there wasn't good. The folk from Alpine Recreation really could have done with a little consultancy from Kyle on how that peaty stuff works, although perhaps it would have been too cold for the worms. But the doors faced away from the main hut, out over the mountains. There was not another soul in these hills, and I found that, if I left the door open, the stench was less severe and, furthermore, the view from the toilet over the snowy mountaintops was spectacular.

I took a bucket of water from the tank and a bar of soap and went up onto the balcony around the back, where nobody could see. It was a unique spot for a wash. At first, stripping off all my clothes in the fresh air made me feel somehow self-conscious. But, really, there was nobody around, and it was wildly liberating to take a shower with an entire mountain range lying at my feet. The snow-covered peaks rose and fell toward the horizon, the silence punctuated only by the occasional booming of a distant avalanche. Two kea flew by and squawked. The bird-watcher within me chirruped in reply.

My wash completed, I went back into the hut, drank a glass of wine, played a game of Scrabble with the others, and listened to Sam and Paulette's tales of life in Korea. They didn't seem to think much of it and were greatly looking forward to leaving and returning to Canada when their year's contract was up. But they had had some interesting culinary experiences.

"There's this fish that looks like a penis," said Sam.

I expressed considerable interest in learning more. How big was this penis fish? What color was it?

"It looks just like a penis. It's the same size and color and everything," Paulette concurred.

Sam and Paulette both claimed to have been very surprised the first time they were presented with a plate of these delicacies in a restaurant, and their Korean hosts had found their astonishment a source of some amusement. I had never heard of this kind of fish before and had to consider that they might lift snorkeling to a whole new level, should one happen to pass a whole shoal of them wiggling by.

"What's the fish called?" I asked.

"I dunno," said Sam. "We just call it the penis fish."

And with that, we all tucked eagerly into the pasta, meat sauce, and vegetables that Roy had concocted for our dinner.

On the second day, we walked a little higher into the mountains, up into the snow, and learned self-arrest techniques with and without the ice ax. The idea is that, when you are climbing in snow and ice, you need to be able to stop yourself from plummeting down a steep slope should you happen to slip. So we spent a happy couple of hours sliding down a snowy slope on our bottoms, gathering speed, then flipping over and standing up, or digging the ice ax hard into the ground where, hopefully, it should act as a brake.

It was in these mountains that one of the most famous of all Kiwi blokes, Sir Edmund Hillary, first cut his teeth, or more accurately his steps, in snow. Hillary grew up just south of Auckland but used to make frequent trips to these very slopes, where he became hooked by the mountains. The solitude must have suited him as much as the actual climbing for, while taciturnity and understatement are accepted traits of Kiwi blokes, Hillary seems to have embraced these qualities even more than most. On learning that he had been knighted, his initial reaction was one of horror.

"My mind flashed to a picture of myself walking around the little town of Papakura, south of Auckland, in a pair of well-stained overalls. My God, I told myself, I'll have to buy a new pair of overalls," he writes in his autobiography, *View From the Summit*.

His skills with women were clearly a little limited: He was so shy about proposing to his first wife, Louise, that his mother-in-law-to-be had to telephone and ask her on his behalf. He also appears to have been a master of good Kiwi stoicism. During the Second World War, he was involved in an accident that left him with second-degree burns over forty percent of his body. In his autobiography he describes the first week in the hospital as "rather miserable"; as for the 140 penicillin injections he was given, "at night they were trying."

Personally, I would have screamed and cried and begged for a morphine drip. I'm a keen fan of anesthesia when the going gets tough, or even when it gets a tiny bit uncomfortable. Let's face it, after my shearing experience, just two sore legs and a couple of blisters had left me laid up on the bed with half the contents of the minibar. A short walk yesterday and I'd downed a good part of the wine box and had every intention of putting in a similar performance tonight after my hard day's wielding of my ice ax. I don't think they have wine boxes on the top of Everest, though, or indeed on any other high mountains, which goes some way to explain why the highest I ever got was to that rewarding point on the Mount Cook range where you know you can easily get back to the Caroline Hut in time for the cocktail hour.

Day three was supposed to be our big walking day. The route out of the mountains, over Ball Pass, should have taken us eight or nine hours. But Roy was worried that our group's progress was too slow. He reckoned it would take us a good twelve hours, by which time we might be grumpy. We might even find ourselves indulging in psychopathic daydreams involving violent acts with the spiky soles of our crampons. So, being a resourceful person, he suggested an alternative: He could take me rock climbing in the morning while the others slept in, and then we could take the three-hour shortcut back down to the van. It seemed like a good option.

I'd never been rock climbing before.

"Were the views good?" Paulette asked when we got back to the hut. They had probably been quite awesome, but I had to confess that, from my position perched on narrow rock ledges, I had been too frightened to look. The only place I had looked during the whole morning's outing was upward, in the direction I had to climb. To look down had seemed like a very foolish idea.

But I loved the rock climbing. In fact, it was the best part of the whole three days. Roy, with his years of experience taking total novices up these pitches, was delightfully calm and humorous.

"Have I gone the wrong way?" I asked as I tried to clamber up a narrow alley between two rock faces. My bottom was wedged against one wall, my feet and knees were splayed inelegantly against the other. I was stuck.

"Well," said Roy, grinning down from above, "there may have been a better way, but rock climbing is a very personal sport."

I nearly lost my nerve altogether when Roy leapt over a chasm between two rocks and landed neatly on the small platform on the other side. The gap was not impossibly wide, but it was certainly a leap, not a step. The drop between the two rocks was seemingly bottomless. I was attached to a rope, I told myself, as Roy climbed a little higher to a safe spot. I was also wearing a helmet. If I fell down the chasm, I wouldn't actually die. But I would almost certainly get bashed about a bit and my confidence would tumble. It was my turn to go. I took one or two very cowardly baby steps toward the edge. I stopped. One part of me wanted to peer over the edge, to see the full extent of the risk before I jumped. The other part of me knew that would be a very bad idea indeed.

"Just walk to the edge and leap!" a voice commanded from high up.

Oh, to hell with it. There was no other way out of here. I did as I was told.

"Has anyone ever fallen down that chasm?" I asked Roy later, over lunch.

"Not yet," he said, unruffled as ever. "But the day will come."

On the final pitch I got stuck one last time, balanced precariously with one foot on a tiny foothold, the other jammed into a crack in the rock, both hands clinging for dear life onto next to nothing. Beneath me, the rock dropped away; to my inexpert eyes it looked sheer. After a minute or so of terrified inaction, I looked up.

"I'm not feeling happy here," I told Roy in as calm a manner as I could muster. He grinned.

"Just persevere," he said, entirely relaxed.

There wasn't a whole lot of choice. After all, there was just me, and Roy, and a bit of rope, and a sheer drop. Down didn't seem like a very good way out of here, which really only left the options of staying on this ledge forever or gathering up my courage and climbing upward.

All right, I admit it, I briefly considered whether I could stay on the ledge forever. After all, if that family up in the kauri forest had survived for fourteen years living in a tree, what was to stop me residing for a while on a rock face? With a bit of work I might be able to fashion a little platform on which to sleep, and it would be only reasonable for walkers from the Caroline Hut to drop vital supplies by every few days. In the end, though, I had to abandon that plan because, I remembered, I was attached by a rope to Roy, and it didn't seem fair to his wife to make him stay there too. So I gathered every ounce of courage, wrenched my now-sore foot out of the lifesaving crack in the rock, and tiptoed bravely along the ledge to a point from which it was easier to climb. And then, probably in much the same manner as Hillary and Tenzing scaled that final face leading up to the summit of Everest, I hauled myself heroically to the top.

A Sad, Sad Day

"D'YOU SHOOT?" ASKED RICHARD.

"Good heavens no," I replied.

"Excellent!" said Richard. His blue eyes lit up; a wide beam stretched across his face. "Come with me," he said, grabbing two rifles that were standing by a cabinet. And with that, he set off through the door.

Inwardly, I groaned. I'd been tramping around the New Zealand countryside for a few months now. From the start, I'd been nervous that somebody was going to try to make me shoot things. Rural New Zealanders are known to like taking a shot at their dinner or, indeed, anything else that moves. I was particularly worried about the bunny rabbits because, although I know they were introduced to the country for the sole purpose of having their brains blown out by hunters and, since then, have bred to a quite indecent degree, I like rabbits. I like their pert little sticking-up ears and their fluffy little tails; I like the way their furry bottoms bob up and down when they run. However vexing a pest they may be, I really didn't think I could bring myself to cold-bloodedly murder a bunny. The mere sight of the poor little one that had drowned in the swimming pool at Christmas had been quite traumatic enough, without adding personal responsibility into the equation. So I muttered a little prayer for the rabbit population of Canterbury and then followed Richard out through the door.

In many ways, Richard was not a typical Canterbury farmer. I had stopped by his farm in Staveley on my way to Christchurch: He was a distant relative of some friends of my family. Several rooms of his house were filled with pile upon pile of books and magazines; he was fascinated by the concept of neurolinguistic programming. In other respects, though, he was Kiwi bloke through and through. His yard was littered chaotically with old machinery; in one pile were heaped countless metal contraptions. These turned out to be a device for tightening fencing wire that Richard had invented. Apparently they were selling very well. And, of course, he liked to shoot.

I asked him how many guns he had.

"Can't remember," he replied as we marched up the hill.

He couldn't remember? How many guns would a person have to own before they lost count? Five? Ten? A hundred? Was that a slightly manic hue I detected in Richard's piercing blue eyes? He was, effectively, a total stranger. Was it a good idea to disappear up a deserted hill in the middle of nowhere with an unknown man carrying guns? To make matters worse, Richard had started wheezing heavily and commented on his heart condition.

We climbed over a locked gate, then up some more. Richard seemed to be really panting now. I was beginning to worry that he might expire altogether before we reached the top of the hill. If he really took a turn for the worse, I didn't think I'd be able to carry him back down. I could roll him, perhaps. Or just run for help, but that would involve leaving him there alone gulping, gasping, and clasping at his chest. It wouldn't be good either way. Finally, just as Richard seemed to be about to breathe his last, we stopped.

"Now," said Richard, recovering his breath as he loaded a rifle. "You can tell there's nobody around, because the stock hasn't been moved from that paddock over there."

He waved his right arm toward a distant hillock where, little more than specks against the green grass, some cattle grazed. His reasoning didn't seem all that convincing. In front of us there was a stretch of open field; beyond it were trees. The fact that a couple of cows were munching grass in a field some distance away didn't really seem sufficient evidence that nobody was lurking in the copse where my stray bullets would inevitably be drawn. It wasn't Richard's fault, of course. I hadn't exactly given him all the information he needed. I had omitted to tell him that the only time before today that I had ever touched a gun, I broke it. I hadn't pointed out to him that I am grotesquely inept with anything mechanical and that I have very poor coordination. I hadn't told him that people who know me well generally avoid pressing lethal weapons into my hands.

But Richard didn't know any of this, and so he was far-too-cheerfully stuffing large, deadly bullets into the chamber. I had visions of myself in the defendant's box in court, dressed in threadbare prison overalls stained with the bodily fluids of incontinent mass murderers who had gone before, my wrists chafing under the cold, cutting metal of the handcuffs, my legs impotent in those shackles they reserve for the most dangerous of psychopaths.

"I'm really very sorry that I killed Mr. Copse-Lurker," I

would say earnestly, "but I thought it would be all right because the stock hadn't been moved from that paddock."

The judge would sardonically raise one bushy eyebrow and purse his hardened lips. The jury would gasp at such evil disregard for human life. Mrs. Copse-Lurker, dressed all in black, would let out a little yelp, weep, and wring her hands. A little row of junior Copse-Lurkers, of which there would be at least six under the age of ten, would sit beside her, lips trembling and tummies rumbling since some idiot had stupidly murdered the breadwinner of the family.

I had just gotten to the stage in my fantastical nightmare when, having been sent by the bushy-browed judge to rot in jail, I was sadistically assaulted when Richard finished loading the gun and saved me from the perils of my imagination.

"This is a rook rifle," he said. It looked kind of old. Parts of it were made out of wood. "It's an antique," he said. "Made in 1870."

Oh, bloody hell. He probably cared about this gun. Honestly, giving it to me wasn't a good idea. It was not beyond the bounds of possibility that, even if there really was nobody else around, and even if I didn't break the thing, I might accidentally shoot him, or myself, or even, in a particularly well-coordinated display of staggering ineptitude, simultaneously finish off the pair of us.

"Now, you see that rock there," said Richard, pointing to an encouragingly large lump of limestone in the middle of the field. "I want you to shoot that rock."

Thank goodness, I didn't have to annihilate Flopsy or Mopsy. I didn't have to try to kill anything more than an old rock, which, very sportingly, was standing still. Richard lined me up, put my feet in the right spot, made sure I was leaning right, and told me to pull the trigger. There was a loud bang, and the rock died a horrible, violent death. The huntress within me stirred.

"So, did you enjoy yourself?" Richard asked as we tramped back down the hill.

"Er, yes, thank you," I replied, a little embarrassed. The problem was, I actually *had* very much enjoyed myself, and I was beginning to detect in myself a tendency of which I didn't entirely approve. Several weeks ago, I had enjoyed catching fish too. I didn't really see myself as the hunting, killing, butchering type. Why couldn't these practical New Zealand folk have ignited in me a passion for flower-arranging, or baking cakes, or some other activity that was wholesome and sweet? They could just as easily have taught me to grow big carrots, I would have thought. Even learning to change the oil in a car engine might have been of some use. So how was it, with all these wondrous activities the New Zealanders could have shown me, the ones that I instantly took to involved killing fish and shooting a rock? Really, I worry about myself a lot. Kiwi blokes may have been turning domesticated, but I, on the contrary, seemed to be bucking the trend by becoming worryingly butch.

It wasn't to last. My adventures were, very sadly, due to end. From Richard's farm I had to ride into Christchurch, and there I had an appointment to keep. I was meeting Ian and his wife, Robin, who were taking my bike away. It was a terrible wrench, an emotional parting, but it was time for the bike to go back to its real family.

Last night I had given the bike a bit of a wash. I didn't want it looking anything less than its best for the big day.

"So that wasn't such a terrible trip in the end, was it?" I had asked it as I lovingly wiped the splayed flies' innards from its headlight. "I mean, I know to start with there were a couple of, well, small hiccups, but didn't you enjoy yourself just a *tiny* bit in the end? I know you were cross not to ride out to Milford but, um, deep down, I think you liked that lakeside spin into Wanaka—didn't you? And didn't you feel just the tiniest flutter in your engine when we came 'round that magnificent bend in the road on the way to Glenorchy?"

The bike had given a little affirmative squeak. At least, it could just have been the way my cloth rubbed on its bodywork, but I had taken it to be a low-key expression of approval. The Suzuki, after all, had never been one to let rip with gushing, clamorous compliments. As I had already seen, disgruntled growls and rabid roars were more its style. That tiny squeak had warmed my heart.

I rode along the highway. It became increasingly busy and dull as the road led inexorably toward the city. Arriving in Christchurch, I rode through the park, over the River Avon, and toward my hotel.

Ian and Robin had already arrived and were eager to move on, to drive up to Hanmer Springs, where their tour group was stopping that night. My gleaming Suzuki was duly loaded and strapped. And then Ian, Robin, and the bike turned out of the driveway and disappeared from sight.

I stood in the driveway and sighed. I stared at the space the bike had occupied just minutes earlier; now I'd never see it again. It seemed incredible, really. There had been times over the last few months when I would have given the wretched machine back without a second thought. Actually, there had been times—that heinously wobbly first day, that gut-wrenchingly gusty ride into Te Anau—when I would have enthusiastically paid good money to anyone who was generous enough to take the bike off my hands. But now that I really did have to give it back, I'd forgotten about those hairy events. All I could remember were the good days: the long, solitary blast up to Karamea with the waves crashing on white sand and driftwood to my left and the dense, lush bush rising into the mists on my right; the ride over the hills between Queenstown and Glenorchy and the astonishing view of the deep-blue lake and the snowcapped mountains as I came around that particular bend; my ride through the Rock and Pillar range down to Dunedin, where the harrier hawks skirted and dived over the golden grasses. During the last few weeks, I'd grown attached to that bike. I'd rather forgotten that it wasn't actually mine.

It had been a long road of terror and jubilation, sunshine and rain—oh yes, and let's not forget that hail—but now I was even, heaven help me, thinking it might be rather nice to buy a motorcycle all of my own back home. The rush of wind, the sensation of leaning around the bend and eventually the speed, the power, the acceleration, the ability to overtake more or less anything, anywhere, with just a nudge of the throttle, put driving a car to shame.

In a couple of days I'd go back to England. I'd be reunited with my car. How dull that would be in comparison. When I drove the car, all I thought about was arriving, finishing my journey, or at best what the DJ on the radio was driveling about. Riding a bike was so much more fun, so much more vital, so much more involving. The bike was an adventure, the journey was an activity in itself. And now, so soon, my trip was over.

All alone, I trundled into Christchurch. I carried out a few mundane administrative tasks. I went to the Air New Zealand office to change my return flight and avoid a ten-hour stopover in LA. The groovy motorcycle leathers were of no use to me anymore and had to be mailed back to London in a large box, given that my luggage had grown so horribly that there was no chance any airline would agree to take it all.

Chores completed, I walked through the park, where men in stripy blazers and boaters punted Japanese tourists down the tiny, shallow dribble that they called the Avon. I wandered through the streets past Christ's College, a private school where teenage boys wear striped blazers, baggy knee-length shorts, and long socks with garters. *Hello?* This was supposed to be 2003, not 1903. Was there some kind of time warp going on here? It was truly bizarre: It was all so "English," but in a way that England hadn't seen for decades. Let's face it, no one in England has dressed like that since the last time they filmed *Brideshead Revisited*.

Now, I know I was in a mean and grumpy mood, but nonetheless Christchurch struck me as a peculiar place. It is, supposedly, a re-creation of an English cathedral town. The Avon runs through the center, punters drift by in their flat-bottomed boats, willow trees duly weep. The cathedral is suitably Gothic. But it didn't feel to me like an English city at all. It was all wrong. It felt like a New Zealand city with an eerie familiarity, because, if it were really to be an English cathedral city, it would have had to be so much older, dirtier, and crumblier. The traffic would have needed to be jammed and congested down tiny streets that were never meant for moving cars, let alone parked ones—but here in Christchurch there was an orderly grid of multilaned streets with traffic lights at each main junction. The river with its willows was flanked in Christchurch by modern bars rather than timbered buildings with leaky walls, uneven floors, and beams you bumped your head on. They were serving artfully presented risotto and chilled white wine where there ought to have been soggy, bread-crumbed scampi, inedible boiled potatoes, and fabulous local beer. Or maybe there oughtn't—this was New Zealand, after all—but if that was the case, why on earth were there men wearing straw boaters punting down the Avon?

I preferred the other cities of New Zealand, which had their own character: Wellington's colorful weatherboard houses chaotically littering the hillside, Auckland's brash, unapologetic Viaduct poseurs, Dunedin's arty, funky youth culture. Christchurch didn't seem, to me, to have any of these things, but rather to be some kind of bizarre theme park: Stratford Towers, Oxfordland, Cambridgeworld. It seemed a lackluster attempt to soothe its founding fathers' homesickness, to re-create a home away from home—but if that's all they wanted to do, one has to wonder: Why didn't they just stay there?

I found a bar by the river and its oh-so-English willow trees, ordered a beer, and jotted down on the beer mat a five-point plan for the reconstruction of Christchurch. I accept that it might seem a little radical to sensitive souls, but it went something like this:

1. Fill in the river. It's an embarrassing little stream, any-way. I thought New Zealanders liked to do things big.
2. Roast the ducks, seeing as their environment has been destroyed in step one.
3. Chop down the willow trees.
4. Stage a ceremonial burning of every punt and boater in the city. (In the spirit of twenty-first-century multi-tasking, the ducks could be roasted on the same bon-fire.)

5. Ban all varieties of ridiculous stripy blazer and pelt offenders with rotten kiwi fruit, barrels of which should be kept handy at all times in Cathedral Square. (Postscript: they can keep the cathedral. Never let it be said that I can't make concessions.)

The strangest thing about Christchurch, however, was not the punts, or the boaters, or the baggy knee-length shorts. It was my hotel.

In keeping with the city's theme, the establishment was rather like an old English guesthouse—perhaps the kind they had in places like Brighton and Blackpool in the 1950s, though I can't be sure because I wasn't around then. But certainly it seemed to date from an era before people did dirty things like have sex on vacation—or at least before they admitted to it—because all the beds seemed to be singles. They featured satiny, floral counterpanes. The long corridors had worn, heavily patterned, deep-red carpets and shiny flocked wallpaper. The communal bathrooms were spartan and eagerly trumpeted "linoleum." There were no telephone jacks in the rooms, just a row of pay phones in the hall. In my room there was a single outlet so that I, child of the techno-age, was unable to use my laptop computer and to recharge my cell phone at the same time.

And the strangest thing about this hotel was that, shortly after seven-thirty in the morning, a PA system kicked into life, loud and clear, and jingle-jangled down the corridors.

Dong-dong-dong-dong-dong, it clamored. I leapt to life beneath my shiny bedspread, nearly falling out of the frighteningly narrow single bed. It was like the school assembly in the *Grease* movie, just before the principal chirps, "Good morning, boys and girls, and welcome to Rydell High"—or whatever it is that she says. But here, instead, a male voice, excessively cheery for the early hour, boomed in.

"Good morning, everybody. It's twenty-five to eight and this is the first call for breakfast, which is now being served in the dining room."

I mean, breakfast wasn't due to finish until a quarter to nine. There were people trying to be on vacation here, for heaven's sake. I hauled myself out of bed and went to eat.

Later that morning, I took a taxi to the airport. My hand luggage went through the X-ray machine; they pulled me to one side.

"Oh no, not another pair of nail scissors!" I groaned, having already donated several pairs to airport stashes around the world.

"No," said the man. "This time it's the wine knife on your corkscrew." (I'd finally invested in one when asking hotel bar staff to uncork my tipples had become too much to bear.)

But Christchurch, being an airport run by New Zealanders who are averse to waste and prone to helpfulness, have found a way around the problem: Just by the X-ray machine is a mail shop replete with Jet-Paks, weighing scales, and those little green customs stickers. You just pop the offending item in a bag and mail it home. Now that is Kiwi ingenuity.

Final Encounter

AN HOUR OR SO later, I was back in Auckland. With a little help from a jet plane, I'd completed the full circle of New Zealand. From here, I was flying home.

There seemed to be an awful lot more people in Auckland than there were last time I was here. Had the place grown exponentially in the last few months—or had my perceptions altered? The traffic! The congestion! The crowds! What happened to the big green garden that I remembered? This place had been transformed into a chaotic urban sprawl. There were so many shops, so many restaurants, such an endless array of sidewalk cafés, it was almost too much to cope with. It took me hours just to walk down Parnell Road, sidetracked as I was into every shop doorway selling paintings, pottery, clothing, rare books. Where was I supposed to start? How could I ever end? How on earth was I going to cope when I got back to London?

But I had one final call to make. I had to go to Gordi's house to pick up all that luggage that I had so heartlessly rejected, abandoned to spend its months in New Zealand in the back of a wardrobe.

Gordi was just making the tea (he has not yet graduated to large plates of three types of cake) when a huge, furry white cat appeared. He was vast and cuddly, the kind of cat you might like to snuggle up with on a cold winter's night. I bent down to stroke him.

"No!" shouted Gordi in horror. "Don't pet Truman!"

From under his bushy white eyebrows, Truman fixed me with an unyielding, don't-mess-with-me stare. His piercing blue eyes hissed, "I'm here for food, not for coddling."

Gordi looked down at the cat with undisguised admiration and added, "Truman's *hard.*"

For while human blokes around him turn new-age and sensitive, Truman stays as tough as a tiger. Truman is a hunter. He comes home with his victims' blood smeared fresh across his fluffy white face.

"The other day he came in and we thought he'd been hit by a car—but then we realized it wasn't his blood but something else's," said Gordi, laughing now.

"What does he catch?" I asked. "Do you have sparrows here?"

"Ah yes, he eats sparrows and blackbirds and stuff, but they're just snacks, like the peppermints you get on the counter in a shop," said Gordi. "What he really likes is seagulls. And the other week he brought home a massive, bloated rat."

Truman hangs out under cars and comes home with oil-stained fur. He plays in the road. He is very, very hairy but takes no notice of his appearance. His coat is continually matted. He bites feet in unprovoked attacks. He beats up the dog.

From down by my feet there was a strange noise. I blinked and looked down.

"Was that a grunt?" I asked.

"Er, well, could have been a hairball actually, but you never know," Gordi ventured.

It was an extraordinary thing, but this cat really was displaying all the characteristics of the real Kiwi bloke, in a way that the so-called real men I'd tried to root out on my travels had never done.

For sure, many of the men I'd met displayed characteristics of the original bloke, some more than others. The shearers drank beer and did stuff with sheep. I'd met men with sheds in which they'd built hovercraft and airplanes. I'd toured farms with guys who shot goats and others who wore black tank tops and gum boots. But there was no doubt about it: This was a species that was mutating beyond repair. Morris may have built his hovercraft, but he was so upset by his pet cat's death that he couldn't bury it for days, and his cattle had to be shot by the neighbor. Two of the shearers had children with them. Dave shot goats—but he wore sunglasses because of his allergies. The men in the pub in Karamea fished for their food—but they went to counseling, for heaven's sake. Aylmer in Wellington may have had biceps the size of my thighs, but could he call himself a true-blooded bloke when he'd set up a support group? Richard had more guns than he could count, but he read books about neurolinguistic programming. Wayne was fit and lithe—but he'd *adopted a baby duckling*.

The fact of the matter was that, for better or for worse, the Kiwi bloke was changing—just as men across the rest of the globe were. In ten years' time, even fewer specimens would be showing the characteristics of the Original Kiwi Bloke, who lived, tough and taciturn, in the bush, or on the goldfields, the pioneer who traveled across the globe to a new land where he learned to build his own home and shoot his own dinner. I'd ridden on my motorcycle across the land in search of one true specimen, but I'd never found anyone who matched the entire description, no one individual who hadn't started to mutate. Until now, when I was just about to go home. At last, I had found the one remaining real Kiwi bloke. He was hairy and hard. He liked cars and killing. He was taciturn, tough, and virile.

He was a cat.

Sources

Future Indefinite/Noël Coward, Methuen Publishing
Voyage of the Beagle/Charles Darwin, Wordsworth Editions
The New Zealand Dictionary/Elizabeth and Harry Orsman, New House Publishers
View From the Summit/Sir Edmund Hillary, Corgi
The Journals of Captian Cook/Penguin Classics
Station Life in New Zealand/Lady Barker, Vintage
A History of New Zealand/Keith Sinclair, Penguin
The Chopper Boys and Helicopter Hunters/Rex Forrester, Penguin
Growing Up Maori/ed. Witi Ihimaera, Tandem Press
Making Peoples/James Belich, Penguin
Paradise Reforged/James Belich, Penguin
Being Pakeha Now/Michael King, Penguin
Pavlova Paradise Revisited/Austin Mitchell, Penguin
The Wild West Coast/Leslie Hobbs, Whitcombe and Tombs
Pighunting in New Zealand/Ken Cuthbertson, Reed
The Ordeal of William Larnach/Hardwicke Knight, University of Otago